Democratic Values
and Technological Choices

Democratic Values and Technological Choices

STUART HILL

STANFORD UNIVERSITY PRESS

Stanford, California   1992

Stanford University Press, Stanford, California
© 1992 by the Board of Trustees
of the Leland Stanford Junior University
Printed in the United States of America

CIP data appear at the end of the book

To my mother, Carolyn Nelson

Preface

IT SEEMS APPROPRIATE as democratic institutions are rapidly gaining new adherents around the world, to turn our attention inward and judge how well the United States fulfills its own commitment to democratic ideals. One of the most important challenges during the post–World War II era has been to ensure that the broad expansion of government services remains in touch with and responsive to citizen wishes and interests. There have been a number of innovations seeking to tighten the link between the government and its citizens as policy analysts have developed and refined methods to measure preferences for public programs and projects. In addition, the procedures of administrative decision making have been reformed to allow greater participation and influence by activists and members of the lay-public.

In no area of policy making is the task of ensuring democratic responsiveness more difficult than with technological choices. It is a demanding task to measure the assessments that different individuals make concerning programs or projects that involve new and complex technologies. The need for specialized expertise limits how much citizens know about the choices before them, and new technologies, in particular, often pose unusual value trade-offs with which most people have little experience. Decision-making procedures must then structure the authority and influence that particular political actors have on the final choice. What level of influence, for example, should the views of the general public carry when compared with administrators and political activists? Who is more capable of judging whether a power plant or a new regulatory program serves the interests of the majority?

How we devise solutions to these procedural problems is structured by our empirical assumptions about the characteristics of the preferences citizens have and the methods of assessment they employ. These assumptions dictate what we seek to measure and reveal who we believe is capable of making these choices—either alone or in concert with others—in a manner that is responsive to citizen interests. If we are to successfully design methods that increase government responsiveness to citizen interests about technological choices, then we must start with a realistic view of how different citizens assess technology.

Policy analysts have typically sought to measure citizen assessments by assuming all individuals have well-defined preferences and follow common methods of assessment in applying those wants to technological impacts. In contrast, participatory procedures give those with extensive background in the technology in question—administrators and activists—an influential role in public deliberations but fail to solicit the judgments of the majority of the laypublic. The purpose of this book is to develop and test a third model of assessment that challenges the empirical premises and methods of *both* approaches.

The type of analysis I propose is not common in discussions of policy analysis and citizen participation. The literature in this field typically works within well-established frameworks to address less global and more immediate needs such as discovering how to incorporate judgments about the value of risk impacts into our analysis or the best manner for resolving long-term disputes. When empirical research on citizen assessment is employed, it is most often used to answer relatively narrow questions rather than to judge the validity of the general models upon which current approaches rest. The work of Herbert Simon and Charles Lindblom is the most important exception to this pattern of inquiry. Over 30 years ago (March and Simon, 1958; Lindblom, 1959) they developed a general descriptive model of rationality that was used to critically evaluate existing methods of policy making. Although this particular work continues to be frequently cited, the method of analysis it represents has, unfortunately, not been developed as an ongoing and integral part of the field of prescriptive methods. This book is an effort to return to and enhance that legacy by evaluating the empirical foundations of prescriptive methods through the building and testing of a new descriptive theory of citizen assessment.

The logic of this argument has led me to consider a number of diverse fields of inquiry, and many people have contributed to my effort, sometimes in ways that they never realized. Before I started this project, Paul Kress, Orion White, David Orr, Duncan MacRae, Bob Daland,

and Kerry Smith at the University of North Carolina raised critical questions in my mind about the relationship between the normative goals of a democratic society and the constraints of citizen assessment. My colleagues at the University of California at Davis showed great patience in giving me the opportunity to pursue such a large undertaking. Larry Wade, Ed Costantini, David Bunch, John Gates, Lloyd Musolf, and Helen Roland patiently listened and offered useful suggestions when I was in the throes of conceptual and methodological uncertainty. The Institute of Governmental Affairs at Davis provided a quarter of release time from my teaching responsibilities at a critical juncture in the development of this project.

To test my theoretical approach I conducted a survey of a sample of the views of citizens and political activists who observed or participated in the controversy over the Diablo Canyon nuclear power plant located near San Luis Obispo, California. I want to thank the Universitywide Energy Research Group within the University of California system for funding this study. They took a chance on an investigation that was far riskier than the norm. John Culver and David George at California State Polytechnic University generously gave their time to help me contact potential interviewers. Susan Hunter provided excellent direction in a training session to teach my interviewers how to conduct an unconventional survey. A random sample of local citizens and many members of the groups who were involved in this dispute—the Mothers for Peace, the Abalone Alliance, and the Citizens for Adequate Energy—should be commended for their willingness to contribute to this research by graciously responding to a long and often taxing in-person survey.

In developing my research design, many questioned whether using students as interviewers was wise. After supervising over 200 interviews and listening to more than 150 hours of surveys on tape, I have no regrets. Overall, these students did an excellent job. I would like to call particular attention to Lauren Nolan, Mary Mitchell-Leitcher, and Daryl Hutchins who put in especially long hours and did far more than was expected in conducting surveys of both the general public and the political activists.

At different stages of this project, Ron Brunner, Stephen Brown, Bill Ascher, and George Downs also provided invaluable feedback on both substantive and methodological issues. Neil Pelkey deserves special thanks for his efforts in setting up a program to test whether the positions I discovered in this survey were significantly different from random outcomes. I have received great support from Stanford University Press. My editor, Muriel Bell, has shown impressive patience and good cheer in trying to entice me to finish this project sooner rather than later. Ellen F. Smith's copyediting helped smooth out many of the rough edges of the manuscript. Finally, my wife, Debra Long, listened to me drone on about this project for many nights long after the dog went to sleep. Now that is commitment. Thanks.

Contents

Figures

Tables

Democratic Values
and Technological Choices

CHAPTER ONE

The Importance of Experience in Technological Assessment

> For me to sit here in Washington and tell the people of Tacoma that [the cancer risk associated with arsenic emissions from a copper smelter] is an acceptable risk would be at best arrogant and at worst inexcusable.
>
> William Ruckelshaus
> *New York Times*, July 16, 1983

A FUNDAMENTAL CONCEPT in modern notions of democracy is that the legitimate exercise of power requires the consent of the governed. Although direct citizen control has not been pursued on a large scale because it is seen as impractical (and, by many, undesirable), democratic institutions in the United States and other Western industrialized states are built on the premise that the actions of government should represent the wishes of the vast majority of the people or some conception of the public good that the majority supports (Pitkin, 1972).

Mechanisms for representation have been steadily strengthened in most modern democracies. It is now possible for an ever larger portion of the populace to participate in politics, and procedures have been created to hold public officials more directly accountable for their actions. The right to vote in the United States, for example, has been extended to wider segments of the society (e.g., women and non-whites), and the obstacles based on property qualifications and literacy have been removed. The direct election of U.S. Senators and the tying of the Electoral College vote for President to the outcome of a state's popular vote have made public officials more subject to popular control. Participatory reforms in administrative procedures have opened more avenues of access so that citizens can directly influence government policy.

The goal of "democratizing" political institutions in this manner is to make what government does—its policies and its actions—more responsive to the wishes of the public as a whole. This objective, however, potentially runs counter to another significant development of modern government: the increasing use of complex, expertise-dependent technologies to provide many of the services that citizens desire.

The Challenge of Technological Choices

Since the early decades of the twentieth century citizens have increased their demands for political institutions to solve a wide range of difficult problems in virtually every sector of society. With increasing frequency government has employed complex technologies to provide better services and to mitigate unintended effects from previous innovations. The construction and maintenance of an interstate highway system, the peaceful development of nuclear power, the removal of hazardous pollutants from the nation's air and water, and the protection of endangered species are just a few of the more notable examples.

Addressing these new and challenging issues, however, demands highly specialized expertise that most citizens and legislators lack. Elected officials have responded by creating new agencies staffed by people with the necessary skills. Legislators typically identify very broad goals and give agency personnel considerable statutory discretion to devise a specific program or set particular regulatory standards (Lowi, 1969; Crandall and Lave, 1981). But, in fulfilling their responsibilities, administrators inevitably face choices that go beyond technical competence, choices that involve weighing ends as well as selecting means. The interpretation of a broad goal in terms of specific technologies necessitates identifying a range of alternatives that may offer very different combinations of impacts. The choice of one course of action over another thus requires, implicitly or explicitly, an assessment of the value of those impacts. The manner in which any alternative is applied to a specific set of circumstances, moreover, sets priorities about the relative worth of different impacts in a given place.

A major new technological initiative, such as an interstate highway or a large waste repository, for example, can offer dramatic improvements in the economic well-being of a particular area by stimulating rapid economic growth and reducing unemployment. The worth of these gains must often be balanced against sizable and even irreversible environmental, social, and economic costs, such as the loss of a rare ecological system, historically important buildings, or older sources of income for a community or region. Some of the most difficult choices concern the degree to which one imposes or mitigates risks to human health from such threats as air- or water-borne carcinogens, hazardous machinery in the workplace, or the possibility of catastrophic accidents.

Because these trade-offs are embedded in the specialized language, concepts, and controversies of producing a particular technological service, the knowledge required to make assessments is seldom part of the everyday experience of the laypublic. As a result, citizens' understanding of possible effects and their ability to offer valuative direction is necessarily limited. The technical training of administrators, on the other hand, does not confer upon them any special knowledge of how to assess these decisions in a way that is representative of the preferences of those who will actually gain or lose.

The need for specialized expertise in technological decision making thus raises a basic problem of representation for modern democracies: How do political institutions close the gap between those who have the most complete understanding of the means—the technical experts—and those who are the final arbiters of value—ordinary citizens? How does one ensure democratic responsiveness in expertise-dependent choices?

The significance of this question for any particular decision will always be a matter of degree, depending on how distant the value choices are from citizens' backgrounds and how high the stakes are. For technological decisions that produce marginal changes for which the trade-offs are reasonably well known or accessible to the layperson, the failure to learn precisely what the polity wants in a specific instance is not of great consequence. Past decisions can provide a general evaluative direction (e.g., widening a highway or fluoridating the water), and because the new choice is limited in its impact, it should not diverge too far from citizen wishes. Adjustments can be made in subsequent choices as individuals react and make their wishes known.

When the government faces decisions that demand high levels of specialized expertise and produce large-scale and lasting impacts, however, the problem of representation is more critical. Citizen assessments are very difficult to infer from reactions to past decisions. A large-scale, complex technology is unlikely to produce the same pattern of trade-offs from one location to the next, nor can citizens be assumed to have similar social and economic backgrounds and values. Moreover, those who are directly affected by a project typically do not have sufficient time to learn about and weigh the impacts before a decision is made. A simple public opinion poll of their reactions, therefore, is not particularly instructive.

Nevertheless, if governmental decisions are expected to be responsive to citizen wishes, we must devise political institutions that draw on the laypublic's appraisal *before* a decision is made. A poor reading of citizens' preferences may result in significant, but undesired, outcomes with which these individuals will have to live for some time.

The Problem of Evaluative Knowledge

The key obstacle to representing citizen assessments of technology is the fact that—as noted above—these evaluations have not yet taken shape by the time decisions are typically made. It would appear, then, that democracies need to learn how the process of citizen evaluation operates and unfolds over time: understanding that *method of assessment* could reveal how *measures of such assessments* might be developed. We could discover, for example, how to speed the process of deliberation for a representative group or how to gauge what evaluations would be reached if there were more time to debate the relevant issues.

The ability to develop reliable estimates of citizen assessments obviously rests on the scope and accuracy of our understanding of the process that produces them, in itself a challenging theoretical task. Consider the diverse questions that must be answered.

Impacts that stretch wide across society and long into the future are usually subject to considerable uncertainty, provoking technical disagreements over the type and level of outcomes. To calibrate what citizens want, we must first ask how members of the laypublic acquire information about and then evaluate technical controversies. Technological choices, moreover, present individuals with impacts that are often new to their experience and have great qualitative diversity. How, then, do individuals judge the relative value of economic, environmental, social, and risk effects, each of which can vary widely in terms of the context in which they arise, their probability of occurrence, and their severity of effect?

Decisions that have substantial and diverse impacts also inevitably affect a wide range of individuals and interests. To estimate what citizens want, we must also take into account *who* will be considered when they make their assessment. Do citizens attribute importance only to their own personal gains or losses without regard for the welfare of others? Or do they take a wider view, by weighing the well-being of the disadvantaged or larger collectivities such as their community or nation or even future generations? If they actively consider these broader interests, in what manner do they assess their relative importance?

Finally, because a broad spectrum of individuals are exposed to these impacts, it is necessary to judge whether there are significant differences in the characteristics of the wants and the methods of assessment that individuals employ. Do variations in social or economic background, for example, shape systematic differences in the specificity and breadth of wants and their methods of application? Or are evaluative procedures so deeply rooted that they are largely immune from worldly effects?

Choices with broad and enduring impacts are the most challenging because they combine all of these dimensions in a single decision: the need to estimate how individuals from different backgrounds judge qualitatively diverse impacts and interests that are subject to considerable technical disagreement. (Examples of such major projects range from more traditional hydroelectric dams, nuclear power plants, or urban freeways to more recent efforts to clean up sources of air and water pollution or to protect endangered species and ecosystems.) A powerful theory is needed to explain the process by which different individuals judge such a broad range of issues and reach their overall evaluations. But this understanding is essential if citizens' views are to be represented in administrative decisions.

Making a choice about a major technology, however, involves more than discovering a means for developing and measuring citizens' assessments. Assuming that this information can be acquired, political institutions must then judge how much weight the laypublic's views ought to carry compared with other political actors. When faced with a choice of substantial scale and complexity, should the judgments of the laypublic "direct" the final outcome or play a secondary role and only "inform" that decision?

These are, in many respects, generic questions that political institutions must address about public policy decisions. Theorists of democratic representation, however, have long disagreed over the most appropriate answers because they start from differing conceptions of the evaluative capabilities of the ordinary citizen compared with the abilities of government officials.

Two Views of Representation

An enduring and widely recognized position argues that public officials are morally obligated to seek instructions, or a "mandate," from their constituents and, as the "agent" of those constituents, to reflect that assessment in public deliberations and actions (Friedrich, 1948).

Each individual is seen as the best judge of his or her own welfare. To act in a manner that does not reflect the wishes of the majority not only violates the duties of being a representative but also fails to serve the best interests of the polity (Birch, 1971; Pitkin, 1972). Since elected officials often shirk this obligation for technological choices by giving government agencies broad mandates, one implication of this line of thought is that the administrators who now must play a central role in making these decisions bear a growing responsibility to consult and act upon citizen assessments (see J. Burke, 1989).

In the quote with which this chapter began, William Ruckelshaus appears to reflect this sentiment. As Director of the Environmental Protection Agency in 1983, he faced the decision of whether to close a copper smelting plant, an important source of jobs (approximately 800) for people who lived near Tacoma, Washington, because it posed a "significant" health hazard from the emission of arsenic (estimated to be an additional two cases of lung cancer per year). By calling it "at best arrogant and at worst inexcusable" for a distant bureaucrat to make this decision, Ruckelshaus implied that such a choice should only be made by the individuals who would actually bear its very significant costs and benefits.

This "mandate" position, however, has been criticized by "independence" theorists, who believe that following the cues of the ordinary citizen in making important government choices does not necessarily serve the public's interests. These theorists argue, as a practical matter, that citizens cannot be as well informed about public issues as government officials because they do not spend as much time learning about the consequences of different courses of action nor do they have ready access to this information. Even if they were well versed in the nuances of policy, citizens are unlikely to provide the clear direction that the "mandate" theorists posit because they usually do not share a single mind on any given topic.

On a more fundamental level, the many issues that the government typically faces are seen as so complex that they demand judgment capabilities the ordinary person does not possess. Some "independence" theorists maintain that average citizens are preoccupied with local or provincial concerns and that to consistently follow their lead would neglect the interest of larger collectivities such as the region or the nation (E. Burke, 1969; Pitkin, 1972). Supporters of this approach view technological decisions as exemplifying these very issues. The impacts of major technological projects are often numerous, requiring an investment of time to learn the type and level of effect. The layperson is not likely to be well informed, nor will different citizens necessarily share the same evaluative reactions. Furthermore, one must question whether ordinary citizens have the ability to judiciously evaluate many of the difficult trade-offs that technological choices raise (e.g., balancing uncertain economic gains against risky impacts) or to consider the interests of larger collectivities that are so often at stake with such decisions (see, e.g., Hensler and Hensler, 1979; Nisbett and Ross, 1980; Mazmanian and Morell, 1990).

In the classic debates over representation, critics of the evaluative capacities of the ordinary citizen maintain that public officials should be given considerable independence in decision making precisely because they do not suffer from the same deficiencies as the laypublic. From this perspective, the public's judgment would at best inform the deliberations of representatives, who would then be free to weigh any factors that the public missed.[1] For the independence argument to apply to technological choices, of course, one must believe that administrative decision makers (and, we should add, organized interest groups that routinely attempt to influence their decisions) can be counted on to exhibit skills in evaluating and promoting the general interest that elected representatives purportedly have.

Both sides of this debate agree on the ultimate goal of representation: that decisions ought to be made in the interests of the majority of citizens. And the decision about who is best able to implement that objective depends, for both sides, to a surprising degree on *empirical* assessments of the capabilities of different political actors. For technological choices, it is clear that the laypublic's lack of knowledge about impacts puts it at a decided disadvantage compared to experienced administrators and interest groups. Yet if this lack can be overcome, and reasonably well-informed assessments by the laypublic can be developed, then the crux of the disagreement really concerns the *quality* of those judgments and, by implication, the process of assessment that produces them.

The questions that must be answered for gauging the quality of citizens' capabilities are essentially the *same* as those that are needed to

[1]The extreme version of the "independence" or "trustee" model of representation would maintain that government officials do not have to pay *any* attention to public wishes, at least until they are voted out of office. The range of debate concerning the proper means to represent citizen interests about technology in the United States does not appear to reach this extreme (see Hill, 1985).

develop estimates of their overall judgments. In both cases, we must explain how different citizens evaluate the diverse impacts, interests, and technical disagreements of major technological decisions. Armed with this knowledge, we can then determine, for example, whether average citizens are, in fact, injudicious in their method of weighing different effects or provincial in how they define their interests.

The comparison of the capabilities of the laypublic with those of administrators and activists can be seen as an expansion of a larger theoretical question, the need to determine what effect, if any, variations in background have in shaping distinct grounds for and methods of assessment. The dramatic differences in experience in technological affairs between the laypublic and veteran political actors only reinforces the need to understand the role that experience plays.

The Significance of Experience

The degree to which experience does or does not have an impact on preferences and their method of application can shape virtually *every* expectation about how the process of assessment operates for *all* citizens. If the experience of events has a systematic influence across a *diverse* population, for example, a *divergent* range of evaluative methods should result. A complete lack of effect, on the other hand, would leave open the intriguing possibility that all individuals share *common* characteristics of wants and methods that remain untouched by the passage of events. Virtually no other theoretical issue offers this power to explain the grounds and methods of assessment—or, by implication, holds such significant consequences for the design of political institutions.

To illustrate, imagine a continuum from which three models of the impact of experience can be derived. At one end, individuals share well-specified preferences and deeply rooted, common methods of assessment that are virtually impervious to outside events; experience has no effect. Estimating an overall assessment of a major project or policy should be quite simple: one measures past expressions of preference for each impact and then uses the knowledge about common evaluative procedures to reconstruct how citizens compare these effects to reach a final assessment. The expectation of similar grounds and methods of assessment, moreover, provides at least tacit support for the position of mandate theorists: that each individual is the best judge of his or her interests. There is no hierarchy of capabilities here. Every person is equally adept because they all share the same approach.

By contrast, in the center of the continuum, experience slowly and methodically shapes preferences and evaluative procedures over time. Length and intensity of exposure are key factors, as the accumulation of experience dictates the specific characteristics of current wants and methods. Those who lack experience are at a loss to respond effectively because their preferences and evaluative procedures are poorly defined and cannot be specified within a short period of time. Reconstructing citizen assessments is now more complex. Individuals who have different experiences with particular technological decisions or impacts will differ dramatically in the methods they employ and in the degree to which they have well-defined or even recognizable approaches. Developing a representative cross section of their assessments is more difficult, because it requires understanding a number of divergent evaluative procedures.

The need to gather detailed information from every group of citizens, however, is less pressing in this model. Because individuals apply the lessons learned from specific choices in the past, veteran public officials and activists on particular issues have a distinct advantage over the laypublic, who typically lack substantive experience. The slow rate at which evaluative skills are acquired, moreover, indicates that members of the general public cannot overcome their deficiencies during the brief time that a particular project is actively debated. It might be prudent, therefore, to give those with more background greater authority in technological decision making.

This "past-structured" view of assessment does not mean, however, that the capabilities of those who have substantive experience should be overestimated. Such individuals, by necessity, are restricted to the characteristics of and lessons learned from the choices that they have commonly encountered. As the variability of the technical and evaluative issues increases with greater scale and length of effect, the profile of the "typical" choice is less likely to conform to the specific attributes of any particular decision. Constrained by the lessons of the past, individuals are unlikely to be very responsive to new information that does not easily fit their preconceptions.

At the other end of this continuum, experience can have a more immediate impact and play an even larger role, particularly for members of the laypublic. Individuals who have extensive backgrounds in a particular area still rely on readily available cues for making future judgments. Inexperienced citizens presented with a choice of substantial scale are likely to try to address their deficiencies by drawing on the positions of more experienced actors to determine how well they apply to the specifics of the case at hand. Thus, preferences and methods are *shaped by the past* for those with background and are more heavily *structured in the present*, during public deliberations, for those who have little or no experience.

Because assessments by the laypublic are developed in response to contending arguments in an ongoing public debate, these positions should be limited in number and reasonably accessible. The importance of participation by the laypublic, moreover, is greater as choices become more challenging. Large, complex decisions, as noted in the second model, are less likely to match the profile of choices experienced actors have frequently encountered. By evaluating how well the positions of these actors pertain to the specific characteristics of a particular decision, the attentive layperson provides a perspective that can complement the capabilities of public officials and political activists.

Each model of the role of experience in citizen assessment differs from the others on several dimensions that are important for accurately measuring and weighing citizen assessments of technology. In addition, each model suggests very different institutional procedures to ensure that technological choices are responsive to citizen wishes and interests. Judging how well existing institutions operate or designing new ones thus requires that we identify the empirical underpinnings for our prescriptive methods and determine which approach we believe is the most plausible. Only then can we begin to distinguish between the real and illusory alternatives facing democratic societies.

The special problems that technology poses for democratic decision making have long been recognized. Analytic techniques have been designed to provide measures of citizen assessments in order to inform decision makers about these judgments in a timely manner. The process of technological decision making in the United States, moreover, has been structured in a manner that weighs the judgments of the laypublic and other political actors in making actual decisions.

These institutional methods assume, implicitly or explicitly, that the process of citizen assessment operates according to the expectations of one of the three models of evaluation described above. When those methods are critically examined, it is striking how much their ability to serve democratic norms directly depends on the validity of their empirical premises and, by implication, the accuracy of their assumptions about the impact of experience.

Prescriptive Policy Analysis

Techniques of prescriptive policy analysis have been developed over the last 50 years to provide decision makers with information about citizens' assessments and to facilitate making the best possible choices. These methods include, most notably, cost-benefit analysis and a variety of methodologies (multi-attribute utility theory, multi-criteria decision making, and interactive forms of these techniques) that can be grouped under the broad rubric of "decision techniques."

These methods are built upon a very powerful model of citizen assessment that draws directly from the discipline of welfare economics and assumes a very limited role for experience, as in the first model described above. The task of reconstructing or measuring citizen judgments is simplified because different individuals are assumed to employ common, stable methods for evaluating a potentially diverse array of choices. This particular approach can best be described as a preference-driven model of evaluation, because assessment is essentially seen as a process of weighing the consequences of particular options in terms of preexisting desires.[2]

Individuals, according to this view, have a complete and precise ordering of preferences for the available objects of choice. They know, in other words, whether a particular quantity of one item gives them greater satisfaction than some amount of another. Even though many individuals are acknowledged to have altruistic feelings towards others, the focus of their evaluative concerns is on serving their own personal welfare or the welfare of their households.

In making specific choices, individuals are motivated to select the option that offers the most satisfaction, because they face a world in which the resources that are available to them are always scarce relative to their wants. The characteristics of preferences facilitate reaching decisions because choice attributes are believed to be easily "decomposable," so that any individual can break down large, complex options

---

[2]The conceptual grounding for cost-benefit analysis and multi-attribute utility theory is relatively well developed (see, e.g., Bohm, 1973; Keeney and Raiffa, 1976). With many multi-criteria decision techniques, however, the assumptions about assessment are implicit in the manner in which information is gathered, and one must infer the underlying theoretical similarity from what is being measured.

into component parts and judge the worth of each characteristic "at the margin." The satisfaction that one receives from each of these attributes is viewed as being readily exchangeable or substitutable in small increments with others. As a result, one can easily compare and make trade-offs among the available items to achieve the greatest gain with what one can afford.[3]

Consistent with the belief that assessment is preference-driven, information about impacts and alternatives is gathered to discover how best to meet one's wants within the constraints of limited resources. In cases where individuals need technical expertise, for example, they use commonly accepted measures of competence (e.g., many years of education and professional experience) to judge whether the benefits of that advice are likely to be worth the cost of consultation.

Reconstructing how citizens from different backgrounds assess large-scale technologies with highly dissimilar impacts is conceptually straightforward. The policy analyst simply assumes that all citizens employ the same method of assessment over the course of deliberations. The methodology of cost-benefit analysis is one of the most direct applications of this model (see, e.g., Bohm, 1973; Mishan, 1976; Haveman and Margolis, 1983; Hufschmidt, 1983). The cost-benefit analyst assumes that every individual who is affected has a preexisting preference for each object of choice. The government's technical experts typically provide estimates of the level of each outcome (i.e., they offer the "best" available information). The analyst divides the impacts of a major technological project into a common list of "discrete" impacts. The value of those impacts is estimated by measuring what citizens have previously been willing to pay in order to gain the benefit or avoid the loss in other contexts.[4] To the basic economic model of citizen assessments cost-benefit analysis adds an explicit normative principle for comparing the assessments of different individuals: if those who gain

[3]The theories of welfare economics and multi-attribute utility recognize that these assumptions are, at times, violated (e.g., "interactive effects" among complementary goods or "kinks" in one's indifference curves). Nevertheless, such effects are usually seen as exceptional compared with the "normal state of affairs." Indeed, this theoretical approach, and certainly its application to government projects, would look very different if one assumed that preferences varied considerably in their degree of completeness, decomposability, fungibility, and breadth of interest across different individuals (see Hill, 1986). Policy analysts now go to great lengths to try to circumvent these problems—or, in many cases, they simply assert that they are unimportant.

[4]Impacts that take place over a number of years, in this view, are "discounted" to determine their "present value." The discount rate is a measure of time preference that indicates how much more present costs and benefits are worth compared to those that occur sometime in the future.

could compensate those who lose and still come out ahead, the venture ought to be deemed worthwhile from the standpoint of society as a whole.

"Decision techniques" have been developed more recently, in part as a response to perceived deficiencies in cost-benefit analysis (see, e.g., Keeney and Raiffa, 1976; Nijkamp, 1980; Zeleny, 1982; Fandel and Spronk, 1985; Saaty, 1990). These methods make limited theoretical changes that seek to more realistically portray citizen assessment (e.g., citizens use multiple criteria) or to improve the process of decision making beyond what might otherwise occur (e.g., weighing uncertain impacts as expected outcomes). In addition, decision analysts directly question particular individuals, such as decision makers and political activists, about their preferences in an effort to more accurately measure intangible impacts for which market measures may not be available (e.g., environmental, uncertain, or redistributive effects).[5]

Despite such differences, all these current policy analytic techniques share the premise that individuals have well-specified preferences and employ common and presumably stable methods for evaluating project and policy choices. While this assumption greatly simplifies the task of analysis, it also raises potentially critical questions about the validity of the information the analyst offers. For *different* citizens to evaluate diverse impacts in the *same* manner, their preferences and evaluative procedures must be insulated from the vicissitudes of experience prior to and during public deliberations about a particular choice.[6]

This assumes, for example, that variations in background do not structure those wants and procedures. Thus, the practice of speaking with and sharing common ideals with others does not significantly broaden one's definition of interest beyond oneself, and how one thinks about the world does not bind particular values together in interdependent systems. Differences in background do not influence the comprehensiveness and specificity of wants. The rate at which one is willing

[5]Individuals in positions of responsibility might differ from others insofar as they have better information or more incentive to consider a wider horizon of interests than does the layperson. The underlying character of their preferences or their method of meeting them, however, is not expected to be fundamentally different from that of the ordinary citizen. Thus, it is not surprising that most of those who adopt the decision-techniques approach also support respecting the sovereignty of individual choice and define the interests of society as the aggregation of individual welfare (see Stokey and Zeckhauser, 1978).

[6]The importance of experience in establishing grounds and methods of assessment has long been recognized in cognitive psychology and theories of bounded rationality (e.g., March and Simon, 1958). The relationship between experience and process of assessment for the laypublic, however, is not well developed.

to exchange or trade-off one item for another is not contingent on one's experience with it or the context in which it has appeared. Differences in experience do not limit the types of choices for which one is willing to rely on the technical expertise of others.

In this view, well-defined wants and common, stable methods must also be impervious to the effects of public deliberations. Once debate begins, listening to contending positions about the relative worth of esoteric impacts or the weight of conflicting levels of interests (e.g., the individual, the community, and future generations), for example, must not further define citizens' preferences about those impacts or interests. Observing how well a governmental agency or its critics have acted in the political and administrative process should not significantly affect judgments about the credibility of those actors.

The validity of the information that policy analysts generate about citizen assessment directly depends on these assumptions. No one checks after the fact, for example, to see if all citizens bring similar evaluative procedures to a particular choice and then disaggregate and weigh its impacts in the manner prescribed by cost-benefit analysis. With an in-depth questioning of particular individuals, decision techniques can capture a few past-structured effects.[7] However, the possibility that preferences and evaluative procedures are structured by and evolve in response to the positions that emerge in public debate has never been seriously considered nor measured by either approach.

Even if experience does structure evaluative procedures, the analyst might still argue that we ought to follow the recommendations of these methods, and this response has merit, provided that the effects of experience are limited to unambiguous problems in the methods of citizen assessment that these techniques then solve or ameliorate. On the other hand, if experience produces extensive changes in the grounds of assessment, this recommendation is far more problematic. Under such circumstances, policy-analytic techniques might well mislead decision makers about what citizens really want rather than enlighten them about how to improve their methods of evaluation.

The Procedures for Technological Decision Making

Institutional procedures in effect in the United States today to weigh the judgments of the laypublic and other political actors employ quite

---

[7]Depending upon the technique, the analyst may check to see if all preferences are decomposable. Or the analyst may assume at the outset that all individuals use multiple criteria rather than judge a project on a single evaluative dimension.

different assumptions about citizens' methods and capabilities than do the premises underlying policy-analytic techniques. The manner in which power is allocated and justified suggests, not that individuals have well-specified wants and use similar evaluative procedures, but that the definition of their preferences and evaluative methods varies with each political actor's substantive background in technological affairs.

Administrative agencies have always enjoyed considerable discretion and influence in technological decision making compared with members of the laypublic. Before the late 1960's the justification for this power was entirely consistent with the premises of prescriptive policy analysis (e.g., Lilienthal, 1963). Administrators clearly had greater technical expertise than did citizens. Because polls and voting behavior indicated that the vast majority of citizens wanted more rapid technological development, administrators could be seen as simply using their expertise to implement those wishes (Haveman, 1965; Ferejohn, 1974).

When consensus on technological goals began to fracture visibly in the late 1960's, these benign perceptions of government agencies also started to change. As popular sentiment shifted towards giving increasing weight to environmental, social, and risk impacts (Milbrath, 1984), federal agencies increasingly found themselves in the role of the technology's promoter, arguing that the "hard" economic benefits outweighed these "soft" intangible costs (see, e.g., Morell and Singer, 1980; Casper and Wellstone, 1981; Nelkin, 1984a). Among a growing segment of political activists, agencies were no longer seen as objective "technicians," but as valuatively "biased" by their past history of technological development and their interest in winning additional appropriations for building more projects. Regulatory agencies were increasingly viewed as being "captured" by their long association with and dependence on the organizations they were supposed to regulate (Mazmanian and Nienaber, 1979; Culhane, 1981).

Faced with such new value conflicts, legislators could have stepped in to make these difficult choices. Instead, Congress decided to leave government agencies with substantial decision-making power.[8] The procedures that govern how administrators make decisions, however, were changed to push them to consider impacts they previously ignored. Under the National Environmental Policy Act (NEPA), for example, whenever a federal agency considers a "major action," it must

---

[8]One of the reasons that administrators were given discretion in the first place was that representatives sought to avoid having to make decisions on particularly controversial policies (MacIntyre, 1986).

prepare detailed impact studies that attempt to predict the type and level of consequences for the "human environment" that are likely to occur, as well as the impacts of the available alternatives. The goal is to learn as much as possible about the effects and then carefully weigh the value of each outcome in reaching a final decision.

NEPA was initially seen by some as another effort at "encouraging" administrators to be comprehensive and objective in their assessments. Administrators are required, for example, to gather more data to ensure that they are *fully* informed (Caldwell, 1982). Other provisions of NEPA and the manner in which it has been implemented and reformed over time, however, reveal an additional purpose. The preparation of in-depth impact statements requires technological agencies to hire large numbers of staff who are primarily concerned with technology's negative effects, and this initiates a process of reform by adding new voices of dissent within the organization (Wichelman, 1976; S. Taylor, 1984). To ensure that important impacts are not missed, NEPA also requires that the sponsor of an impact review solicit the views of other federal and state agencies and private organizations that have an interest in the decision (U.S. Council on Environmental Quality, 1979). More internal information, thus, is combined with the expertise and political pressure that external organizations, such as environmental groups and government agencies who are established to protect the environment, can bring.

The formal role for these new participants is still advisory; the impact statement does not bind agency action. By vigorously raising issues that have to be addressed in a public document, however, this wider group of players can bring greater pressure on agencies to give more consideration to deleterious effects they might otherwise ignore (see Andrews, 1976; Liroff, 1976).

The role of the laypublic, which has no organized involvement in technological affairs, by contrast, remains essentially passive and symbolic. The process of policymaking is open to inspection, as it is for other government and activist organizations.[9] Yet lay input is not solicited. No effort is made, for example, to actively encourage the involvement of a representative cross section of the general public. Instead, there is just the opportunity to speak at public hearings—one of the least effective methods for influencing government decisions (Arnstein,

[9]The Government in the Sunshine Act (1976) and the Freedom of Information Act (1976), for example, require that agency meetings be open to the public and that citizens have access to government information and documents.

1969; Checkoway, 1981; Cole and Caputo, 1984). The implication is clear: although members of the laypublic have a right to be heard, their views are not actively sought because they lack the substantive background in technological affairs to make a distinctive and meaningful contribution (see Gormley, 1989).

Current decision-making procedures thus clearly differ from the assumptions underlying policy-analytic techniques. All individuals are not expected to follow the same method of evaluation. There is a clear ranking of ability—from administrators, who have the most experience in technological assessment, to interest group activists, who supply needed background in a neglected area, and to the unorganized members of the laypublic, who have virtually no substantive experience and nothing to offer but mere "opinion."[10]

Although past-structured assumptions provide a pecking order of capabilities, they also limit what we can expect from those who are most skilled. No individual or organization is expected to be comprehensive or synoptic in its assessments. Administrators do not consider all impacts nor do they judiciously weigh them. In a past-structured world rationality is "bounded" by one's background. Acquiring more substantive experience expands those limits, but only slowly, limiting involvement to those who have the prerequisite experience. Creating a process in which partisans of different backgrounds confront one another, therefore, can be seen as an attempt to avoid the worst pitfalls that would occur if any particular individual or organization were allowed to act unilaterally on its own limited perspective.[11]

This procedural response for technological decision making is still reasonably new. The sobering assessments of individual capabilities that underlie its development, however, raise doubts about whether this "solution" is adequate to the task. A defining characteristic of major technological projects and policy initiatives is their variability: in tech-

---

[10]As William Gormley (1989) has argued, by the mid-1970's there was a move toward "responsible representation" that placed great emphasis on participants having experience and expertise. Court interpretations of NEPA provide additional support for this hierarchical ranking. Although federal agencies are faulted for failing at times to conform to NEPA's procedures, the courts have yet to seriously question their evaluative expertise for judging the relative worth of competing impacts such as environmental and economic effects (see Baram, 1980; Caldwell, 1989).

[11]NEPA, from this perspective, is quite consistent with the more academic analyses of Charles Lindblom (1959, 1979, 1990) and Herbert Simon (March and Simon, 1958). Because of the cognitive limitations of any particular individual, Lindblom argues that democracy is "intelligent" insofar as its decisions are the product of multiple partisans trying to influence the outcome from very different perspectives.

nologies with large-scale and enduring effects, each new proposal combines different and often novel values and technical requirements. The challenge of assessment is to identify and carefully weigh each somewhat unique package of value choices. Past-structured skills, however, center the attention of veteran political actors on impacts that they frequently encounter rather than on effects that are unusual or idiosyncratic to the choice at hand. Because administrators and activists often bring widely divergent political backgrounds (e.g., technological administrators and environmental activists) to any given decision, they also focus on a limited set of the effects (e.g., economic or environmental) and weigh them in a manner that consistently produces conclusions of either support or opposition. It is not surprising that long, heated battles result, for there is little middle ground for compromise. *Taken alone*, the evaluative abilities of political veterans are not particularly well calibrated for identifying and carefully weighing the variable impacts of major initiatives.

Representative members of the laypublic might appear to be prime candidates for correcting at least some of these deficiencies. They are likely to be far more concerned with the characteristics of the particular project before them and to seek to weigh those impacts with values that are less extreme than the judgments of activists and administrators. By representing the views of the majority of the body politic, they could provide a political incentive for resolving these disputes in a more timely manner.

From a past-structured perspective, however, such optimism is not warranted. Average citizens are held to lack the substantive background needed to contribute effectively. Because evaluative capabilities tend to develop slowly, they are unlikely to overcome their limitations during the time span allowed for public deliberations (see Lindblom, 1990).

The State of Current Research

The prospect that members of the laypublic might react to public debate in a responsive and effective manner challenges the empirical foundations and methods of *both* prescriptive policy analysis and current institutional procedures. Neither approach anticipates that citizens develop their assessments by drawing on the arguments of political veterans and evaluating how well they apply to the particular characteristics of the choice at hand. If the "present-structured" thesis that I advance in this book is valid, no current method of policy analysis accurately reconstructs or represents citizens' assessments, nor does any present method of providing for citizen participation take advantage of the lay-public's special skills and political clout to moderate between widely divergent interests.

Two questions stand out then as particularly significant for research. First, we need to know whether experience systematically specifies the grounds and methods of assessment that citizens bring to public deliberations and whether it structures evaluative procedures during public debate for citizens who lack extensive background. Second, if experience does have one or both of these effects, we need to know *how* it shapes evaluative methods, so that we can critically evaluate the empirical assumptions underpinning current institutional procedures. At the present time, no theory of evaluation is sufficiently powerful or well enough substantiated to fully answer these questions. Variations of preference-driven theories have enjoyed success at predicting the short-term outcomes of decision making (Ajzen and Fishbein, 1980). Yet they have consistently failed to accurately reproduce evaluative procedures, which is precisely what is needed in this case (Hastie, 1986).

The most promising approach uses generic concepts about information processing from the study of social cognition in psychology (Fiske and Taylor, 1984) and argues that past experience should structure current evaluative procedures at least through the initial stages of public deliberations. The reason is simple. All individuals must cope with a limited ability to process and manipulate the vast amount of information to which they are exposed. Consequently, they have a strong incentive to draw heavily on their own direct experience and on trusted individuals to construct readily accessible knowledge structures, or "schemas," that aid in dealing with the contingencies of daily life (Conover and Feldman, 1984).

Political scientists and scholars in related fields have also examined the impact of experience, as we will see below, but typically in narrower theoretical terms. The results of their investigations, however, are surprisingly consistent with a very similar expectation: the past structures the grounds and the methods of assessment that different actors apply to political choices through the early stages of public debate.

The effects of experience are, of course, clearly evident in the procedures of veteran political actors. Both political activists and administrators have reasonably well-defined skills as a result of their formal training and organizational background. Interest group activists, for example, are considered to be politically "sophisticated" (Putnam, 1976; Pierce and Lovrich, 1980; Aberbach, Putnam, and Rockman, 1981). Their positions on a number of issues are logically consistent with prevailing liberal or conservative ideologies, and they can defend their views by drawing on considerable issue-specific information. Administrators also learn decision-making methods that identify specific options, sources for data, and means for analyzing real-world decisions. Their organizational experience teaches them not only how to solve substantive problems but also how to coordinate larger, more complex programs and to recognize and respond to external political threats (March and Simon, 1958; Allison, 1971).

This research reveals that the past not only imparts skills but also limits the range of one's response. Political activists, for example, seek out new knowledge that supports their preconceptions but discount or ignore data that does not help their case (Sabatier, 1988; see also McGraw and Pinney, 1990). Frequent encounters with those of like mind only encourage activists to focus on information that is consistent with the views of the group (Rajecki, 1982). In the same manner, administrators do not necessarily review the full range of possible alternatives or the "best" sources of information. Instead, they employ the decision-making procedures that their organization has used repeatedly in the past and that are consistent with its perceived "mission" (Halperin and Kanter, 1974). Information that falls outside this habituated scope of analysis produces little or no immediate change in their behavior (Mazmanian and Nienaber, 1979; S. Taylor, 1984).

Although the available findings are humbling for political veterans, members of the laypublic, by comparison, are even less well-prepared. Indeed, there has been a long debate over whether most citizens have *any* defensible belief system for evaluating political choices. The pessimistic view, drawing on several decades of data from national election studies, argues that the vast majority of citizens are poorly prepared for any form of political participation. Average citizens know little about politics and are unsophisticated in their methods of political reasoning. They do not link multiple issues together into coherent conservative or liberal ideologies, nor do they use abstract belief systems for making judgments about specific policy choices. Instead, their sense of political direction is poorly defined, governed by simple notions of group benefits, allegiances to political parties, or ephemeral feelings for how good or bad the times are (Berelson, Lazarsfeld, and McPhee, 1954; Campbell, et al., 1960; Converse, 1964; Jacoby, 1986; Smith, 1989).[12]

Lacking the background to understand the ideological terms of political debate, most citizens pay relatively little attention to issues. They focus on less substantial concerns, such as the personal characteristics of the candidate, or they follow the dictates of enduring partisan loyalties (Converse, 1964; Page, 1978). When members of the general public do examine issues, most choose the easy problems for which they have strongly held values rather than attempt to reason through policy questions that are cognitively complex (Carmines and Stimson, 1980).

Studies of technological assessments support many of these findings. Citizens know few "facts" about technological impacts (Hensler and Hensler, 1979). They are "intuitive scientists" who must rely on a narrow range of experience that inevitably causes systematic "biases" and errors in assessing uncertainty and performing many basic tasks of reasoning (Nisbett and Ross, 1980; Kahneman, Slovic, and Tversky, 1982). Simple political loyalties or cues explain many of their judgments of complex choices (Kuklinski, Metlay, and Kay, 1982). Citizens' responses to technological risks, in particular, are far more likely to be dictated by their perceptions of whether they can exercise personal control in the event of an accident than by the careful weighing of the worths of uncertain outcomes (Fischhoff et al., 1978; Slovic, Fischhoff, and Lichtenstein, 1980). Some seek to avoid any technological risk nearby—the NIMBY or "not in my backyard" syndrome (Kraft and Clary, 1991).

An alternative, more optimistic line of research challenges these findings, arguing that such findings on belief systems are surprisingly narrow and even misleading. Although the available evidence confirms that the laypublic does not think about politics in terms of liberal and conservative ideologies, it fails to determine whether there may be other general orientations that do not conform to these labels. Conventional surveys and statistical methods reinforce this conceptual limitation because they are not designed to identify and reproduce alternative frameworks.[13] Research tools that are intended to address these prob-

[12]Norman Nie, Sidney Verba, and John Petrocik (1979) found that up to 33 percent of the electorate could be described as ideologues in 1972, a particularly contentious year. Their measures, however, have been criticized on both conceptual and methodological grounds.

[13]Statistical surveys require, for example, that the designer of the survey preselect the stimulus that he or she *thinks* is potentially important for a *national* sample. Given the breadth of individuals who are interviewed, the survey may fail to identify what is actu-

lems suggest that most citizens have at least some preparation for political decision making. They are certainly not as sophisticated as political veterans, and they do not have general orientations that combine many beliefs in a logically consistent fashion. Yet it appears that their stands on specific issues can be explained by more general core values, broad symbols, or common orientations (Jackson, 1983; Conover and Feldman, 1984; Peffley and Hurwitz, 1985; Hurwitz and Peffley, 1987; Feldman, 1988). Moreover, their skills in evaluating candidates may be reasonably astute, because they use instrumental assessments of competence and integrity rather than rely on superficial, "cosmetic" judgments (Miller, Wattenberg, and Malanchuk, 1986; Popkin, 1991).

Scholars have also questioned whether ideologies of the left or the right readily explain citizens' responses to technological impacts. Many argue that other political, cultural, and social value dimensions might account for judgments about risk effects in particular (Otway and Kerry, 1982; Douglas and Wildavsky, 1982; Fischhoff, Watson, and Hope, 1984). In this view, the role of procedural judgments cannot be reduced to a simple questionable desire for personal autonomy and may reflect broader, more defensible judgments about the decision-making process (U.S. Environmental Protection Agency, 1979; Vlek and Stallen, 1981; Popper, 1983).

The optimists thus partially rehabilitate the laypublic by examining broader notions of reasoning and assessment. Concepts from social cognition have played a particularly important role in articulating how this alternative view operates (Lau and Sears, 1986; Miller, Wattenburg, and Mallanchuk, 1986; Hurwitz and Peffley, 1987). Generic ideas about the way information is processed and stored ask us to look beyond preconceived and often rigid ideas about the role of particular ideologies to functional patterns of political thought and evaluation. Social cognition is also helpful in providing a common explanation for this broad range of findings in its fundamental premise—that our ability to process the vast amount of information we confront daily has definite cognitive limitations. The findings reveal that *all* political actors both use and are constrained by the limited range of their past experience and their cognitive abilities to manipulate information.

---

ally significant to the subjects (see Bennett, 1977). In addition, issue coherence or "constraint" is typically measured by calculating statistical correlations among the subjects' responses to discrete questions. Because each item can appear in very different places in the survey, the analyst can easily fail to reproduce the paths of reasoning by which the respondents combine their belief about these issues in a logical fashion (Nelson, 1977; Bennett, 1977).

An explanation of assessments that is based on social cognition, moreover, predicts that varying levels of background produce consistent differences in methods. Individuals, such as activists and administrators, with considerable experience in a particular area develop more abstract and well-integrated knowledge structures that actively guide their perceptions and expectations in the future. These "schemas" reveal, for example, how events are expected to unfold or how particular people ought to act under a given set of circumstances. They also explain how substantive issues in a particular area of politics interrelate or how procedures for decision making are expected to operate. Members of the laypublic, who spend much less time dealing with and thinking about political issues, inevitably suffer from leaner orientations. Their ability to perceive and analyze the various dimensions of comparable issues, as a result, is necessarily far more limited. It is not surprising that most citizens rely more heavily on procedural schemas, because this type of cognitive structure can be applied to many different situations, from political decision making to committee work at the office.

At the beginning of public deliberations on a major technology, then, the veterans are at a decided advantage. They are able to identify key issues, reach an initial assessment, and even develop arguments to persuade others relatively quickly based upon their past "cognitive investment." By comparison, members of the general public know very little and react in terms of rudimentary orientations. What happens beyond this point in time, however, is not clear. Previous studies have not analyzed from this theoretical perspective choices involving a major technology that has high stakes and provokes an extended debate. If the laypublic's response is minimal and confined to past-structured judgments, the empirical foundation of current evaluative procedures remains relatively secure. As we saw earlier, however, the prospect that the typical citizen may react in a responsive and effective manner raises basic normative questions about how a democratic society represents and weighs citizens' assessments. At the present time we have no empirical test of the methods that different political actors use to evaluate a "mature" or well-developed technological controversy. Unfortunately, the available data tell us very little about the likely response from most citizens or even the methods those actors are *capable* of using as public deliberations unfold.[14]

[14]This is not to suggest that the impact of debate has been entirely neglected. There have been efforts to understand the role that debate plays or ought to play when political elites face difficult policy decisions (see, e.g., Adelman, Stewart, and Hammond, 1975;

Some scholars might argue that there has been a wide range of empirical findings about citizen assessment over the years. For example, Eric Smith (1989) recently reexamined the data from the national election studies and maintains the results reveal that most of the laypublic is cognitively incapable of judging political issues of even modest complexity in a sophisticated manner. The implication is that they are therefore unfit for the more demanding rigors of technological assessment.

Reactions to national elections, however, are a poor test for measuring the possible range of citizens' methods and capabilities. When the nation chooses its political leaders, the polity is exposed to a large number of diverse issues in a limited period of time. The presentation of coherent arguments and rebuttals about any particular issue is rare. Presidential "debates," for example, ask candidates to respond to a long list of disparate questions on which there is very little direct interchange (Kraus, 1979). Polls reveal, moreover, that many individuals are not highly motivated to pay attention because they do not believe that the outcome of elections substantially alters the course of political events, certainly not in a way that directly affects them or the things that they treasure (Niemi and Weisberg, 1984).

By contrast, a major technology raises the prospect of transforming the very character of one's community. Consequences of this magnitude frequently provoke long and heated discussions among government administrators and political activists that are closely followed in the local print and electronic media. While this interchange rarely conforms to the guidelines of a formal debate, members of the general public are nevertheless presented with an extended set of arguments on a particular policy decision. The issues, moreover, are among some of the most complex that government faces.

Learning how citizens respond when the incentives are unambiguous, the arguments are well developed, and the questions are extremely challenging is a far better test of citizens' methods and capabilities than elections, in which it is difficult to argue that these conditions hold (see Downs, 1957; Popkin, 1991). In addition, by comparing the laypublic's process of assessment with the procedures that veteran political actors employ, we should gain a much better measure of the relative capabilities of these actors.

Mitroff and Mason, 1982; and Majone, 1989) and when the laypublic is exposed to particular polarizing national issues such as the Vietnam war (Zaller, 1991). Unfortunately, this literature does not tell us what the capabilities of the laypublic are or how they compare with that of political veterans.

The Argument

The purpose of this book is to use the concepts from social cognition to construct and test a more accurate explanation of citizen assessment. Based upon this understanding, I will critically evaluate the validity of the information that prescriptive techniques provide and the empirical premises that underpin current procedures for public participation in technological decision making. Using my "social-process" theory of citizen assessment, I will then identify alternative empirical assumptions that suggest a more active role for the laypublic in making the most difficult technological choices.

My thesis is simple: experience structures the methods of assessment for all citizens prior to public debate, and during the key period of deliberations, it shapes the evaluative procedures of those who lack extensive background. As a result the method of evaluation employed by the laypublic, in particular, significantly differs from the empirical expectations of either prescriptive policy analysis or current institutional procedures. This argument, developed in full in later chapters, can be summarized by revealing how my theoretical alternative broadly compares with the empirical assumptions of existing evaluative procedures.

As we have seen, prescriptive analytic techniques assert that individuals bring well-defined, "unstructured" (i.e., readily divisible and substitutable) preferences to technological choices and, as a result, have little need to specify their judgments based on positions developed in public debate. Because of the limits of citizens' past experiences, I will argue that their wishes are poorly specified for many key technological outcomes. Any standards that are well-defined are likely to be highly structured by direct experience with the multiple attributes of particular places and people. When faced with large-scale technological choices, citizens should be particularly responsive to the evaluative arguments *and* the procedural actions of political veterans as a means for overcoming the deficiencies of their own past.

Current methods of citizen participation in technological decision making are far more realistic than prescriptive analysis, because they recognize that experience shapes evaluative procedures. Government administrators and activists frame new choices in terms of the enduring lessons learned from earlier decisions. Their past-structured skills, however, are not well calibrated or very responsive to the case-specific variation that characterizes major technological choices. I argue that the laypublic complements the methods of the political veterans by judging how well their arguments apply to the substantive impacts of the choice before them and by evaluating how responsive they have been to those issues. Enduring substantive and evaluative expertise from the political veterans, thus, is balanced by a focus on procedural and case-specific issues from the general public.

The propositions that this new perspective offers are wide-ranging, and it is impossible to investigate all of them in one study. The central issue that separates past-structured assumptions from a social-process perspective, however, is the manner in which different actors respond to an extended debate over a high-stakes project. To test the thesis that the laypublic's methods are present-structured, I selected a technological choice that presented local citizens with strong incentives to engage a well-defined set of arguments about a nuclear power plant. The controversy focused on whether the Diablo Canyon nuclear power plant, located near San Luis Obispo, California, should be allowed to operate.

This facility promised local citizens a very significant contribution to the local tax base, as well as additional sources of electrical power for the state of California when energy was in particularly short supply. The safety of nuclear power, however, became a prominent topic of national debate during the time this plant was being actively debated from 1972 to 1985. Moreover, the Diablo Canyon facility was inadvertently sited near an earthquake fault and then suffered numerous criticisms over the quality of its construction. The most costly and glaring mistake was the initial failure to properly retrofit the plant so that it could withstand a sizable earthquake. The escalation of rhetoric for and against the plant provided strong incentives to engage in a long and well-developed public debate.

Designing a study that can accurately gauge citizens' evaluative procedures for such a difficult choice is a methodological challenge. I chose a package of methods by which I could directly measure citizens' procedural and substantive schemas (multiple Q sorts) and then estimate their interrelationships (path analysis). Lengthy structured interviews were conducted among a random sample of 147 members of the general population, followed by open-ended surveys with representative individuals. For the purposes of comparison, 45 interest-group activists who were involved on both sides of this dispute were interviewed in the same manner.

The specific results of this investigation, as we shall see, are striking.

The implications, however, go well beyond the particular lessons. Examining and testing the empirical assumptions of current institutional procedures challenges the prevailing philosophy underlying approaches to both prescriptive analysis and decision-making procedures. The fields of policy analysis and institutional design place high value on methods that claim to improve individual and collective decision making, yet, as I have suggested, they give remarkably little attention to developing a basic understanding of actual methods of citizen assessment. This, I argue, is a critical omission, because how citizens judge difficult choices literally defines the options that we have for measuring and weighing their assessments. Most analysts appear to believe that we know enough about citizens' methods to get on with the tough task of improving them. I believe that we know much less. This study represents a first step toward overcoming that limitation so that we can learn about the real rather than illusory options that now lay before us.

I do not seek to offer yet another set of prescriptive techniques. Instead, I hope that this work will contribute to a broader recognition of the critical importance of first improving our empirical understanding of citizen assessment so that we then can do a better job of plotting fruitful changes in prescriptive techniques.

My argument is developed in full over the following seven chapters. In Chapter 2 I return to a more extended review of the preference-driven approach that underpins current policy-analytic techniques—cost-benefit analysis and decision techniques. It is an appropriate place to begin my analysis, because this is the most explicit and well-defined theory of citizen assessment used in present evaluative procedures. By arguing that different individuals use common methods over time, this model provides a clear baseline against which to consider the impact of experience.

Chapter 3 presents my theoretical counterpoint to this approach. The social-process view of citizen assessment builds directly on concepts from cognitive social psychology to construct a path model of decision making for the laypublic. The contrast with the model of common, stable methods from policy analysis techniques is highlighted. The social-process theory is then applied to administrators and political activists in Chapter 4. The capabilities of these veteran political actors are directly compared with the skills of the laypublic for contributing to technological decision making.

A research design to test this new theoretical perspective is set forth in Chapter 5. The methods employed are characterized so that those who do not have a strong background in quantitative techniques can follow the logic without a great deal of difficulty. Chapter 6 presents the results from both the structured and the open-ended interviews with members of the laypublic who live near the Diablo Canyon nuclear power plant. In Chapter 7 these findings are compared with the methods from the interest-group activists, and the empirical results are summarized. Finally, Chapter 8 develops the implications of this research for changing how we think about prescriptive analysis and improving the democratic process of technological decision making.

CHAPTER TWO

Prescriptive Policy Analysis

ANY THEORY EXPLAINING the process of citizen assessment necessarily simplifies reality. Yet theory, especially practical theory for informing policy actions, would be of little use unless it summarized what is important in our surrounding world. As a result, an inescapable tension arises between the brevity of our explanations for why things happen as they do and the diversity and complexity of actual events. This chapter presents an assessment of how accurately prescriptive techniques currently in use in policy analysis—cost-benefit analysis and decision techniques—measure citizen wishes. My purpose is not to ask whether the preference-driven model of assessment that underlies these techniques captures the vagaries of evaluation in their totality; even the most ardent supporters do not make such sweeping claims. Instead, the relevant questions are *how* does this model simplify the process of assessment and *what support* does it offer for the theoretical choices that are made? Does the theory capture what is essential, or does it miss factors or processes that seem particularly important for the purpose at hand? Only after identifying those characteristics of the world that the theory takes in account can one assess whether it accurately measures citizens' wishes and improves on their method of assessment for addressing present or foreseeable circumstances.

Prescriptive policy analysts, of course, believe that they do capture the essential characteristics of the individual's preferences and the method of applying those wants to difficult choices, including the complex and often controversial choices about major technological projects. Any divergence from real-world methods is limited and typically seen as improving the process of assessment in a manner that the majority of the public would endorse. Theoretical power is achieved by deducing a model of assessment from the premise that preexisting preferences drive and order the evaluative process. Individuals know what they prefer, but they face a world in which resources are limited relative to their wants. They maximize their satisfaction by following the same "rational" method of assessment, a method that can be applied in almost any choice setting.

Prescriptive policy analysts, however, have never argued that they can explain how these preferences—or the ready willingness to defer to the expertise of others that characterizes this view of assessment—are developed. What is even more striking about this model is that its assumptions about preferences and expertise are expected to apply uniformly to *all* individuals and to remain stable over time, even during the course of an often dynamic and contentious public debate. In other words, this theory in its purest form excludes the possibility that experience systematically shapes the character of evaluative standards or the view of expertise over time. Indeed, its predictive value is contingent upon that exclusion. I will argue that their failure to provide a systematic defense of the validity of their theory of preference and choice on this dimension leaves serious questions about how well these policy-analytic techniques represent citizen preferences unanswered.

Cost-Benefit Analysis

Cost-benefit analysis is the oldest and most widely used prescriptive analytic technique. Now employed to assess almost any governmental initiative, it was first applied to technological decision making: in 1936 Congress mandated that cost-benefit analysis be used in judging water control projects. Since that time, technological projects in a wide variety of areas (e.g., weapons systems, transportation projects, power plants, and water projects) have been among the most frequently analyzed policies (Merewitz and Sosnick, 1971; Rhoads, 1985b).

Cost-benefit analysis draws its intellectual inspiration from the larger discipline of welfare economics, building directly on the economic premise that individuals seek to maximize satisfaction through their decisions because they face a world in which resources will always be limited relative to their wants. The cost-benefit analyst hypothesizes that, because all individuals are driven by this common motivation, they will tend to follow the same method of assessment, regardless of their individual desires. Since each individual is believed to know best what he or she wants and to employ similar evaluative methods, judgments of collective welfare are gauged by measuring and aggregating the assessments of each individual.

Deference to Expertise

From the viewpoint of cost-benefit analysis, individuals use their cognitive powers to fulfill their desires: to gather perceptions of the world or acquire more formal knowledge to better identify the most appropriate means to a given end. In addition, they seek to anticipate with greater precision the consequences of alternative courses of action in order to judge the potential gain or loss from a particular decision. Highly technical and esoteric choices, however, may exceed the cognitive abilities of the layperson. In order to get the most return from limited resources, therefore, individuals are usually willing to rely on the expertise of those whose specialized skills can help them overcome their cognitive constraints.

One of the first tasks of the cost-benefit analyst is to draw on the knowledge of experts to identify the probable outcomes of a given technological project. An expert's capabilities are judged by his or her technical credentials in the relevant field of inquiry. In most government agencies expertise is supposed to be developed and available "in-house." Although it is rarely stated explicitly, the analyst assumes that those who will be affected should be willing to defer to experts because of their specialized knowledge. Disagreements over estimates of the type and levels of effects, therefore, become a question for those with the appropriate skills to resolve, using technical criteria.

The Attributes of Preferences

The content and intensity of preferences are expected to vary among individuals. The characteristics of preferences, however, are held to be shared and stable over time.

Decomposability. Just as the gathering of information is part of an effort to maximize one's satisfaction, so is the manner in which individuals judge the consequences they perceive. The world of choice is readily "decomposable," or divisible, into separate, component parts. Decision making always takes place at a single point in time "at the margin," by selecting between amounts of distinct and irreducibly small increments or attributes of value. The motivation for such fine discrimination is that the individual wants to carefully calibrate what *each* expenditure of scarce resources will add to his or her relative sat-isfaction when compared with the other possible options at a particular set of prices.[1]

Individuals' preferences are "revealed" by their observable choice behavior and measured by their willingness to expend some amount of their limited resources for a particular quantity of an item or attribute at a given price. Applying the premise of decomposability, the cost-benefit analyst assumes that this expression of value—one's willingness to pay—refers only to the item in question and does not incorporate the context in which it is found. A desire for a particular good, there-fore, should not be situation-specific but should remain stable from one context to another (assuming that price and income remain the same).

The assumption that choices—and, by implication, preferences—are decomposable directly guides the method by which cost-benefit analysis estimates citizen assessments of major technological projects. A large-scale project typically comes as an interdependent package of values that will stimulate a distinctive pattern of development in a cer-tain location (e.g., from building a major airport, highway, or water control project). For the purposes of evaluation, however, cost-benefit analysts—seeing themselves as replicating the process that citizens would follow—separate the project from its surrounding environment and then break it down into a single list of discrete costs and benefits. The stimulative effects that the technology generates and the pattern of development that results from its construction are of little evaluative concern: they are reducible to divisible impacts that are simply being transferred from one place to another, without creating any net gain for society. Only when the analyst believes that the relocation will lead to the utilization of additional resources, such as unemployed workers, are secondary effects considered (Haveman and Weisbrod, 1983).

Decomposing a project in this manner implicitly assumes that the individuals who are affected have not acquired, from their past experi-ence, a particular evaluative interest in the type of technology, in a spe-cific combination of impacts, or in the pattern of development gener-ated. The information that experience offers is used to fulfill rather than change or influence one's wants. Once again, economists generally be-lieve, and the cost-benefit analyst operates under the premise, that pref-

[1]These assumptions are drawn from both standard treatments of welfare economics and the methodology by which those assumptions are applied to policy choices. A sum-mary of those principles can be found in Steven Rhoads's *The Economist's View of the World* (1985) or any current microeconomics textbook.

erences are stable and that when value change occurs, it is for the most part arbitrary and has no systematic relationship to past experiences and choices.[2] This expectation is reinforced by the belief that personal judgments are not shaped, to any large extent, by the views of others who may be in the same choice environment. Under conditions of perfect competition, for example, the cost-benefit analyst assumes that the evaluation of a single individual does not independently influence group behavior.[3]

The theory of welfare economics recognizes that there are times when the assumption of decomposability is inappropriate. For example, when two items complement one another, the satisfaction received from one is not independent of the level of the other. This interaction effect (e.g., the desire to have lemon with iced tea or gin with dry vermouth) will be missed by measuring complements separately. When preferences are isolated from experience, however, this type of value interdependence is rarely acknowledged, because most individuals have not drawn tight evaluative associations between many objects of choice.

The expectation of decomposability also serves an important practical purpose. It offers the analyst a supposedly realistic appraisal of how much each impact is actually worth to a broad range of individuals, by measuring revealed preferences (i.e., past expressions of willingness to pay). Of course, the past context in which those wants were expressed may be far different from the circumstances surrounding the current project. But since experience is not assumed to shape situation-specific desires, the cost-benefit analyst can use evaluative estimates that have been revealed in very different settings, so long as the constraints of prices and budget are the same.

[2]What is frequently perceived to be a change in values is attributed by some in the discipline to an "investment" (e.g., the ability to appreciate music) or "disinvestment" (heroin addiction) in one's "human capital" to produce a desired outcome (Stigler and Becker, 1977). A few resource economists have based their analysis on changing preferences (Krutilla and Fisher, 1975). Their work, however, simply starts from the observation that Americans appear to desire more "wilderness experiences" at this time; they posit no systematic theoretical reason for why or how this takes place, thereby limiting the ability to anticipate where or when value change will occur in the future.

[3]The individual's evaluative isolation is by no means viewed as absolute, at least within the broader discipline of economics. For example, altruism is acknowledged in family relations (and other settings), and the "bandwagon effect" is recognized by some to have a role in the attraction of certain "fads" (Leibenstein, 1976). Evaluative interdependence among individuals, though, is clearly rejected as an organizing principle of microeconomics.

For example, technological projects can cause health hazards that are roughly similar in their level of risk (e.g., increasing the mortality rate for a given population by several deaths in 100,000 lifetimes). The particular conditions under which this risk is incurred often differ widely in terms of an individual's personal ability to perceive and respond to such a hazard. The expectation that individuals divide the world into discrete outcomes suggests that, so long as they are aware of the degree of danger, the extent to which they can exert personal control over a hazard is inconsequential and should have no value independent of the final result. Preferences are not contingent on the specific situation in which outcomes are found or on the way in which choices are made about them.

Continuous substitutability. Having identified a single list of costs and benefits and sources of data that indicate where similar preferences were revealed in the past, the analyst then estimates the relative worth of these gains and losses. In theory, once complex choices are decomposed to particular items or attributes, the act of evaluation is simply a matter of determining whether one wants more or less or is indifferent to the relative amount one has of those goods. Consistent guidance across all objects of choice is provided by a person's "indifference curves," which specify the rate at which an individual substitutes varying amounts of any two items at different levels of income. Indifference curves are usually portrayed as varying smoothly and continuously across their length, so that the loss of each increment of one desired object can be made up by some correspondingly small gain of another item. The premise is that an individual's evaluative reaction to the external world, as gauged by the rate at which he or she substitutes one item for another, comes in small, fungible increments.

The significance of the assumption of continuous substitutability can be seen in the manner in which preferences are "revealed." If all indifference curves vary smoothly and continuously, then given a choice about how much to consume of any two items, one moves to the curve that represents the highest level of satisfaction one can afford: the point at which one's marginal rate of substitution is equivalent to the ratio of prices or the external rate of exchange for the items under question. Assuming this process takes place across all possible choices, all individuals adjust their relative consumption to the prevailing ratios of all prices.

The task of estimating the comparative value of any two items for different individuals, therefore, has a straightforward solution. One need not assume that dissimilar people have the same preferences, only that they have smoothly continuous indifference curves, so that all individuals adjust their marginal rate of substitution to the same set of relative prices. Prevailing market prices, therefore, represent a minimum evaluation for all individuals who face those costs. Some people, however, may have been willing to pay a higher price than they are required to in the marketplace. The cost-benefit analyst calculates this "consumer's surplus" by using past-choice behavior (i.e., longitudinal and/or cross-sectional data) to estimate how much of an item would be consumed at progressively higher prices.

This view of preferences can be easily extended to impacts that do not appear in explicit marketplaces but are frequently found in technological choices. Theoretically, individuals should also have indifference curves for these nonmarket choices reflecting how willing they are, for example, to incur risks to their mortality or to breathe polluted air. Therefore, these preferences can be measured in terms of the "shadow prices" for these impacts. The expectation is that individuals respond to shadow prices when they accept a hazardous occupation at a particular level of remuneration or buy a house at a reduced cost in a smog-filled environment (Hufschmidt et al., 1983; O'Riordan and Turner, 1983).[4] Following the same rationale, items for which physical substitutes are not available, such as a historically important building or an ecologically unique area, can be seen as having attributes of value (i.e., how old or how unique), the potential loss of which can be thought of in terms of judgments such as "option," "bequest," or "existence" value (Krutilla and Fisher, 1975).

The relative weights that market or shadow prices reveal allow the analyst to compare the worth of very dissimilar impacts, by assuming that individuals have already calibrated these weights and expressed them through the allocation of scarce resources. Notice, however, the implicit premises that a revealed-preference argument makes about experience. Guided by the evaluative judgments embodied in their indifference curves, citizens continually observe and adjust their consumption in light of the prevailing prices, even for the more esoteric and intangible nonmarket items. Moreover, the smooth continuous shape of these indifference curves suggests that, regardless of the diverse back-

---

[4]When shadow prices are not available, the cost-benefit analyst can use specially designed questionnaires to measure demand curves for a particular item.

grounds of different citizens, experience with or shared values about particular objects of choice does not consistently produce "lumps" or "kinks" in the trade-offs that individuals are willing to make.

Completeness. Cost-benefit analysis also presupposes not only that individuals know what they want in making these judgments, but also that their judgments are comprehensive and specific. The consumer in applied welfare economics is "sovereign" in his or her assessments. Yet consider the amount of evaluative information that this particular theory of evaluation requires of each individual. At a given point in time, an individual must have preferences that gauge the relative worth of *every* object of choice, no matter how mundane or obscure. Preferences must also be calibrated across all possible amounts of those objects for the diverse range of effects (e.g., gaining another attribute of historical significance for an increased risk of 1 in 10,000).

The clear implication is that preferences do not vary in their level of definition or specificity with experience. Since a person's desires are already global in their coverage and finely gauged in their application, the individual has no need to spend time learning about and then developing more refined evaluative reactions to those objects of choice with which they have little background. This expectation is particularly important for technological projects because citizens are presented with impacts that they do not normally encounter in the choices of their everyday life (e.g., weighing the worth of additional decibels of aircraft noise or irreversible changes in an ecological system). The presumption of cost-benefit analysis, however, is that not only are individuals well aware of what their preferences are for these items, but they have already revealed those wants, in most cases, by their past choice behavior.[5]

Self-interest. This portrayal of evaluation has focused, thus far, on the method by which individuals judge impacts, without identifying *whose* interests they consider in their assessment. An action of large scale, such as a major technological project, necessarily affects a large number of people, and the question naturally arises about whose welfare individuals are typically concerned with when they make this type of evaluation.

Most discussions of this question decompose interests much as they do impacts and usually begin by distinguishing between a person's self-

[5]The position argued here is not that individuals do not know what they want; instead, the question is how precise their judgments are and whether these assessments are calibrated, in part, by experience.

interest and feelings of altruism toward others. Individuals define their personal welfare, for the purposes of evaluation, as separate from the well-being of others, and then they judge how to best allocate their scarce resources between what they personally receive and what they are willing to spend to fulfill their altruistic desires toward one or more individuals or collectivities. Cost-benefit analysts typically assume that for governmental policies and projects, most citizens are primarily worried about what they personally gain or lose as opposed to being concerned about the consequences that others face.[6] Since preferences are isolated from experience, the expectation of self-interest is not surprising: there is no mechanism in this theory of preference that consistently orients the attention of individuals toward the well-being of others.

Efforts to recognize some degree of altruistic concern have not yet resulted in procedures to identify or to estimate the intensity of this desire in a theoretically consistent manner. One approach starts from the premise that a given increase in income should be "weighted" more—that is, be considered more desirable—if it goes to the poor rather than the rich, because the less-well-to-do are closer to the margin of subsistence. An unambiguous basis for calculating what those weights are, however, has never been established (Haveman and Weisbrod, 1983). Another perspective maintains that citizen preferences for this effect—aiding the poor—can be measured in the same manner as any other want, by how much citizens are willing to pay—in this case, for the benefit of knowing that they have helped the needy (an expression of this concern is exemplified by giving to charitable causes; see Hochman and Rodgers, 1969; Harberger, 1983). The computational problems of this approach are severe, and, as Ezra Mishan (1972) has pointed out, the reasoning behind it is circular. How much a person is willing to pay for a change in the present distribution of resources is contingent, in part, upon how much that person can pay, which is a function of the prevailing distribution of resources.[7]

The inability, thus far, to develop a means to measure and incorporate the individual's or society's desires to redistribute resources to the

---

[6]In a more general frame of reference, Gordon Tullock recently argued, "Most economists having observed the market and government for some time tend to think that most people, most of the time, have a demand curve, the overwhelmingly largest component of which is their own selfish desires" (1982, p. 167).

[7]There has also been some discussion of altering the rate at which future costs and benefits are discounted to achieve redistributional objectives. The argument has been made that government agencies, for example, should use a lower discount rate than the

poor or other deserving groups has led a number of proponents of cost-benefit analysis to simply advise decision makers of what these distributional impacts are likely to be. It is then left to that person to decide what weight, if any, to give to these effects (Stokey and Zeckhauser, 1978).

Judging Social Welfare from Hypothetical Exchange

Up to this point, the analyst closely follows the expectations of positive economics by reconstructing the manner in which citizens are expected to evaluate the impacts of a project. To judge the value of the project as a whole, however, the analyst introduces an explicit normative standard of how the assessments of different individuals *ought* to be compared. The approach is a straightforward extension of the underlying model of assessment. Imagine a hypothetical process of exchange between those who are affected by the project. If the "winners" could, in theory, compensate the "losers," based on their willingness to pay for the gains that they receive, and still come out ahead, the project is generally evaluated as being worthwhile. This social assessment is calculated by aggregating the present values of the costs and benefits (i.e., discounting the worth of later impacts to discover what their value is today) to yield a summary figure of net gain or loss. By portraying collective decision making in this manner, the analyst does not contend that this is what actually takes place; instead, it represents an "ideal" way to resolve interpersonal differences that can be used to inform the judgments of decision makers.

One might argue that this hypothetical process of exchange is a simplified view of the actual negotiation and bargaining that often occurs in political decision making. Yet it is interesting how other elements of that process are not included in estimating this summary assessment. An integral part of the politics of technological decision making, for example, is the debate that frequently takes place between supporters and opponents of a particular project or policy. When a proposal is first made, the agency or company that wants to build and manage the technology usually dominates early discussions by describing for the lay-public what the effects will be and why, in its view, most citizens are likely to benefit. After some period of time this characterization is challenged by prospective opponents. They typically question the accuracy

---

marketplace would indicate is appropriate in order to represent citizen desires to provide investments for future generations. The difficulty, of course, is to determine if and to what degree this preference exists.

of the technical estimates, based on either the testimony of their own experts or doubts they have about the motivations and past track record of the technology's sponsor. In addition, opponents often maintain that the impacts should be weighed differently (e.g., give more emphasis to environmental and social values as opposed to economic effects) and that other interests than those named by the project's supporters should be considered (e.g., the welfare of this particular community or future generations) in judging the project's worth. Once these initial positions are laid out, each side responds to the major contentions of their opponents in an effort to swing the assessment of the public in their favor. Over time, the debate tends to focus on the issues in which the differences between the two sides are the greatest and which strike the most responsive chord among members of the general public.

The response of cost-benefit analysis to the questions raised by a public debate is not to ignore them but to have the practitioner double-check the accuracy of the calculations that have already been made (see Ackerman et al., 1974). For example, does changing the assumptions about the expected level of particular impacts affect the overall conclusions? If substantial uncertainty about the outcomes is identified, the analyst can assess whether the project's rate of return is sufficiently high to pay, as compensation, a "risk premium," much as a speculative private investment must provide greater earnings to attract investors (Hirschleifer and Shapiro, 1983).[8] In addition, the analyst may examine whether the conclusions are sensitive to alterations in the assumptions about the value for certain intangible effects and can consider alternative measures, if they are available.

Consistent with the basic precepts of this model of evaluation, however, the analyst *does not* measure the evaluative reaction of citizens to the political debate. Since experience is not held to influence preferences, listening to this interchange should not alter the judgments of citizens about either the impacts or the interests that they affect. Moreover, since most members of the general public lack a high level of technological expertise, they are not in a position to evaluate the disagreements on technical grounds. As noted above, they should instead be willing to defer to the "best" available technical judgment.

Applied welfare economics presently enjoys considerable support

[8]An alternative approach maintains, however, that no public project should pay this sort of premium, because when a project's sponsor is as large as the federal government, the risk of any particular undertaking is "pooled," or averaged, over many projects (Arrow, 1966).

and widespread use because it provides a theoretically simple and powerful model for estimating citizen evaluations across diverse impacts and individuals. If one accepts the basic premise that individuals live in a world in which resources are always seen as scarce relative to wants, one can anticipate how individuals, motivated by affective desires, will weigh the value that each discrete object or attribute adds to individual satisfaction at a given cost when compared with all other possible choices. The structure of dividing, weighing, or substituting and then recombining one's assessments follows logically from this effort to maximize personal utility with limited resources.

This theoretical power, however, requires making a very strong assumption that, in most discussions of cost-benefit analysis, has not been explicitly recognized: each of the basic principles of this model of assessment is directly contingent upon the proposition that experience does not systematically affect preferences, interests, or methods of evaluation over time. In the context of a choice about a major technological project, the analyst makes at least four assumptions based on this premise, to which I have already referred. First, citizens' backgrounds do not influence degrees of comprehensiveness or specificity of their wants. Second, experience does not bind citizens' values together in more or less interdependent systems or structures. Third, the rate at which individuals are willing to exchange or trade off one item for another is not dependent on their experience with it or the specific context in which the choice is made. Fourth, the practice of speaking with and sharing common ideals about the world with others does not significantly broaden individuals' definition of interest beyond the well-being of themselves and their households. As a result, the analyst also believes that these attributes and preferences, as well as citizens' deference toward the technical knowledge of "experts," are not appreciably changed by listening to and reflecting upon the debate about a given project and those who are managing it.

Reliability

The reliability of cost-benefit evaluations has been criticized for many years by applied welfare economists. The debate, however, has primarily focused on the problems that arise in calculating estimates or applying this theory in a manner that is consistent with its assumptions. Cost-benefit analysts readily admit, for example, that it is difficult to generate reliable empirical estimates for all of the impacts that they face. Controversy surrounds estimates for the more exotic impacts of technological projects that have no explicit market indicators, such as non-work time, noise, various forms of human pain and discomfort, recreation, aesthetic concerns, and almost any other unpriced "externality" (e.g., compare Bishop and Heberlein, 1979, with Schulze et al. 1981). Even value estimates for which market prices can be found often do not conform to those necessary in a theoretically sound analysis. Unemployment, inflation, administered prices, and taxes, among other factors, can distort observable prices, requiring the analyst to adjust these measurements before judging what price would be set if ideal conditions prevailed. Moreover, indicators of consumers' surplus are often problematic, because at any single point in time the analyst only has a single empirical referent that reveals what a given population is willing to pay for a certain value change.

Many, particularly those in the discipline of economics, have been aware of these issues for quite a long time (compare Lipsey and Lancaster, 1956–57, with Krutilla, 1981). Yet what is often ignored in this discussion is that the frequent lack of empirical measurements for individual preferences emphasizes how dependent the analyst is on the integrity of the model of choice from which estimates are generated.

Imagine a hypothetical project with a 20-year life span whose cost-benefit assessment indicates that the benefits clearly exceed the costs. Relying entirely on this finding, the relevant decision maker approves the project. A skeptical sort such as myself may want to judge whether or not the analysis was correct. In 20 years can I look back at the costs and benefits that actually occurred and compare them with what the analysis predicted? It is unlikely. Where am I to find the measure for the surplus that consumers actually enjoyed? What was the real value of the leisure time saved or the reduction in noise levels? Did the analyst grasp the true competitive market price? How am I to know? These calculations are theoretical constructs without direct empirical referents in a real marketplace, either now or in the future.

One might argue that this is a problem of degree, of potential variation within the bounds set by the theory. Two disputants might not agree, for example, on the specific price to set for the recreational value per user-day of a newly created reservoir, but a judicious application of the model would certainly limit the range of disagreement and provide some parameters for debate. As the field develops better empirical measures, one might expect the upper and lower bounds of estimates to converge.

Such confidence, however, must ultimately rest on the adequacy of the model of citizen evaluation from which these calculations were originally generated. To see why this is the case, let us assume, for the purposes of argument, that once the project is implemented, there are empirical referents against which to check the full range of one's present and future calculations. Would this provide a good test of the power of this approach?

The answer, I would suggest, is no. The empiricist tradition in economics emphasizes that one should measure actual choice behavior—preferences that are revealed under real-life constraints in which individuals are forced to choose how much of their scarce resources they allocate between two or more highly valued goals. By this standard one could not place much credence in cost-benefit calculations, because no individual ever views the project as a whole and divides it up in the manner in which the analyst hypothesizes, nor are individuals necessarily willing to continuously substitute and additively recombine the objects of choice, so identified, at the rate that was estimated. Their subsequent choice behavior, after the project is built, is not relevant for answering this question because the circumstances of choice are now fundamentally different. Public decision makers have set into motion an action of such scale that it is essentially irreversible from the perspective of any single individual or group of people who did not find their concerns accurately addressed in the original decision.

What is at issue here goes well beyond contesting the limited changes that the analyst makes to improve the process of decision making. Few find fault with the practice of constructing a more careful and complete process of individual assessment than the average citizen is likely to follow (e.g., identifying and evaluating *all* possible impacts). In addition, the calculation of net benefits, as a summary of a project's worth, is such an explicit normative standard that it is hardly considered by most to be an unacceptable intrusion of the analyst's ethics (MacRae, 1976). On the other hand, if cost-benefit analysis *systematically* fails to measure what citizens want, then the recommendations from this technique may be useless.

Surprisingly enough, it is difficult to find a spirited defense by policy analysts that this *is* how individuals actually make decisions. Indeed, because the vast majority of economists seem seldom to doubt the plausibility of this view of assessment, they find little need to empirically defend its accuracy or utility.[9] For the uncommitted, however, this lack

[9]As Amartya Sen (1980) has argued, most economists perceive that their first interest is not to describe and explain but either to prescribe or to predict. Yet if one's prescrip-

of defense offers little reassurance that the theory reflects how individuals would actually choose if they were given the opportunity.

Cost-benefit analysis has also been found lacking by prescriptive policy analysts for other reasons. They criticize its inability to measure both assessments of intangible effects for which shadow prices are not readily available and the desire by some citizens to redistribute resources to other individuals. In addition, cost-benefit analysis is not very sensitive to political contingencies that decision makers face, such as the need to be responsive to the political power that interest groups can wield. These pragmatic limitations are reinforced by a greater willingness among policy analysts to question whether particular theoretical propositions of a preference-driven model of evaluation need to be qualified or redefined because they no longer appear to be realistic.

Decision Techniques

In recent years a number of "decision techniques" have been developed that supporters maintain can potentially overcome many of the limitations of applied welfare economics. The purpose of these decision techniques is to provide prescriptive advice on how to improve decision making when individuals wish to select the best possible course of action within given constraints (e.g., time and money). Typically, the new methods focus on complex decisions, where the benefits of a systematic approach are believed to be particularly apparent. Major technological projects such as power plants and airports are examples of this type of decision (see, e.g., Haimes and Chankong, 1985).

These techniques clearly differ from cost-benefit analysis in terms of their methodological approach. To gain measurements of citizen preferences for the full range of diverse impacts that various projects and policy choices raise, decision analysts intensively interview one or a few individuals about their preferences for all of the relevant effects. Rather than being constrained by the availability of wants that have been revealed in the face of often elusive shadow prices, the analyst directly asks the respondent how much he prefers one item to another.

---

tions are going to carry normative weight, they cannot consistently diverge from citizens' real wishes without an explicit defense. Arguing, as Milton Friedman has, that the accuracy of the assumptions about decision making is of little consequence so long as the premises accurately predict behavior is not helpful for cost-benefit analysis because one lacks observed behavior under the actual conditions of choice. Therefore, the policy analyst must do more than contend that individuals are acting "as if" they were utility maximizers (see Friedman, 1953; Stokey and Zeckhauser, 1978; Boland, 1979).

The decision analyst also typically surveys decision makers who bear formal responsibility for a project choice and often those individuals who may have an important but indirect influence in making that choice (e.g., interest group leaders or local citizen activists). By focusing on the desires of citizens who have the power to affect the course of decisions, the analyst hopes to have a greater impact on political outcomes than is possible with cost-benefit analysis (Voogd, 1983). Presumably, individuals who hold important public positions are motivated by a sense of responsibility as well as by self-interest (i.e., the desire to retain their job or influence within their group) to represent the citizens who are not directly involved in the political process.

In addition, these decision techniques propose various conceptual alterations in the model of assessment employed by cost-benefit analysis. One approach argues that the principles of a preference-driven theory of assessment are sound, but they have not been applied rigorously enough or fully extended to deal with the contingencies of complex policy choices. Another viewpoint maintains, in contrast, that analysts need to reconsider the generality of certain theoretical propositions. Consequently, a number of methods have been developed, based on making conceptual changes within the framework of this approach. Indeed, it appears that, with these alterations, some policy analysts are increasingly recognizing the possibility, at least implicitly, that experience may have an effect on the evaluative process.

Multi-Attribute Utility Theory

The decision technique that draws most directly from the intellectual tradition of welfare economics is multi-attribute utility theory (MAUT). The policy analyst begins from two now familiar assumptions: that individuals seek to maximize their utility among the choices available to them and that the process by which they consider different trade-offs can be portrayed in terms of indifference curves at varying levels of consumption (Keeney and Raiffa, 1976). The method of assessment for large-scale technologies tends to follow the familiar procedure of dividing, substituting, and additively recombining one's assessments of a project to yield a summary evaluation.

To derive accurate value estimates for a range of diverse impacts, however, the MAUT analyst argues that one needs to actually measure the decision makers' complete utility function, including the relevant indifference curves for the type of project being evaluated, such as a power plant, airport, or highway. This involves identifying all of the general objectives relevant to the particular technology, no matter how intangible the aims might be (e.g., minimizing environmental and social disruption in addition to maximizing economic gain). From these objectives, more specific attributes are selected so that one can estimate the respondent's evaluative reaction to the full range of possible impacts that could occur with any given site for a particular project. Consistent with the basic precepts of a preference-driven approach, outcomes are described to the decision maker in abstract terms based on the implicit assumption that preferences are not typically context-specific.

Unlike applied welfare economics, however, the MAUT analyst does test to see whether the assessments of these abstract consequences are independent of one another for the purposes of evaluation. If it appears that these outcomes are evaluatively separable, the analyst then poses to the respondent hypothetical trade-offs between two impacts at varying levels to determine the person's rate of substitution.

Cost-benefit analysis has long been criticized for its failure to measure accurately a decision maker's preference for dealing with uncertainty. To overcome this limitation, MAUT also attempts to gauge an individual's willingness to take risks by identifying when he or she is indifferent between an assured result and hypothetical lotteries in which there is a probability p of achieving one outcome and a probability of $1-p$ for the alternative result. The theoretical expectation is that, faced with uncertainty, a rational decision maker wants to maximize expected utility (the probability of an event multiplied by its outcome) by choosing the option that would produce the greatest benefit if the decision is repeated over many iterations.

From these hypothetical questions about trade-offs, the analyst calculates "weights" or scaling factors to determine the worth of each attribute as it changes from its worst to best value. Having measured the complete utility function for every impact, the analyst then estimates the expected utility of each alternative by weighing the value of its predicted outcomes and combining the total in a summary figure. This assessment only reflects the evaluation of the decision maker. Proponents of multi-attribute utility theory maintain, however, that the wants of the general public and of particular interest groups can be represented in the significance that a decision maker gives to different attributes or objectives. Thus, if a community's strong desire for environmental protection is greater than the decision maker's own preference in that area, the decision maker would simply increase the weight of the environmental assessment to reflect the wishes of the local populace. These preferential weights can also be changed in response to the relative political power of different interest groups or a desire to treat all parties in a fair or equitable manner (Keeney and Raiffa, 1976; Keeney, 1980). Alternatively, preferences for citizens' groups can be directly elicited from representative members of those organizations (Keeney, von Winderfeldt, and Eppel, 1990). These assessments, however, still have to be evaluated and scaled by the person responsible for making the final decision.

Multi-attribute utility theory, thus, builds on and extends the preference-driven model of evaluation that is the heart of cost-benefit analysis. On theoretical grounds, the analyst expects to find a complete preference ordering of decomposable wants that are continuously substitutable. Unlike applied welfare economics, however, this approach actually tests to see whether the relevant outcomes are divisible and what the shape of the decision maker's indifference curve is. This more intensive effort to measure desires could capture, to some degree, the potential influence of past experience, but the effect would be limited because the responses measured are to abstract outcomes and hypothetical risk-taking situations. The analyst could thereby miss evaluative reactions that a particular setting or combination of conditions might evoke from the decision maker's past.

Multi-Criteria Decision Making

Clearly, MAUT does not challenge the key theoretical principles on which the prevailing model of evaluation depends. Indeed, the effort to measure wants more accurately only reinforces the impression of the model's prima facie plausibility. Proponents of other decision techniques, however, adopt a more critical stance. Although they do not question the overall theoretical framework of a preference-driven view of assessment, these analysts have raised doubts about particular propositions and have proposed techniques aimed at overcoming what they see as conceptual weaknesses. This alternative "multi-criteria" approach to decision making (MCDM) appears to be attracting an increasing number of supporters (Zeleny, 1984).

Proponents of this broad, diverse class of decision techniques argue that a major limitation of both cost-benefit analysis and MAUT is the contention that individuals attempt to fulfill only a single objective of utility or satisfaction maximization.[10] From the perspective of MCDM, however, most decisions involve more than one criterion because there is no common objective scale to measure the worth of the available objects of choice. For example, in making even a simple decision between different apples at the grocery store, one must consider a range of criteria such as size, freshness, tartness, and aroma, as well as price. For technological choices, categories as broad as social or risk impacts cover potentially many more objectives.

Ideally, the decision maker should find a solution or set of solutions that is better than any other alternative on all of the relevant criteria (e.g., monetary cost, environmental protection, and the reduction of unemployment). What makes multi-criteria decisions particularly difficult, however, is that the criteria frequently conflict, insofar as the values that one can obtain on one dimension may well preclude gains on another (e.g., economic growth and environmental quality). The task of evaluation, therefore, is to select the alternative that simultaneously maximizes several often incompatible and diverging standards. The final choice is seen, within the constraints of uncertainty and the limited capabilities of judgment, as a "compromise solution" among competitive criteria rather than a judgment about how well a particular option meets a single ultimate objective (Nijkamp, 1980; Fandel and Spronk, 1985).

The methodology of many multi-criteria techniques follows directly from these premises. For choices about major technological projects, in which the possible sites and technological options are already known, the analyst has the decision maker identify all of the important objectives and then specify how well the attributes of particular alternatives fulfill the relevant standards. Only those impacts that are similar in their effect (e.g., are they economic or environmental consequences) are directly compared and evaluated relative to one another. The manner in which impacts are assessed depends upon the subject matter and the level of difficulty in quantifying the decision maker's assessment. For example, the analyst might use cardinal measures of dollars and cents for monetary costs, but for "softer" environmental effects an ordinal ranking might be seen as more appropriate.

If a single option is judged better on every dimension, then it is the

---

[10]These critics contend that a single overall objective requires all dimensions of evaluation to be "compensatory," in the sense that a small value on one objective can be offset by a large value on one or more other dimensions of assessment (Yager, 1978).

obvious first choice. As a practical matter, this rarely happens. Consequently, the analyst asks the decision maker to set priorities among the criteria to reveal their relative importance (Nijkamp and Van Delft, 1977; Nijkamp and Voogd, 1985). Another, less rigid method is to elicit the levels that one would like to achieve on each dimension and then measure how close an alternative comes to each of these ideal values (Zeleny, 1982).

The expectation that individuals have distinct "multi-criteria" represents a major qualification of the preference-driven model. Dissimilar objects of choice can no longer be directly compared and evaluated. Why individuals cannot equate two very different effects in *subjective* terms, however, is never fully explained. Yet some analysts point to empirical findings that suggest at least the possibility that past experience might have shaped the areas or "domains" within which individuals consider certain choices (see, e.g., Yu, 1984, 1985).

This effort to maximize gains simultaneously on several dimensions, moreover, indicates that there may be a limit to how much a person is willing to give up on any particular criterion. As a result, the trade-offs that a decision maker agrees to may not change in small continuous increments, especially when he or she is faced with the prospect of dropping considerably below a given threshold amount for meeting a specific objective.

Interactive multi-criteria techniques carry this revision one step further by arguing that individuals need to consider *specific* examples of possible objectives and alternatives in order to properly define the decision criteria that they use—in other words, preferences cannot be clearly established in the abstract. The decision maker needs, in many cases, to "learn" about his preferences by moving back and forth between options and objectives through several sessions with the policy analyst. Many of the multi-criteria techniques (e.g., goal programming and penalty models) can be used in this interactive manner (Hannan, 1984; Nijkamp and Voogd, 1985). An excellent example is the theory of the displaced ideal (Zeleny, 1982), which starts from the theoretical premise that the individual's "ideal" option is informed and calibrated by the *specific attributes* derived from the real-world alternatives under consideration. Thus, if one option has especially benign or even positive environmental effects relative to the other possibilities, this is the desired goal or "anchor value" on that dimension. For each of the relevant criteria, the analyst follows a similar process and elicits the best attainable value. The task of decision making, then, is to choose the particular option that comes closest to fulfilling this multifaceted end.

Through an interactive review of the available means, the decision maker learns what is feasible. Options that are clearly inferior on a number of dimensions can be excluded from further review. For the remaining choices, there are programming techniques that can be used to help measure which alternative is nearest to the final multi-dimensional goal. If one or more criteria cannot be satisfactorily met at the desired level, a search can be initiated for new options to try to overcome this constraint.[11]

Interactive techniques are interesting on theoretical grounds because they suggest that preferences are not subjectively considered as abstract entities. The possibility that background or shared values might shape those wants over the long term is not excluded, but "interactive" analysts believe that preferences are not changed as a result of considering a specific decision. Instead, they propose that a decision maker simply comes to a clearer understanding of his or her wants by reviewing characteristics of real options.

This description of MCDM has assumed, thus far, that there is one single decision maker weighing alternatives. Advocates of multi-criteria techniques recognize, however, that this is often not the case, and they have developed proposals for resolving value differences among several individuals. This process of reconciliation follows from the view of evaluation. For example, the analyst can have all the individuals who have a formal or informal role in affecting a decision judge the available alternatives, using one of the multi-criteria techniques. Those options that receive consistently low rankings across the full range of criteria and individuals are eliminated from further review. Through the use of scaling techniques, the analyst can then identify the alternative or alternatives that minimize the distance among the assessments of these individuals and comes closest to being the most highly ranked consensus choice.[12]

Analytic Pluralism

Proponents of decision techniques thus appear willing to critically judge and alter at least some of the central assumptions of the prevailing

[11]These same ideas have been extended to considerations of risk in which the decision maker seeks to choose the alternative that combines the lowest achievable risk with the highest achievable expected return (Zeleny, 1982).

[12]The analyst can also construct interactive procedures among the participants so that when each provisional solution is proposed, these individuals can vote or bargain to ex-

view of evaluation. Although the role of experience in shaping assessment is never systematically addressed, the alterations and qualifications of key premises allow for its possible influence, as we have seen in the preceding discussion.

The ability to capture the effects that experience might have had in the past, however, does not cover all of the factors that could potentially contribute to citizen assessment. The sensitivity to context of at least some decision techniques evidently applies only to judgments about substantive outcomes and is not extended to questions dealing with procedure. For example, the analyst does not ask those who are interviewed if their assessments depend upon whether they trust those who have formal responsibility for decision making and management. Nor does the analyst ascertain the importance respondents assign to the degree to which they can exert personal control over different impacts in the future.[13] In addition, no decision technique anticipates that there will be marked or consistent changes in evaluative standards or in an individual's willingness to rely on technical expertise *during* the course of public deliberations. For example, interactive methods, as noted above, assume that individuals use specific examples to trigger preexisting preferences and that wants tend to be stable. Moreover, decision techniques certainly do not seek to measure how procedural judgments might evolve in response to public deliberations about a specific project.

In sum, when one compares decision techniques with cost-benefit analysis on theoretical grounds, one finds general agreement that evaluation is preference-driven. Where decision techniques differ is allowing for the chance that experience and reflection have a limited influence on some attributes of preferences in one's past (e.g., decomposability and substitutability). The possibility that experience might play a more systematic role over time, particularly during the period that a project is under active discussion, has not been developed.

The Problem of Representation

In addition to the conceptual disputes with applied welfare economics, decision techniques, as a group, represent a distinct methodological

---

press their approval or disapproval and so provide a basis for considering additional options (Nijkamp, 1980).

[13]This is not to argue that analysts employing prescriptive techniques believe that project analysis will, or even should, remain untouched by political debate. To their credit every approach emphasizes the importance of being open and explicit about one's as-

alternative. By directly measuring the preferences of decision makers, the policy analyst attempts to provide more accurate estimates of assessments and to increase the political relevance and use of analysis. The strategy of focusing on the preferences of one or a few individuals carries with it the opportunity to develop a much more in-depth understanding of each person's wants and desires. For practitioners of decision techniques to claim that they also represent citizen preferences, however, they must believe that the person interviewed has the capability to develop a fairly accurate reading of the preferences of those who will be affected by a proposed project. If there is a single decision maker, that person should know roughly what proportion of individuals support or oppose the technology in question, what reasons led them to their conclusions, and how strong their convictions are. The decision maker must also be able to weigh and amalgamate citizen assessments to reach an overall evaluation, hopefully in a manner that is seen as justifiable to those who are affected.

Supporters of this methodological approach recognize that this places an important and difficult responsibility for gathering and analyzing a great deal of information on a single individual (see Keeney, 1980). Involving representatives of several people from different political groups presumably makes this task more manageable.[14] Yet some determination of the general public's distribution of preferences is still necessary to ensure that the most vocal or well-organized groups do not drown out the positions of the population as a whole.

The task of representation is easier if citizen assessment conforms to the expectations of a preference-driven model, with its assumption that citizens' preferences are well defined and stable. The decision maker should at least be able to estimate the broad outlines of what their assessments are likely to be, based on past choices. But if those judgments are contingent on the escalation of public debate, as individuals further specify their wants and refine their assessments of the credibility of the principals, then decision makers could miss how the laypublic's assessments develop over time and so fail to be responsible in representing its wishes.

---

sumptions and calculations, so that the product of analysis can hopefully be improved by outside input and critical review. But it is quite a different matter to suggest that the assessments that the analyst seeks to estimate will change in a systematic manner in response to that debate; this question has yet to be addressed.

[14]An interest group leader, on the other hand, would presumably have to know the preferences of the organization's members, ranging from the people with whom he or she has personal contact to those who simply pay their dues and receive a newsletter.

The quality of the information the analyst receives, therefore, depends upon the ability of those who are interviewed to accurately perceive the preferences of their particular political jurisdiction or constituent group. Among proponents of decision techniques, however, there has yet to be a critical examination of how well the individuals who are selected perform this task. One might excuse this omission by arguing that the capacity to represent is not as important as the fact that certain individuals have the *power* to make administrative and political decisions. From this perspective, the role of the policy analyst should be to attempt to improve the rationality of that process *within* these practical political constraints. The problem with this argument is that if a person does a poor job representing the preferences of others, then developing better and more complete measures of that person's idiosyncratic wants can hardly be seen as an improvement over the status quo and might actually make matters worse.[15]

Alternatively, if one believes that citizens suffer from important evaluative deficiencies and that administrators are able and willing to overcome the limitations to perceiving what is in citizens' interests, then agency personnel *may not need* a precise estimate of the laypublic's assessment. For this argument to be persuasive, one would have to believe that the technical and organizational background administrators and activists bring to these choices gives them a distinct advantage not provided by the varied histories of ordinary citizens and that this advantage tends to persist over time. To date, supporters of decision techniques have not addressed this issue in a systematic manner.

Theoretical Accuracy

Even if these questions of representation can be answered, there is a second and potentially more serious issue that needs to be addressed. When one reviews the manner in which decision techniques are applied in particular cases, it is impossible to determine how well these analytic tools succeed in accurately measuring the evaluations of the individuals who are interviewed, much less of those who are not consulted. Unlike methods that indirectly measure preferences, decision techniques actively intervene in and attempt to structure decision making. The purpose is to improve that process, so that a better decision is more likely

[15]Ralph Keeney (1980) maintains that the public is frequently uninformed about what impacts are likely to occur and that it is therefore difficult to measure what their preferences are. This is no doubt true with highly complex projects. The possible divergence I

than would otherwise occur. The difficulty comes in verifying these claims.

The actual use of decision techniques does not provide an answer to this question because, by becoming directly involved, the analyst does not know and cannot know *what would have happened if the technique had not been used*, whether the results were better, worse, or about the same as proceeding without intervention. If one is going to prescribe how to improve the process of decision making, therefore, it would be helpful to understand, first, exactly what one is seeking to improve. In other words, what is the baseline—even in a general sense—against which one's purported gains should be measured? Does a technique recognize and then seek to build on the underlying rationality of the method that individuals would "normally" use, or does it act in a manner that is contrary to the logic of this approach? If it does diverge from the process that would otherwise occur, what is the justification, and is there general agreement that this rationale is defensible?

Every decision technique is deduced from some theoretical premises that imply a particular view of decision making. Proponents of different methods often assert that their approach is more "realistic" or does a better job of incorporating a wider range of issues than other methods. Supporters of multi-attribute utility theory, however, have yet to defend their approach in terms of the larger descriptive literature about decision making or the findings that are increasingly available about technological assessment in particular. In contrast, some of the best-known advocates of multi-criteria decision making have begun to point out how key theoretical premises are consistent with selected findings (Zeleny, 1982; Yu, 1985). Indeed, this method of defense tends to be used in seeking to justify a major disagreement with the procedures of other techniques, such as cost-benefit analysis and MAUT.

This defense of premises shows an encouraging turn in the development of the models of evaluation employed in prescriptive policy analysis. Thus far, however, it has not been applied in a systematic manner. The exceptions that decision analysts acknowledge suggest that there may be more serious theoretical problems than those that they presently recognize. If one's preferences are situation-specific or consistently reflect a concern for interests beyond oneself, the natural ques-

---

have identified between the public and decision makers, however, is not due to differences in knowledge, and there is no reason to assume that, if the public and decision makers were equally informed, their positions would therefore be similar.

tion is why? What would produce this variation, and does it imply that a more thorough revision is necessary?

To argue that policy analytic techniques should be informed by empirically grounded theories of evaluation is not to maintain that prescriptive procedures must then mimic that real-world process. Research could reveal weaknesses in the method of evaluation that decision makers and/or citizens employ that most would agree ought to be corrected. Without developing a fuller understanding of how the process of technological assessment actually operates, however, it is virtually impossible to make this judgment in an informed manner.

In addition, given the difficulty that is increasingly encountered in reaching a timely and amicable resolution to choices about major technological projects, a descriptively accurate view of assessment might help to better identify the sources of contention and the means of addressing those issues in a political context. Thus, the development of a theory of how citizens actually evaluate complex governmental projects or policies can potentially speak to both the normative and pragmatic concerns of policy analysis. The task of the next chapter is to begin this process.

CHAPTER THREE

The Social Process of
Citizen Assessment

DESPITE THE GREAT intuitive appeal of a preference-driven understanding of assessment, I have argued that its validity rests on strong and debatable expectations about the effects of experience. As we have seen, the latest developments in prescriptive techniques allow for the possibility that the past does have some impact on evaluative procedures. Yet no current technique anticipates or seeks to measure whether citizens draw upon the deliberations of public debate to specify their assessments of technology. (Indeed, these techniques suggest that citizens have little incentive to be responsive to the evaluative arguments of public debate, because they come fully prepared, with well-defined wants for a broad range of substantive choices.)

Understanding how past and present experience might influence the grounds and process of assessment, therefore, is absolutely critical for judging the degree to which prescriptive techniques accurately represent citizens' assessments. By learning the methods of evaluation that different political actors employ, we can also determine how the laypublic's approach differs from that of veteran players in the political process, what the rationale for such differences is, and what role is therefore appropriate for the laypublic in the decision-making process.

The review of the available empirical evidence in the first chapter suggests that changes in prescriptive techniques are well-advised. Past experience in fact has very significant effects on the content and the method of citizen assessment. The literature on political belief systems, however, does not explain *how* the past influences the judgments of different actors for the wide range of evaluative issues that technological choices pose. More importantly, there has been remarkably little attention directed to explaining what effect an extended public debate may have on the process of citizen assessment. Consequently, we have neither the theoretical understanding nor the empirical test that can reveal how the evaluative capabilities of the laypublic compare with the methods of political veterans.

The purpose of this chapter is to use concepts from social cognition to develop an explanatory model of the process by which the laypublic evaluates the most difficult technological decisions. Key concepts will be reviewed and then extended to explain how this method of technological assessment operates. At each step of the argument the preference-driven assumptions of prescriptive techniques are critically compared with the expectations of this new theoretical alternative. Special attention is given to understanding the impact of public deliberations.

Theoretical Premises

In contrast to the expectation that individuals share preferences with common attributes and methods of application, a long line of research stresses the importance of cognition and experience in shaping evaluative standards and procedures. Herbert Simon's model of "bounded rationality" and his collaborative work with James March on administrative decision making (March and Simon, 1958; Simon, 1979b), for example, have helped to explain organizational behavior by examining how the administrative environment shapes decision-making routines. Building on the findings from cognitive psychology, social psychologists have constructed an even more generic set of concepts and research findings (e.g., Neisser, 1976; Rumelhart and Ortony, 1977; Hastie, 1981; Taylor and Crocker, 1981; Fiske and Taylor, 1984).

Experience is critically important from the view of social cognition. The reason is simple. All individuals have a limited capacity to process and manipulate the great amount of information that is available to them in any given environment (S. E. Taylor, 1981). As a result, the lessons that they learn and the interpretations that they share with individuals whom they trust from their past are used in dealing with future circumstances. As experience accumulates in particular "domains," or areas of knowledge, individuals construct prototypical views of people, roles, or activities that they commonly encounter. These knowledge structures, or "schemas," are defined as "organized prior knowledge, abstracted from experience with specific instances" (Fiske and Linville, 1980: 543). Schemas explain how the attributes and characteristics of the world are typically related to one another in particular contexts (Taylor and Crocker, 1981; Rumelhart, 1984).

Faced with far more stimuli than one can perceive or understand, one employs schemas to actively structure what is seen and how it is interpreted. These schemas direct where we look for relevant material in a given situation or what information we retrieve from memory to address a particular problem. When important "facts" are not provided, this type of knowledge structure can fill in "default values" (Rumelhart and Ortony, 1977). With greater experience, a more general framework is constructed within which specific cases or attributes are categorized and understood (Taylor and Crocker, 1981). The more developed a schema becomes, the more instructive it is in the future, as it allows a person to take in and interpret more detail.

Because schemas set our expectations of how events will unfold or individuals will act in particular circumstances, they frequently trigger evaluative or judgmental reactions based on how closely these expectations are met (Fiske, 1982). Individuals may also develop strong affective feelings about the prototypical activities or people (e.g., mothers, politicians) that schemas explain, and the degree of "fit" or match that an individual perceives in a specific instance, for example, can determine the extent to which those feelings are engaged (Fiske and Taylor, 1984; Fiske and Pavelchak, 1986).

Because of cognitive constraints, new choices or events are not encountered or evaluated as a collection of discrete attributes that are readily substitutable with one another.[1] Instead, they are perceived and judged in terms of how they fit larger interpretive patterns learned from specific experiences. For arenas in which one has a great deal of background, the characteristics of the world are seen and assessed as well-defined packages of attributes from particular organizational or place-specific environments.

Direct experience alone, however, is far too narrow a base from which to draw for dealing with the wide range of contingencies of daily life. Because of their limited background, individuals have a strong incentive to take cues from those whom they trust. The more frequently such cues are taken from a particular person or group, the more likely an individual will invest in and begin to adopt these more widely shared

---

[1]A cognitive schema includes "factual" information, or declarative knowledge, bound together by "associational knowledge," which specifies the relationships among these characteristics of the world and their connection to specific instances or events (Rosch, 1975; Rumelhart, 1984).

interpretations. Thus, schemas are typically *social* products (Fiske and Kinder, 1981).

Having to rely on the cues or the interpretations of others requires that individuals develop the capacity to determine *whom* they trust. In a world of competing interpretations, it is reasonable that individuals construct "procedural" schemas to help them determine under what circumstances they are willing to follow another person's advice and what characteristics are important in judging someone's veracity and competence.[2] Politics, in particular, poses a daunting array of complex issues for which no individual can be fully prepared. Citizens must rely on a social stock of political interpretations and knowledge if they are to impose order on such a challenging and dynamic arena (see Eisenstadt, 1954; Campbell et al., 1960; Brady and Sniderman, 1985). When well-defined substantive predispositions are unavailable, procedural judgments about the "players" and the process serve as a means to assess whose claims are more worthwhile.

The many contingencies of daily life demand that every individual maintain a large number and diverse topical range of interpretive structures. The use of any particular schema, however, is facilitated by organizing common areas of subject matter under more general cognitive and evaluative structures. Schemas thus are constructed and operate at various levels of abstraction (Taylor and Crocker, 1981). Higher, more abstract levels integrate more specific ways of thinking and evaluating by synthesizing the lessons learned from a longer period of time and the social judgments drawn from a broader and often more diverse base of individuals.[3] This general framework facilitates finding specific sche-

---

[2]Some authors in cognitive psychology postulate that there are "content-free" procedural schemas, which act like processing rules to link bits of information together in hierarchical or causal orderings (e.g., Tsujimoto, Wilde, and Robertson, 1978; see also Taylor and Crocker, 1981, for a review), but this is not the meaning that I intend here. "Procedure" refers to judgments about the manner in which decisions are made rather than to the methods by which one relates items of information. Moreover, my assessment of procedure goes beyond evaluating how "fair" the process has been (see Tyler, 1986); it also includes a judgment about the competence of the collective decision makers for dealing with highly complex, technical issues, their truthfulness in communicating relevant information to the polity, and their commitment to acting in terms of the larger interests of the citizens who are affected.

[3]In dealing with political issues, for example, one might draw from viewpoints one shares with particular interest groups at lower, more dynamic levels in order to develop judgments about specific policies, but these conclusions will often be framed within broader divisions based on party identification or ideology (Kuklinski, Metlay, and Kay, 1982; Sears, Huddie, and Schaffer, 1986).

mas and provides a basis for judgment when more precise guidance is unavailable.

Because schemas at higher levels address the welfare of ever-larger social groups, they typically frame issues in terms of collective rather than individual interests. To the extent that individuals adopt these wider perspectives and identify themselves as supportive of their interpretations and ideals (e.g., being an American, an environmentalist, a conservative, a booster of a particular community's future, etc.), they judge particular actions in the terms and at the breadth of interest these schemas provide. The hierarchy of structures, from general to specific, indicates that individuals bring multiple, overlapping levels of interest to their assessments of specific choices. Expectations of narrowly defined self-interest find little support when one examines how individuals actually think about their political world.

In the construction of schemas to address new areas of activity, the balance of influence between more general past orientations and current social interpretations depends on the level of one's previous investments in more abstract perspectives. The development of judgments in a new policy area, for example, is structured by whatever general judgments about politics one brings to a discussion, as well as current interpretations one shares about the issue with others. For those with more past experience and reflection, an abstract schema immediately offers what has been reliable direction in previous choices. Consequently, there is less need to take the time for gathering and evaluating social cues of indeterminate value. To use the terminology from belief systems, the more "horizontally constrained," or coherent, a general level is, the more likely specific schemas within that topical domain are "vertically constrained," or logically consistent, with those premises. On the other hand, if more general orientations are poorly defined, the construction of new schemas is heavily shaped by present interpretations of the specific issue or choice at hand. Of course, this requires potentially heavier investment in procedural judgments to determine whom one trusts in these new circumstances.

By examining the relative role of past and present experience, one can explain the procedures by which different political actors judge policy choices. Having accumulated long experience, veterans have belief systems that are horizontally constrained on multiple levels of politics—global, organizational, and policy-specific. The focal point of development within this system varies with background and political role (e.g., a legislator invests in an ideology with a broad horizon while an administrator specializes in a particular policy; see Pierce and Lovrich, 1980; Glazer and Grofman, 1989). Specific schemas about particular policy issues are developed and vertically constrained or structured by this broader and more enduring framework (Sabatier, 1988). Participation in past political conflicts defines procedural expectations about what is likely to occur when a new choice is placed on the political agenda and how one should act if one's views are to prevail.

Thus, veterans' past experiences provide direction for identifying and weighing the characteristics of a particular choice in greater detail. If there are going to be extensive public deliberations, veterans' background should indicate the "script" that they believe events typically follow. The arguments they hear from the "other side," for example, have little impact because these views are already anticipated based upon what has unfolded in the past. The veterans' own conclusions, moreover, tend to be reinforced over time as they gather additional evidence that is consistent with their expectations from members of their organization, who examine the new choice in terms of very similar schemas.[4]

Members of the laypublic come to policy choices with much less experience. They have multiple "levels" of political assessment, but their global perspectives are fewer in number and far more limited in terms of content, internal consistency, and impact in sharing lower-level interpretative structures. Most do not have well-defined schemas for particular areas of policymaking. Their procedural schemas, on the other hand, are relatively more developed than most of their schemas for substantive judgments, because these provide a common means of determining whom one trusts across a broad range of issues.

At the beginning of public deliberations about a new policy choice, the judgments of most citizens are going to be poorly defined. Only in a relatively small number of cases where they have background with the policy issue or experience with the particular place or event that is

[4]This "persuasive-arguments" explanation challenges an alternative and older line of investigation that maintains polarization of this type is due to social comparison. According to this latter view, more moderate individuals in a group setting move to stronger stands on issues because they feel "released" from the fear of being seen as extremist or because they desire to compete with those who hold more extreme positions. The result is a group-induced "risky shift." Proponents of this explanation now acknowledge that persuasive arguments play an important role in producing this shift, but they still hold to the belief that social comparison is an important and complementary factor (compare Sanders and Baron, 1977, with Burnstein and Vinokur, 1977).

at issue can they respond with clarity of judgment. Otherwise they must rely on general, common orientations and limited social cues that offer vaguely specified assessments. If a particular choice is of limited consequence, public attention soon turns elsewhere, and no further cognitive investment is made. With large-scale, controversial decisions at stake, however, most citizens should move beyond simply taking social cues and begin to construct choice-specific schemas from the arguments they hear in public debate. Lacking well-defined prior expectations about the policy area, they have considerable schematic "slack" to select *which* arguments and issues are important to them. Motivated by the debate about a specific choice, they are likely to focus on *its* characteristics rather than on arguments or evidence about the general policy. In the face of contending claims about prospective effects, procedural schemas are formed for determining which side seems more truthful and competent as a result of examining their credentials and actions in arguing the choice which is at issue.[5]

Assuming they are motivated to pay attention, there is no theoretical reason to believe that a significant portion of the populace lacks the capability to perceive or understand those arguments. Rival positions in public deliberations typically make claims based upon evidence that is justified or "warranted" in commonly identifiable ways (Toulmin, 1958). Perceiving the content and logic of these arguments is in most cases no more challenging than the cognitive tasks that individuals face in dealing with the contingencies of everyday life (e.g., managing a family, learning the fundamentals of language and mathematics in grade school, etc.). Individuals do relatively well in solving problems of logic and reasoning when those issues arise in familiar circumstances (compare Wason and Johnson-Laird, 1972, with Griggs and Cox, 1982, and Cheng and Holyoak, 1985). Certainly there is no expectation that a large portion of individuals cannot comprehend and then construct coherent or logically constrained positions among the multiple attributes

---

[5]This view of the development of technological assessments places considerable emphasis on the role of experience in shaping evaluations over time. It differs to some degree with a line of research that downplays the importance of debate and "issue-relevant" thinking. Robert Zajonc (1980), for example, believes that simple affective processes (e.g., exposure) shape attitudes without a great deal of conscious mediation. This approach, however, has been applied and tested primarily in situations where there is no explicit "advocacy," as there is in a heated debate over a controversial technology. I would agree with Richard Petty and John Cacioppo (1986) that the influence of experience grows when individuals have a strong incentive to engage in such a debate. On the other hand, the more primitive affective processes should dominate when that motivation is low.

of political arguments. Indeed, individuals are highly predisposed to acquiring information if it is already packaged, or "chunked," in a familiar pattern (G. A. Miller, 1956).

This "social-process" approach thus differs from the basic expectations of preference-driven assumptions about all political actors, but particularly members of the laypublic. The level of specificity of assessment varies dramatically with how much experience an individual has with a particular issue. When expectations are well defined through past experience, they are highly structured and tied to particular places or contexts rather than divisible and easily substitutable. Because members of the laypublic lack detailed background for most areas of policymaking, public deliberations are a critical period, as average citizens draw upon the evaluative arguments they hear to address the deficiencies of their experience and understanding.

The degree to which the expectations of a social-process approach diverge from perspective-driven assumptions depends on the characteristics of the choice. The key features that a social-process perspective identifies are not going to be particularly important for small-scale, familiar government initiatives that provoke little controversy over the level or value of impacts. As size of impact increases, however, a choice is more likely to engage schemas citizens have constructed about particular places that may be transformed by the project. Larger scale and more complexity also mean greater diversity of effects, for which most citizens lack the necessary background to make evaluations and so, again, they must draw on public debate for evaluative tools. Finally, when the effects are controversial, procedural judgments are increasingly important to disentangle whom one believes and why. Major technological projects are distinctive in having *all* of these characteristics.

This theoretical overview of the social process of citizen assessment suggests very broad differences with the assumptions of preference-driven theories and current prescriptive techniques, differences that should be particularly important for technological decision making. To understand more precisely where the expectations of these models diverge for technological assessment requires examining the full range of evaluative issues that these choices raise. Given this theory's emphasis on the impact of experience, it is appropriate to begin a more detailed study with the limited number of impacts for which citizens are likely to have extensive background and well-defined schemas.

Single-Value Impacts

The impact of past experience and social interpretations in informing schemas suggests that the assessment of particular objects of choice
is often defined by the specific context in which they appear. The most
obvious items of value that acquire special status are those with which
individuals have the longest and presumably the most positive experience, such as one's home, friends, and neighborhood. Research on the
determinants of community attachment and satisfaction, for example,
reveals that in Britain the most important factor is the length of time
one has lived in a particular location (Kasarda and Janovitz, 1974; see
also Higgins and King, 1981). Results from the United States also indicate that length of residence can be the most important factor, at least
for small communities (Goudy, 1982). Increasing size and density of a
city, however, appear to erode satisfaction, in part, one could argue,
because the possibilities for interaction that produce place-specific attachments decline (Wasserman, 1982).

Because major technologies often require large amounts of land and
heavy construction, their pattern of development may conflict with
place-specific attachments. Schemas that are structured by a particular
context and group of people present two problems for the use of prescriptive techniques and for cost-benefit analysis in particular. First, the
use of market price and current methods of demand-curve estimation
to calculate the worth of these values measures how much *others* are
willing to pay for the attributes of a piece of land, a home, or a business.
That estimate does not indicate the subjective meaning that actual residents attach to these values because they are never "forced" to reveal
these preferences.[6]

For example, when the Roskill Commission was searching for a site
for a third London airport in the early 1970's, commission members
encountered, much to their surprise, a rather dramatic illustration of
this type of evaluation: 8 percent in one survey and 38 percent in another claimed that no amount of money would compensate them for
the loss of their homes, location, friendships, and the like (cited in Lovins, 1977). The commission dismissed these results arguing that either
these people were being dishonest and seeking to better their bargaining
position or they were irrational. One can certainly argue about whether

[6]If one could identify these subjective values, the "cost-benefit" answer to this problem would be to estimate a place-specific demand curve through the use of questionnaires.

such a large number really felt that *no* amount of money would compensate them. Nevertheless, the general direction of the judgments—that is, there were very strong attachments to one's home and locale—is consistent with social-process assumptions and the findings on community satisfaction. The latter are especially instructive because they cannot be interpreted as expressing a self-serving reaction to a pending policy decision (see also Wilkening and McGranahan, 1978). Indeed, values other than one's home (e.g., a neighboring park, community organization, or building to which residents are attached) might be expected to attract the same type, if not intensity of, concern (Kirschenbaum, 1983).

Another difficulty of starting with the *a priori* assumption that judgments are generally discrete and readily substitutable is that the cost-benefit analyst may not even look for time- and place-specific judgments. The Roskill Commission only made its discoveries when it went beyond traditional methods; having made the discovery, it dismissed the results based on prior premises.

This second limitation is particularly important for decision techniques. If the analyst directly identifies and measures a person's preference for an outcome in a specific context (e.g., a park in a particular neighborhood as opposed to a hypothetical park), this problem can potentially be avoided. However, because the normal procedure is to select a very limited number of individuals and because that selection process is not informed by a theory of how project-relevant preferences develop, the decision analyst can easily miss an evaluative response simply by failing to interview those who hold it.

Multiple Values or Attributes

Schemas represent an effort to discover coherence in the different domains of one's experience. The world is seen in terms of patterns of attributes rather than a series of numerous, isolated stimuli. Thus, the interpretations that one develops and shares with others can produce evaluations based on interrelated bundles of values.

This can be illustrated in the way one thinks about and judges environmental values. Landscape features, for example, vary systematically from place to place in terms of qualitative type and arrangement. A vista in the Southwest obviously differs from one found in New England. Moreover, within these broader regions there are patterns that are more or less unique to particular places. If one believes that stimuli are evaluated as discrete items based on stable, non-context-specific preferences, then one would predict an individual's response by adding up his or her judgment of each attribute such as the number of trees, the variation in elevation, colors, and the like. On the other hand, if the manner in which one assesses a physical environment is strongly influenced by one's direct experience and by group interpretations, then a particular package or pattern of attributes often holds a meaning that is greater than the sum of its parts. Environmental psychologists have discovered, for example, that the meaning people attribute to the "molar" environment, or a place taken as a whole, cannot be consistently derived from its "molecular" parts. Apparently, there are "emergent properties" with wider levels of perception and evaluation (Ward and Russell, 1981a, 1981b).

Imagine a picturesque valley. One can think of each attribute of the valley as a piece of a larger puzzle. If each part is viewed alone, one can predict that the aggregation of these separate judgments would not anticipate the breathtaking impact of seeing the valley as a whole. For the viewer there is an "interactive" effect when these specific characteristics are combined. Moreover, one can anticipate that the significance of this interaction often grows with repeated viewings, as one learns to appreciate the nuances and subtleties of this mosaic and shares that appreciation with those of like mind. By the same token, if one degrades one piece of this interdependent puzzle, say spray painting graffiti on a large granite bluff or erecting a multistory building in the valley, it detracts from the other surrounding visual attributes, because these parts cannot be separated from the whole.

Although environmental impacts are useful for illustrating the possibility of interaction among multiple values or attributes, the same process can take place when other desired objects or activities are brought together in distinctive patterns that individuals learn to appreciate (see Higgins and Rholes, 1976; Fiske and Pavelchak, 1986). Any inhabited spatial setting, such as one's neighborhood, community, city, or even state, is a potential candidate because it combines a limited number and type of values (employment, aesthetic, social, etc.) that are spatially ordered in some fashion within certain geographical boundaries (see MacRae and Carlson, 1980).

Based on past experience, we might expect individuals to develop an attachment to a particular combination of attributes or a "way of life" that exists in a given area. It is not surprising that cities frequently try to maintain their identities by channeling and limiting growth in a particular manner. In the late 1970's, for example, San Francisco enacted a massive use of transfer development rights so that what the mayor called the "essential character" of the city would not be destroyed by unregulated skyscraper development.

A preference for a package of values, however, does not have to be place-specific. As an example, Fred Hirsch (1976) argued that many migrants to the suburbs in the 1950's and 1960's shared a common ideal about the meaning of the suburbs, as a distinct entity, which shaped their evaluation of its component parts. Hirsch maintains that the original "essence" of the suburb was its strategic location between the jobs, cultural opportunities, and entertainment of the city and the relatively unpolluted air, inexpensive land, and open space of the countryside. By moving en masse from our urban centers to these outlying regions, Hirsch contends, we may have inadvertently degraded both city and suburb beyond what most would have chosen if they had had the opportunity to perceive and act upon these changes ahead of time.[7]

On the face of it, the immediate problem that Hirsch identifies is a very old and well-recognized economic issue: the "tragedy of the commons," where uncoordinated individual action destroys a common property resource. The "commons" that Hirsch identifies, however, is different from the usual one, which is typically a factor of production such as a fishery or a segment of grazing land. What is at stake is not a level of physical output, nor is it the destruction of a number of desired items that are considered separately. Instead, it is a coherent package of values that defines or gives meaning to the city and suburbs as distinct entities.

Migrants who have moved out of the city and suburbs also have, according to surveys, fairly well-ordered ideas of the rural or exurban way of life that they seek (Zuiches, 1981). The underlying structure of values is apparent in Louis Ploch's summary of what recent migrants to Maine want to realize: "a simple life style, slow pace of life, peacefulness, serenity, friends, relatives in Maine, qualities of the people, general environmental quality, lack of pollution, natural beauty, and the ocean coast" (1978, p. 300).

To what extent such multiple-value structures matter is open to debate. Once again, market price often fails to reveal the intensity or even the existence of this type of concern. Present residents, for example, may place a premium on a particular combination of values found in

[7]Consistent with this expectation, it appears that subsequent migration to rural and exurban areas was fueled, in part, by dissatisfaction with what the suburbs had become (Blackwood and Carpenter, 1978; Coleman, 1978; Campbell and Garkovich, 1984).

their community which is not revealed by the amount that the last person who moved there was forced to pay (i.e., a "holistic" consumer's surplus). In addition, even if the aggregation of individual actions is moving in a direction that present residents dislike, the transaction costs of perceiving future trends and coordinating individual actions to produce a pattern of development more consistent with their desires may have prohibited action in the past. A technological choice, however, is likely to present an opportunity in which those trends can be perceived and the costs of collective action are more manageable.

Imagine a group of individuals who desire the combination of values X, Y, and Z that are found in a particular town. In the case of the migrants to Maine, these might be slow pace of life, lack of pollution, and the ocean coast. Imagine then that an oil refinery is proposed for that community and will negatively alter all three of these values. Harbor development affects the aesthetics and degree of pollution of the ocean coast. Increased air pollution degrades what was previously pristine air, and the secondary development from the project "quickens" the pace of life with rapid in-migration of outside workers.

With the simultaneous reduction of the qualitative level of each interdependent attribute, what is distinctive about this place for these individuals is increasingly threatened. Therefore, their rate of substitution for any single value is dependent upon the level of the other two values. Adding up these impacts fails to predict this interactive effect, at least for those who share this meaning structure (see Tribe, 1972, for a different example of the same type of problem). Decision-analytic techniques can easily miss this effect if they fail to interview a wide range of individuals and to test for interaction among project-specific impacts. Though the latter is done in some cases, decision analysts do not typically select and interview a rigorously representative sample of the general public.

The Social Construction of General and Specific Schemas

The vast majority of citizens are poorly prepared for judging many technological impacts. They usually lack background in the large scale and wide topical range of effects that a major project produces. Technical disagreements over the level and types of effects seem able to be resolved only with a highly specialized expertise that few members of the laypublic can claim. Without well-defined schemas to guide them, most citizens react, at least initially, based on more general interpretive structures. Socially shared political symbols, ideologies, or common orientations mitigate the worst effects of cognitive constraints and limited background by giving average citizens the evaluative direction to identify the side of the debate to which they are predisposed.

This "assessment," however, contains virtually no information about the particular project in question or, in many cases, the type of technology involved. It is based on the most general views about politics, technology, and the environment (see Kuklinski, Metlay, and Kay, 1982). If the debate continues and the rhetoric raises the prospect of very large-scale effects, citizens have a growing incentive to pay much closer attention to the competing positions they hear in public deliberations. Their more general predispositions offer a framework for gathering and judging these positions to construct their own project-specific schemas.

Common or symbolic orientations, however, provide limited grounds or direction for careful selection and assessment. Most citizens have previously made few investments in thinking about or observing technological or environmental affairs at more abstract levels of analysis. Because their "priors" about the particular type of technology involved are not well specified, citizens can be expected to selectively focus their attention on the specific characteristics of the project before them.

This process of assessment can be represented by a path diagram. As shown in Figure 3.1, the direction of influence typically flows from older and more general schemas to more current and specific interpretive structures. (Patterns of internal influence are represented by unbroken lines, and the external effects of public debate are portrayed by a dashed line drawn to the recently constructed schema for substantive effects.) Thus, citizens' common orientations directly shape their overall evaluation of the debate on the substantive effects of a project and determine which side's arguments will be used in developing a new, project-specific schema to make their final assessment.

Recent research reveals that common orientations are very powerful predictors of citizens' positions across a number of specific policy choices, including technological decisions (e.g., Kinder and Kiewiet, 1979; Sears, et al., 1980; Kuklinski, Metlay, and Kay, 1982; Sears and Citrin, 1982; Jackson, 1983; Conover and Feldman, 1984; Peffley and Hurwitz, 1985; Hurwitz and Peffley, 1987). These broader judgments vertically constrain specific judgments and positions. However, the degree to which they contain much substantive content that is

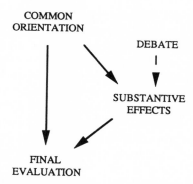

Figure 3.1. The basic path diagram of assessment in technological debate.

internally coherent and horizontally constrained has not yet been resolved.[8]

Measures of past willingness to pay are unlikely to register either the direct or indirect effect of common orientation. Large technological projects are usually built to maximize economies of scale. One consequence is that, for any particular area, most individuals do not have a clear-cut opportunity to express a past "ideological preference" that would differentiate between technologies, because they are only offered one choice, in the present time. Indeed, benefits from these projects are most often measured in a generic form (e.g., kilowatts of electricity or gallons of water) that does not even allow one to immediately tell from which source it came. At times, however, citizens can indicate a judgment, implicitly or explicitly, about particular impacts (e.g., how land values vary by distance from an oil refinery). The limitation of these measures is that it is difficult to generalize from one place to another, because the analyst typically does not know to what extent these past evaluations were dependent on variations in common orientation (e.g., see Blackwood and Carpenter, 1978). In addition, individuals' past expressions of willingness to pay in other contexts are not going to represent the judgments of local citizens about the specific project before them and how their schemas for judging develop over time. One

[8]Because the methods that were used in previous investigations suffer from important limitations in their ability to measure schemas, it is presumptuous to reach very strong or broad conclusions. Nevertheless, there is no theoretical reason to believe that citizens' predispositions about a policy area just beginning to attract sustained political attention would be well developed.

of the virtues of public debate is that new information and evaluative arguments can be raised and considered at any time before, and even after, construction begins. Past measures of market price obviously cannot reflect these new developments.

Problems in using decision techniques are no less troubling. If the analyst directly measures a person's preferences in the early stages of decision making, the results are not likely to include important shifts provoked by new discoveries in the outside debate or to describe the manner in which that person thinks about and evaluates the project's impacts in light of a general orientation toward politics and technology.

Indeed, thinking of a person's higher-order values as combining values and beliefs into interpretive structures significantly differs from decision techniques, in which values alone, usually considered separately (e.g., economic, environmental, and social impacts), identify the evaluative weights or priorities that are applied to specific effects. Thus, a major limitation of decision-analytic estimates is that they do not necessarily reveal the meaning that particular impacts (e.g., the different effects from nuclear- and coal-powered plants) have for the person being interviewed in terms of his or her common orientation (e.g., ardent environmentalist or proponent of an unregulated marketplace). If the growing amount of evidence about the importance of this integrative outlook is correct, this is a potentially important omission.

Procedural Judgments

The focus, thus far, has been how project-specific schemas develop to evaluate substantive impacts. Technological choices, however, also raise important issues of procedure, because this type of decision is outside the control of ordinary citizens and often subject to considerable controversy. Citizens affected by the decision depend upon the commitment and ability of collective decision makers to acquire the best available information, to follow socially defensible methods in weighing the value of impacts, and, if the choice is to proceed, to manage or regulate the technology in a responsible manner.

Citizens' dependence on others in every facet of their lives provides a strong incentive for them to develop expectations about the manner in which personal and collective decisions are made. The "procedural" schemas they develop over time offer a means for defining the types of choices where individuals are willing to rely on the judgment and expertise of others. They also provide criteria for assessing how much one trusts the information that another person provides. Assessments about the process of decision making, however, go beyond this, to include standards of how decisions *ought to* be made. Through their relationships with others, individuals develop identities as actors who make choices in a particular manner within the different domains of their lives (e.g., their degree of autonomy from, dependence upon, or commitment to others). The extent to which one's procedural standards are fulfilled in particular circumstances can become an end in itself (see Thibaut and Walker, 1975; Tyler, Rasinski, and Spodick, 1985).

Personal control. A concern for personal control reflects an individual's desire to perceive, react to, and exercise control over particular facets of his or her life, such as technological risks. In a market society and a liberal political system that extol the virtues of individual autonomy, it is not surprising that citizens place great importance on personal control, even if it comes at the expense of outcomes. Past research in the United States, for example, has found that a sense of self-respect and control over one's life rivaled material possessions and income as an independent predictor of subjective well-being (A. Campbell, 1981).

Technology often challenges norms of personal control. Powers of eminent domain are typically employed by the state to acquire land needed for construction. Once in operation, a major project can also impose significant externalities on local residents over which they have no direct control. Some impacts such as health risks are not only involuntary but also imperceptible to the user during the time of exposure, potentially increasing the perceived loss of autonomy.

I would argue that if a particular technology is seen by local residents as limiting their exercise of personal control, this procedural judgment is likely to shape their overall assessment in at least two different ways. First, citizens who highly value individual control tend to be skeptical of positive estimates of substantive outcomes to the degree that they cannot independently verify the estimates (e.g., a situation when one does not know when or if one may be exposed to a risk such as a carcinogen in the water). This sensitivity to circumstances in which information is scarce is a "rational" reaction to the world, if one assumes that individuals are aware of their limited cognitive abilities and those of others. The second, and more direct, effect bypasses evaluations of substantive effects altogether. Individuals may very well withhold support for a project precisely because something they value— personal autonomy—has been constrained. In other words, personal control is judged *as an end in itself* rather than as a means to some other

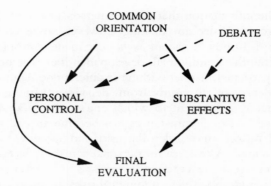

Figure 3.2. The role of personal control in technological debate.

end (see Tribe, 1972, 1973). Both these possibilities are illustrated in Figure 3.2.

Although risk-benefit researchers have not yet broken down this issue in these terms, they have gathered evidence that provides preliminary support for both of these propositions. Research reveals that the circumstances in which one takes a risk associated with a technology—such as the degree to which the risk is perceptible or voluntarily chosen—are crucial, at least in hypothetical circumstances, to its acceptability among the general populace (Fischhoff et al., 1978). For some individuals, this can be the most important factor in their evaluation (Thomas et al., 1980). Furthermore, it appears that there is wide variation by place and political outlook, indicating the importance of common orientation and local groups in influencing the value placed on personal control (U.S. EPA, 1979; Lindell and Earle, 1983; Fischhoff, Watson, and Hope, 1984).

Notice the contrast with the expectations of applied welfare economics, which presumes that individuals seek to maximize the value of discrete substantive outcomes when they face risks, regardless of the specific manner in which a hazard is incurred. Based on this assumption, one can come up with estimates of risk compensation from other places and circumstances (e.g., differential pay scales in hazardous occupations) so long as the *level* of the risk to which people are exposed in each place is the same. In defending this stance, the proponents of cost-benefit analysis argue that as a matter of social policy, it is economically inefficient to judge the outcome of a particular incremental increase in the risk to the life of one person to be different from that of another (see Schulze and Kneese, 1981).

This position, however, neglects the possibility that *how* one chooses has value to the individual as an end in itself, beyond the issue of what consequence results from that decision, an omission that is also made by decision analysts. This possibility was shown in Figure 3.2, in the direct link between personal conflict and final evaluation. If the goal of economic efficiency is to maximize the satisfaction of individual ends, then ignoring this preference would be counterproductive.

Furthermore, the path from personal control to substantive effects suggests that, given the opportunity, not all individuals would be willing to accept the common estimates about substantive effects, especially those that are difficult to verify. Prescriptive techniques discount the role of this path by implicitly assuming that individuals are or should be willing to depend upon the expertise available to and used by political decision makers. The empirical validity of this premise, however, rests on the actual manner in which citizens judge collective decision making.

Procedural judgments and trust. Whether one is supportive or skeptical of a project's worth also depends on how much one trusts the veracity, technical competence, and commitment to the "public welfare" of the agency responsible for managing the technology. The evaluation of that organization and the actions it takes in proposing and defending a technological initiative are informed by the common orientation one brings to the decision and by the theory of collective decision making that one holds. For example, do citizens believe that highly centralized or decentralized institutions are more trustworthy or more capable? Are past actions by government or industry personnel reliable indicators of future efforts? Surveys indicate that most individuals have distinct views on issues of this type, and these views have been integrated into their common orientation of the world and can potentially inform technological choices (Huntington, 1981; Vlek and Stallen, 1981; Lipset and Schneider, 1983).

Judgments about particular procedural issues depend on one's assessment of the motives of those in charge and the ability of established regulatory processes to monitor and control their activities. No one can trust, for example, the information that organizations provide, their technical competence, or their willingness to respond to new issues if there are substantial doubts about the interests they seek to fulfill. Any breakdown in the capabilities of the regulatory process only reinforces these fears. It is not surprising, therefore, that a perception of missteps in the process of collective decision making can lead to large and rapid shifts in citizens' overall assessment of a project. For example, case studies gathered by the U.S. Environmental Protection Agency (1979) on efforts to site toxic chemical dumps reveal that a failure by the disposal firm to inform local citizens and their representatives on the complete scope of proposed plans is interpreted as behavior that is indicative of future actions. Or, if it is revealed that an agency or firm has been unreliable in fulfilling its commitments, this can also result in significant changes in local evaluations.

In such cases, skepticism about a project's sponsor could lead one to directly discount that organization's substantive claims (see the path procedural judgment to substantive evaluation, Figure 3.3). In addition, the degree of trust one has in collective decision making could either heighten or ameliorate one's concern for personal control in a given case, and this then has an indirect effect on one's judgment about substantive effects.

Accurate information about impacts, for example, is often scarce and subject to dispute. External indicators of the primary benefits, such as increased electricity production, are relatively unequivocal, but there can still be substantial disagreement over how much it costs to generate the power. "Soft"-value impacts, such as degradation of the environment or health effects that may take years to appear, are typically much more difficult to reliably monitor, even for experts in these fields. Since those affected cannot independently verify consequences, their sense that they can maintain personal control may well rest on their judgment of the credibility and capability of the project's sponsor. Thus, there is both a direct and an indirect path by which procedural judgments about the collective decision-making process could influence estimates of the project's substantive effects (procedural judgment to final evaluation and procedural judgment to substantive evaluation to final evaluation in Fig. 3.3).[9]

Cost-benefit techniques do not even purport to gather this type of information, because the task of estimating the level of impacts is seen as clearly separate from the evaluation of those effects. Thus, one asks

[9]An important line of research has discovered that perceptions of the level of risk are guided in one's daily life by several very general "heuristic principles" (e.g., how memorable a risk is or how representative a risk is of a larger class of hazard) that draw on past experience to predict the likelihood of future events (Kahneman, Slovic, and Tversky, 1982). This approach also builds from assumptions that individuals must continuously cope with cognitive constraints. However, the exact manner in which these principles operate in particular contexts with different types of choices has not yet been fully defined, theoretically or empirically. My path model can be seen as an effort to specify the general process by which a citizen arrives at a judgment about the level and significance of a risk, as well as other impacts, associated with a major technological project in a contentious political environment.

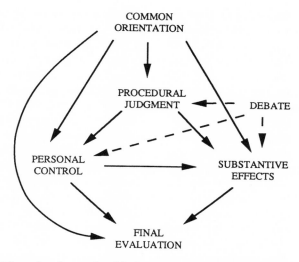

Figure 3.3. The role of procedural judgment in technological debate.

those with technological expertise (e.g., engineers and cost account-
ants) to calculate what will occur, and the analyst estimates citizen judgments of those effects from preferences revealed by past choice behavior. Once again, however, position tends to underestimate the importance of political and organizational factors to which citizens are often
responding.

A large-scale technology, for example, not only offers economies of
scale but also commits local officials and residents to a long-term contract and working relationship with a particular agency or corporation
(e.g., by building a water control project that is anticipated to have a
useful life of 100 years). Once construction is complete, government or
industry personnel know that it is very difficult, if not impossible, to
break this contract, even if the technology does not live up to its ad-
vanced billing. As a result, there is a well-known and well-documented
incentive to inflate the level of benefits and underestimate the costs to
win acceptance for what may be a "pork-barrel" project (Haveman,
1972; Ferejohn, 1974). Moreover, given the limited ability of others to
accurately measure impacts, a project's sponsors probably also enjoy
considerable discretion in the level of efforts that they expend in fulfilling each of their substantive commitments.[10] To point out these possi-

[10]There are many examples of an organization's selective attention to goals. Recent
newspaper reports revealed that the Bureau of Reclamation has spent considerable time

bilities is not to argue that they occur in most cases. Since they *are* there, however, it would be surprising, and to some extent irrational, if citizens did not want to critically assess the project's sponsor and the manner in which their interests were being represented in a specific case.

A further complication is that procedural judgments about collective decision making need not be limited to an assessment of the project in question. For many localities, the siting of a large-scale technology project is a more complex and far-reaching decision than those that are typically made. The project's sponsor can, in many cases, become an important and influential actor in subsequent decisions that go beyond the immediate choice at hand (e.g., school or mental health services). Moreover, a large project may very well represent a decided victory for a certain set of political principles (e.g., "public power"). The demographic changes stimulated by the project can influence the direction of substantive political decisions for many years to come. These potential changes in the direction of decision making may well produce an evaluative reaction among citizens that goes beyond a judgment of the particular project (see Bish et al., 1975; Singer, 1980).[11]

While the differences with cost-benefit analysis are clear, this perspective on the role of procedural judgments also offers critical insights that are relevant for decision techniques. Although these techniques try to be politically sensitive by measuring the preferences of the influential and by providing the opportunity for incorporating political constraints (e.g., differences in group power), they neglect an extremely important political judgment for technological decision making: whether or not one trusts the people who are in control and has confidence in the technical competence of their estimates of the substantive outcomes. An assessment incorporating these questions could produce wide variation across the individuals interviewed, because they can potentially shape a person's judgments for *all* of the impacts that a project produces.

Indeed, for many technological disputes trust is the most important obstacle to achieving a negotiated agreement between contending groups. Without some degree of trust, the incentive to reach a mutual

trying to maintain low prices for water for agricultural irrigation but has devoted much less effort to monitoring and cleaning up the deleterious side effects of selenium.

[11]Citizens' overall assessment of a project may also be determined by the degree to which they believe that the procedures followed in the case at hand are open and fair. Thus, for example, if the process were seen as "rigged" ahead of time for a particular outcome—and thus, by procedural judgment, illegitimate—one might oppose the project, regardless of what one thought about its outcomes.

accommodation declines, because neither side feels it can depend on the other to bargain in good faith or to keep future commitments. Knowing the preferences and power of the politically influential can be important ingredients for understanding the role of politics in policy analysis, but it is hardly a complete explanation.

Levels of Interest

To judge a large technological project citizens not only have to decipher which claims they believe have more credibility but must also decide whose interests they consider in making that assessment. For example, are individuals concerned only with what they personally gain or lose, or are they also worried about the fate of other individuals who are affected by a project of substantial scale? If they do consider and weigh the welfare of others, how does this process operate? The answers to these questions are obviously important if an analyst wants to gain an accurate understanding of citizen evaluations.

From the perspective of a preference-driven model of evaluation, there is an incentive for the individual to carefully distinguish one's personal stake in a political decision from the effects on other individuals. As described earlier, in a resource-scarce world, interests are decomposed in a manner that is similar to disaggregating the objects of choice, so that one can calibrate what weight is given to a preference for one's individual well-being when compared to more altruistic motivations toward others. The most common expectation is that self-interest is far more important than altruism in the calculations of most—but not necessarily all—individuals. The problem from the view of prescriptive techniques is how to estimate the significance of these relative weights and include them in a project analysis.

The social-process theory does not challenge the proposition that personal well-being is extremely important in citizen evaluation, but it does argue that collective interests are going to play a different and, in some respects, a more important role than prescriptive approaches assume. The expectation is that individuals typically bring multiple levels of interest to any political choice. The general rhetoric of political analysis focuses on the well-being of collectivities, such as communities, states, or nations, and individuals usually also think of themselves as members of broader social groupings. Since the public debate about government-sponsored or regulated technologies tends to address the merits and liabilities of these projects in collective terms—what will this project do for our community or nation—one can expect that a large-scale project frequently engages more than one level of collective concern for a single individual, as well as his or her distinctly personal assessment.[12]

A political ideologue, for example, tends to ask to what extent a specific action will support or impede the general political principles to which he or she is committed. A conservative might be interested in the degree to which an energy project relieves the nation's dependence on unreliable foreign suppliers of oil; an environmentalist might question what effect the project's waste products will have now and in future generations. Assuming that these same individuals are also long-term residents, and attached to their community, we can anticipate that they are concerned with the local economic and environmental effects. Finally, to the extent that individuals see their personal welfare as separate from these larger collectivities, this self-perception will be used to judge consequences that are identified as specific to one's self (see Conover, 1984, 1985).

A characteristic of collectively constructed levels of interest is that they can be inclusive as well as exclusive of a person's own welfare. For example, if a political conservative believes that an energy project supports his conception of the national interest, then this assessment includes an evaluation of his fate, as a citizen of that nation, with all others who share that status. Thus, levels can overlap in a manner that drawing boundaries between oneself and others for the purposes of evaluation would not anticipate.

The significance of a particular social or personal orientation depends, in part, upon how well developed its particular level is. Given the importance of one's self-schema in most decisions (Markus and Smith, 1981; Fiske and Taylor, 1984), effects specific to particular individuals are likely to weigh heavily in their final evaluation. Yet the structure of a value and belief system suggests that perceptions of self-interest alone are not likely to produce the most strident evaluative reactions that concern government choices about technology. Research in

[12]The view that individuals are concerned with a range of interests is not new. Social psychologists and political scientists have recognized, for example, that perceptions of "fairness" and "justice" in the distribution of resources can be at least as important as an assessment of outcomes considered alone (see Scheingold, 1974; Tyler, Rasinski, and McGraw, 1985). The position developed here, however, extends this understanding by revealing how these wider concerns arise and are applied to specific choices over the course of public debate.

social cognitive psychology, for example, reveals that the strength of one's evaluative position grows as the number and consistency of the arguments that one is aware of increase (Burnstein and Sentis, 1981; Rajecki, 1982). A lack of uniformity in these contentions, on the other hand, is believed to temper one's judgments (see Linville, 1982). Thus, simple agreement in the arguments that one accepts about a prospective project helps fend off nagging doubts about reaching an unequivocal conclusion.

A concern for consistency among levels of interest should be particularly significant in the context of a public debate about the collective consequences of a technology. One can expect that individual citizens feel more justified in taking a strong political stand—in effect, accepting or rejecting the value claims made by others—when they believe that these broader interests enjoy or suffer a fate similar to what they face. The person who is the most convinced and committed should believe that his or her own destiny with this project is replicated on every level that the debate addresses. Inconsistency weakens this political resolve, even for those who estimate that the personal stakes are high, if they cannot find redeeming arguments beyond their own singular welfare. Levels of interest, in this manner, can "vertically interact" because the weight that a particular evaluative concern has on one's final evaluation is not independent of the importance given to another.[13]

Collective assessments, however, are not only significant in the process by which interests are combined to form an overall evaluation; they can also be particularly important in the manner in which citizens judge impacts that are uncertain and subject to political dispute. Under these conditions, the individual does not know, at least in the beginning, what the personal effects of a project are. Public debate typically does not directly identify these impacts for each individual. Moreover, when the general level of effects is subject to doubt and disagreement, the citizen must first determine which collective estimates and interpretation to believe. Only then is one in a position to personalize a social judgment in terms of one's own individual circumstances. As a result, collective judgments come *before* and to some extent *mediate* and *shape* calculations of self-interest.

[13]This expectation is based on the belief that individuals want to think positively about themselves (Tesser, 1986) and that one's self-conception draws, in cases such as this, from public symbols and images (Wicklund and Gollwitzer, 1982). Since pure self-aggrandizement is not likely to receive a great deal of social reinforcement, it will not be the rationale that most adopt.

For example, based on discussions with others, an individual might first accept and support the view of one side of a dispute that a project is likely to bring substantially more jobs and increased economic activity to one's community. Having settled on this social evaluation, the citizen then attempts to estimate whether or not it is likely that his or her personal interests are included within this larger gain.

An important implication of this analysis is that as the distance between the collective and individual levels grows or as the uncertainty about the social effects increases, the ability of the individual to predict personal consequences necessarily declines. Consequently, the link to individual welfare is more difficult to establish. In extreme cases, this leaves *only* a collective judgment as the basis for assessing the worth of a project's substantive impacts.

In the literature on voting behavior, there is an interesting line of research that provides some support for this argument. Investigators have discovered that perceptions of previous personal economic gain or loss are poor predictors of political preferences in Congressional and presidential elections, while judgments about the economic well-being of the nation as a whole are good predictors (Kinder and Kiewiet, 1979, 1981; see Markus, 1988). This finding is consistent with the previous analysis because, first, it points out the important role of collective judgments in citizens' assessments of potentially far-reaching political choices. In addition, since the connection between national economic policies and trends and an individual's personal financial fortunes is subject to great uncertainty for most citizens, it is not surprising that this personal level of interest does a poor job of predicting one's national political preferences.

A socially informed value and belief system reveals, therefore, that collective assessments play a systematic role in the process of citizen evaluation and that this role differs from the expectations of affective models in several respects. First, the emphasis is on "levels of interest" that do not necessarily distinguish between one's personal welfare and the concerns of others, because the definition of the self is variable and multifaceted. More important, in a highly contentious political environment, one's overall evaluation is contingent on the degree of consistency across the evaluative concerns one supports, as well as the weight one places on each level of assessment. Finally, when uncertain impacts are subject to political disagreement, judgments about collective effects not only precede but also mediate estimates of self-interest.

A Dynamic Model of a Social-Process Theory of Assessment

The dynamic changes that the social-process theory of assessment anticipates directly challenge the validity of key theoretical underpinnings of a preference-driven approach and the findings of prescriptive techniques that rest upon those propositions. As we have seen, the attributes of schemas that individuals bring to a major technological choice do not necessarily conform to the expectations of well-specified and primarily self-interested expectations. Wants are not readily decomposable and substitutable with other preferences, nor do individuals necessarily share a general willingness to defer to the specialized knowledge of others.

Because of the limits of citizens' past experiences, their wishes are poorly specified for many key technological outcomes. Those standards that are well defined are likely to be highly structured by direct experience with the multiple attributes of particular places and people. When faced with large-scale technological choices, citizens should be particularly responsive to the evaluative arguments and procedural actions of political veterans as a means for overcoming the deficiencies of their pasts.

Perhaps the most important difference between the social-process theory and preference-driven approaches is that the latter fail to recognize and measure changes in evaluation that occur during public deliberations. It would be useful to know *how* important these "newly" developed judgments are in shaping citizen evaluations. What weight are they likely to carry, either alone or in combination? How strong is the evidence for these "present-structured" judgments? Because both the role of public debate and project-specific judgments themselves develop over time, an understanding of their importance requires reconstructing the stages through which a technological dispute typically evolves. The concepts of social cognition are used to explain how citizens would evaluate a project at each stage.

Pre-decision

Prior to the announcement of a proposal for a major technological project, citizens have accumulated a set of socially shared general predispositions—however vague—toward the substantive and procedural issues that are raised. Based on these prior judgments, individuals can be placed on a continuum that reflects their initial tendency to either support or oppose a sizable new project.

In the last ten to twenty years, technological choices have attracted sufficient attention and disagreement that contending positions about their merits have emerged and become widespread in the United States and Western Europe (Inglehart, 1981; Milbrath; 1984). The perspectives of most citizens toward technology and its impacts are highly abstract and not well differentiated. (The exceptions are projects such as toxic dumps that are seen as producing only negative risk impacts [Kraft and Clary, 1991]). In contrast, general judgments about collective decision making and personal control are probably more highly developed and exhibit greater divergence, because they are encountered and used more frequently across a number of issues in politics and daily life.

To the extent that individuals have substantive predispositions, most tend to be generally supportive of technological development because they believe that, in net, the benefits far outweigh the liabilities. Technological risks are seen, from this perspective, as a necessary cost of continued economic growth, but a cost that needs to be monitored (Martin, 1981). Whether these expectations are reinforced by a belief that collective decision makers are both competent and truthful about technological choices is not clear, because there has been little research on the manner in which substantive and procedural expectations are linked (Hill, 1985). In contrast to the prevalence of these "materialist" assumptions, an opposing position has emerged that, according to some analyses, supports "post-materialist" values and beliefs (Inglehart, 1977, 1981; Milbrath, 1984). This position questions the need for a rapid pace of technological innovation and developments and espouses greater citizen influence in government and corporate decision making. Thus far, only a relatively small proportion (10–15 percent) of the populace endorse this critical perspective.

Many technological projects can thus be assumed to begin with fairly widespread support. Whether that backing is sustained in specific cases depends on characteristics of specific projects and the dynamics of public deliberations.

The "Process" of Technological Assessment

First stage: Promotion. Discussion about a major technology typically starts with an announcement and a defense by a project's sponsor that a proposed project serves the general interests of the local community and is consistent with broader political objectives. The government may be responsible for either building the technology or regulating its impacts. At the time that the proposal first becomes public knowledge

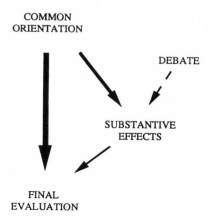

Figure 3.4. The first stage of public reaction: common orientation. A factor's relative influence is represented by the width of its arrow.

there is relatively little specific knowledge about its characteristics and potential impacts. As Figure 3.4 (recalling Figure 3.1) indicates, individuals react for the most part based on their common orientation toward technology by identifying the side of the debate to which they are predisposed. As individuals acquire more information about the technology's attributes, they begin to form simple project-specific judgments about the substantive effects. Because the project is not well differentiated in the minds of local residents, the contribution of this nascent schema to an individual's overall assessment is small compared to the effect of the common orientation, as the relative width of the arrows shows.

At this early stage, most people think of and assess the project in very general terms and at collective levels of interest (e.g., "economic growth" for the "county"). Even large-scale effects produce limited reactions, because they have not been interpreted in a concrete and easily intelligible way. Only those who live in immediate proximity to the proposed site or who have unequivocal information that they will be directly affected begin to consider what the personal consequences might be. Their judgments for or against, however, can be expected to vary considerably, depending upon how they interpret these impacts (Otway and von Winderfeldt, 1982).

Second stage: A credible challenge. The incentive to pay closer attention increases substantially when a group or groups who have some local credibility challenge the sponsor's positive portrayal. By inter-preting the same consequences in a fundamentally different manner (e.g., "rapid economic growth" becomes a "congested and polluted way of life") or by identifying negative impacts that supporters "under-estimated" or failed to mention ("negligible risks" become "untested hazards"), the new opponents motivate many to begin to look for more specific reasons to justify their initial and vaguely defined assessments. Because most citizens have few preconceptions about the policy area, they are far more interested in learning about and evaluating the char-acteristics of the specific project before them.

Citizens give the largest *possible* impacts the closest scrutiny. The scale of effect in particular topical areas such as economic or environ-mental impacts defines the stakes that are at issue. It is no surprise that health risks attract the greatest attention, because the consequences could so adversely affect specific people, as well as general principles (sanctity of human life) that most hold dear. As the scale of effect grows, uncertainty also tends to increase about the chances that either positive or negative effects will actually occur. To contend with ques-tions of uncertainty about substantive impacts, particularly health risks, individuals construct and increasingly rely on project-specific proce-dural evaluations.

Because they require less information, judgments about personal control are developed earlier than assessments about the competence and trustworthiness of decision makers. Reaching an initial appraisal about personal control requires learning about the characteristics of the substantive effects, usually one of the first topics of public discussion. The initial exchange between the principals, for example, is likely to reveal whether there is the possibility of large impacts on the local econ-omy or sizable externalities such as additional pollution or risks to pub-lic health over which individuals will have no direct control.

In contrast, judging the integrity and ability of collective decision makers typically requires more time and information. Just discovering who the principal actors are and what their relationship to one another is can be difficult. (For example, which federal, state, and local agencies are involved and what is their connection to the sponsor of the project?) More importantly, strong judgments about decision makers require some passage of time in which they establish a "track record" of behav-ior that instills either trust or doubt, based on the citizens' views of how responsible decision makers should act.

Citizens' first efforts at choosing between the arguments of sup-porters and critics, therefore, should be dominated, as Figure 3.5 (re-

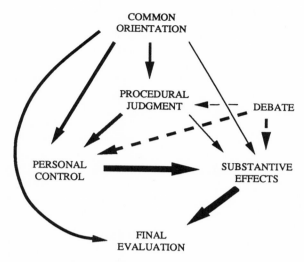

Figure 3.5. The second stage of public reaction: personal control and procedural judgment. A factor's relative influence is represented by the width of its arrow.

calling Figure 3.3) indicates, by their initial conclusions about personal control and, to a lesser extent, by their perceptions of the credibility of those who are in positions of authority. Because the debate is still new and the principals have had little time to act, procedural judgments are limited in scope and are largely confined to gauging the likely scale of the substantive impacts. A project supporter, thus, could weaken or even change his initial assessment if doubts are raised about the credibility of the sponsor or if he learns that he would be unable to perceive negative health effects at the time of exposure (e.g., releases of carcinogens in the air or water). With a more clearly articulated set of competing positions about substantive effects, the level of interests at which the project is evaluated becomes less abstract for an increasing number of citizens. Perceptions of what the community or even the neighborhood might win or lose gain definition.

Third stage: Escalating controversy. The debate is now fully engaged. The principals have laid out contending positions on multiple levels of interest, and each side has had a chance to respond to the arguments of their opponents. The rhetoric focuses on a limited number of specific impacts whose scale of effect and intensity of evaluation is subject to considerable dispute.

Motived by the possibility that high stakes are at issue, the majority of citizens are now aware of the positions on both sides of the debate. They have constructed their own assessments by selectively choosing and weighing the arguments they believe are particularly significant and cogent for judging the choice before them. The positions they choose are limited in number because they are socially defined by the poles of public deliberations and the common predispositions that the population as a whole brings to the dispute. Indeed, by having observed what is now a substantial and often heated exchange, they can place themselves on a social continuum of positions between the supporters and opponents. The increased impact of public debate and reliance on project-specific schemas is portrayed in Figure 3.6. The width of the arrows in the lower part of the path model reveals the extent to which assessment is now present-structured.

Further movement toward support or opposition can come from new discoveries about the project itself or from actions taken by the principals in the debate. New "events" affect both substantive and procedural judgments. A report by an outside "objective" organization, for example, might challenge perceptions about the scale of effect and alter one's substantive assessment. Because the positions of the protagonists are now well defined and widely disseminated, new information also influences perceptions about the competence and integrity of the principals—whether one side has been consistently proven to be right or wrong, for example. The manner in which supporters and opponents conduct themselves during the debate gives further definition to procedural judgments. (Notice how the significance of procedural judgment has expanded at this stage in Fig. 3.6.).

A change in the assessment of collective decision makers can heighten or assuage doubts about their ability to understand and respond to the risks that the project poses. As the level of concern about personal control increases, driven by questions about the credibility of the decision makers, this issue is increasingly seen as an end in itself rather than a means to an end. Early in the debate, perceived threats to personal control are assessed in hypothetical terms, as something still indeterminate. With the final decision close at hand, however, the perceived loss of autonomy is more apparent as individuals realize that the project might well be built, even though they do not trust those who will construct or manage it.

Slower more subtle shifts in a person's overall evaluation also take place as citizens think through their own interests and the levels of eval-

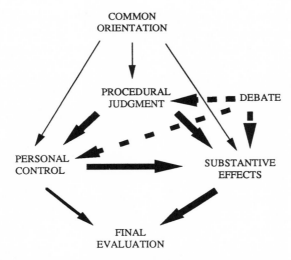

Figure 3.6. The third stage of public reaction: procedural judgment and public debate. A factor's relative influence is represented by the width of its arrow.

uative concern that they share with others. By using procedural judgments to contend with uncertainty, individuals are now more assured of their collective estimates and assessments of the project's impacts. As a result, they are better able to personalize these general assessments of the technology's effects in terms of their own circumstances. If a citizen concludes that the personal effects are significant, this strengthens the evaluative conclusions reached at a broader social level (typically the community or some part of it). With more time to debate the issue, the number of levels of interest increases, as each side tries to build its case and claim the support of the widest possible range of interests. To the extent that these arguments are accepted as consistent and mutually reinforcing on all levels, the populace becomes more divided, as greater numbers move to the extremes of support or opposition.

Concluding Thoughts

Seen in broad overview, what is striking about this process of technological assessment is the extent to which the schemas that develop *during* public deliberations increasingly dominate citizen assessments. The predispositions that individuals bring to a choice provide only a general orientation toward impacts that they have not frequently encountered before. As the dispute becomes more contentious, individuals have a growing incentive to draw and reflect upon the more specific substantive assessments offered in public discussions. The specific actions of the principals play a potentially important role as they become the focal point for determining whether this project is well managed and likely to produce the outcomes they claim. The collective terms of this ongoing debate "cue" the broader interests individuals developed in the past, and help define the evaluative importance of those interests.

Thus, ironically, the very factors that prescriptive-analytic techniques omit from consideration appear to be the most significant for particularly difficult and contentious technological choices, precisely the situations in which some estimate of citizen assessment is most needed. But how accurate is this new view of citizen assessment? Studies of technological and political assessment certainly provide partial support for particular propositions. For example, the investigation by Kuklinski and associates (1982) discovered a pattern of vertical constraint quite similar to the path model in the first stage (Figure 3.4). Other studies support more limited propositions about the second stage, such as the importance of procedural factors, collective interests, and exposure to new information (see, e.g., Fischoff et al., 1978; Kinder and Kiewiet, 1981; Markus, 1988; Zaller, 1991).

The most basic propositions about the impact of public debate and the construction of project-specific schemas, however, have not been tested. These theoretical propositions push well beyond current expectations. There has to be a high level of collective attention to and reflection on public deliberations for a continuum of social positions to emerge among the general public. Even the more optimistic views of the laypublic's methods have only supported the belief that there are reasons—however vaguely defined—for its judgments (i.e., they are vertically constrained; see Hurwitz and Peffley, 1987). The more enduring view of belief systems strongly argues against the prospect that citizens are likely to perceive and construct coherent, multi-attribute positions. Some scholars doubt whether the laypublic even has the capability to respond in this manner (Smith, 1989).

I believe that the concepts from social cognition lead us to expect a very different reaction *if* citizens are given sufficient motivation and information, a reaction that directly challenges the prevailing assumptions underlying *both* prescriptive techniques and current empirical models of citizen assessment. Without an empirical test of how the public responds to an extended debate about a major technology, the past literature remains inconclusive. After a review in Chapter 4 of the models for assessment used by political veterans, we will turn in Chapter 5 to a study that begins the process of such an empirical test.

CHAPTER FOUR

Political Veterans and Their Past-Structured Assessments

THE SOCIAL-PROCESS view of citizen assessment dramatically diverges from the expectations of preference-driven theories, as we have seen. It argues that citizens are not well prepared in advance for evaluating most political issues—certainly not complex technological choices. The process by which they develop their judgments, moreover, is fundamentally social in character, a product of public debate about both procedural and substantive issues. This new theoretical perspective on citizen evaluation not only challenges the accuracy of current prescriptive techniques but also raises the difficult question of what weight *ought* to be placed on the laypublic's judgments. In a world in which experience systematically shapes the grounds and methods of evaluation, it is no longer possible to believe that political actors share the same evaluative skills. To judge who is best qualified to make a decision, we need an assessment of the relative strengths and weaknesses of the various participants.

The actual procedures for making technological choices have long operated on the assumption that experience shapes evaluative procedures. Government administrators who have extensive technical and evaluative backgrounds are seen as having impressive decision-making skills and, as a result, have always enjoyed considerable autonomy. By contrast, the role of the laypublic is essentially passive and carries little or no weight except through the actions of organized groups.

The capabilities of agency personnel, however, have been reassessed in recent years. As noted in Chapter 1, administrators have been faulted for their failure to understand or take into consideration a wide range of "soft" impacts. Critics have argued that agency personnel have neither the interest nor the expertise to identify and judge environmental, social, and historical values. As a result, government agencies are now required to gather information about the full range of effects of any "major" federal action. Individuals who have the appropriate interests and skills are asked to participate in the impact analysis to improve the quality of the information and to pressure the bureaucracy to give neglected effects their proper weight in reaching particular decisions.

Much of the work of scholars and political reformers now focuses on discovering new means to improve the operation of these decision-making procedures. Analysts are concerned with learning how to better "mediate" misunderstandings among contending groups or between political activists and government agencies (Amy, 1983; Bingham, 1987). Others investigate formal methods of bargaining so that compromises that are acceptable to all groups can be more easily discovered (Bacow and Wheeler, 1984). The more current work in prescriptive techniques is consistent with these trends because it seeks to measure the preferences of representatives from opposing groups.

Surprisingly absent from these new developments, however, is any critical debate about whether the circle of "players" in this latest series of reforms is adequately defined (Fiorino, 1990). This is not an idle question. Technological choices are particularly challenging because of the broad range of evaluative issues that must be carefully weighed to reach a final decision. Major projects usually have large-scale and enduring effects and present combinations of impacts that vary widely from one choice to the next. Those who are responsible for making or influencing the overall assessment need well-calibrated skills to balance competing interests.

The purpose of this chapter is to extend my explanation of citizen assessment to include administrators and political activists, so that their methods of assessment can be critically evaluated in light of the demands of technological choices. With such an analysis of the strengths and weaknesses of political veterans, we can begin to judge whether the laypublic's method of assessment, as described in Chapter 3, can make an effective contribution to technological decision making. My analysis builds directly on the key concepts introduced in Chapter 3. Administrators and activists share the same cognitive limits as the general public. Where they differ, and differ enormously, is their level of experience with particular technologies and technological impacts. We must begin, therefore, with their past if we are to understand how they reach judgments in the present.

Noticeably absent from this examination are elected officials. One might imagine that they are obvious candidates for making these difficult choices. They have the resources to learn what the impacts are, and through their control of the budget and the appointment process, they can influence, if not direct, how the bureaucracy exercises its statutory authority (see Moe, 1984; Bendor, Taylor, and Van Gaalen, 1987). They have certainly used this power on many occasions in the past, and their background presumably prepares them for representing their constituents' interests. The current role of elected officials in making the most difficult choices, however, is largely passive, as they respond to the actions and arguments of others.

The willingness of elected representatives to use their power over the bureaucracy largely depends on how a particular choice is likely to be perceived by constituents. If a new technological initiative enjoys strong popular support or if representatives can infer that it would win approval based on past choices, they can be expected to move administrators in that direction. The incentive to act, however, declines as the perceived benefits become more ambiguous. The prospect that a decision might spark strong but conflicting assessments is only likely to dissuade legislators from becoming more directly involved. The irony is that elected representatives have the strongest motivation to provide evaluative direction for the "easiest choices," in which citizen or interest group assessments are well defined and tend strongly toward either support or opposition.

It is not surprising then that as technological decisions became more controversial, Congress did not step in to resolve these disputes on a case-by-case basis. Instead, representatives constrained the administrators' discretion by reforming and politicizing the decision-making process.[1] By observing how a particular issue develops, an elected official can, based on the likely political consequences, choose to become involved or not. For the purposes of this analysis, then, it seems reasonable to leave elected officials in the background.

Administrators

The political actors with the greatest amount of technical training and evaluative experience in making technological decisions are the ad-

[1]There have also been other changes that limit administrative discretion. The courts are now much more willing to review the actions of "expert" administrative agencies on both procedural and substantive grounds (O'Brien, 1986). Moreover, as a response to escalating budget deficits, the Office of Management and Budget has been more aggressive in identifying policies that it considers to be wasteful or to have detrimental economic consequences (Andrews and Sansone, 1984).

ministrators who work in federal, state, and local agencies. These agencies have the resources to hire persons with specialized knowledge in their respective areas of responsibility. Those who work at the highest levels of these agencies, moreover, have directly faced the problems of weighing the value of technological projects and policies on a more frequent basis than any other political actor.

While this extensive background provides administrators with impressive skills, a list of formal credentials or an account of an individual's past history of decision making does not reveal the manner in which that experience and education is actually used. No one could possibly retain or apply this massive amount of information to each new decision faced. James March and Herbert Simon (1958) have argued that, as a means of cognitive economy, administrators must simplify decision making into more accessible patterns that draw directly from their organizational experience.

According to this view, complex decisions are made more manageable by breaking them down into smaller components, which the organization assigns to particular offices or departments. Rather than examine all possible alternatives and their associated effects, the decision maker examines one or, at most, a few familiar options and selected impacts. Administrators are hesitant to base their future on uncertain outcomes and, when forced, tend to employ fairly simple models to predict, based on their past expectations, what is most likely to occur. Standards of evaluation are defined by what the organization has found to be "good enough" in a particular situation. The first alternative found that satisfies this standard is chosen. When decisions are repeated over time, predictable routines that offer guidance for each step are developed and shared with others (Simon, 1957; March and Simon, 1958; and see also March and Olsen, 1989).

There is a strong incentive to draw on and use preexisting procedures. Lower-level jobs are performed with little conscious deliberation by relatively simple standard operating procedures. At higher levels, less precise, but still identifiable, "programs" and "repertoires" exist to ensure the coordinated actions among departments or divisions involved in a common task. For major decisions, differences in background and approach among broad segments of an organization produce predictable strains that must be "negotiated" on a case by case basis.

Individuals within a government agency, however, tend to share common predispositions about their organization's primary role or "mission," and these act to limit the range of disagreement (Allison, 1971; Halperin and Kanter, 1973; see also Light, 1983; Kingdon, 1984). The development or regulation of particular technologies or classes of technological activities typically requires a high level of functional interdependence (e.g., research, development, construction, inspection, and maintenance), and this "integrated" background provides a well-defined sense of purpose. Administrators learn to focus their attention on one or a few means of solving a particular problem and on the importance of the benefits that those options produce. Certain agencies, such as the Nuclear Regulatory Commission and the National Highway and Safety Administration, are literally built around a given type of technology and its particular demands. A similar though more general focus can be seen in the Air Force and the Army Corps of Engineers (see, e.g., Mazmanian and Nienaber, 1979).

Internal decision-making procedures are primarily concerned with matters of substance, such as the means of constructing or regulating a particular technological enterprise. Under federal and many state laws, however, agency personnel are required to hear from outside interest groups and the public on specific policy and project decisions. Administrators' general view of the public's role in decision making reflects a belief in their agency's particular mission and confidence in their expertise to make these decisions in a socially responsible manner. It does not preclude public participation and "input" on particular choices, but it does seek to limit that involvement to specific areas that agency members deem legitimate. Thus, outside challenges to an agency's central mission or its ability to estimate and weigh the value of technological impacts, broadly considered, are strongly resisted. On the other hand, suggestions for limited changes in specific impacts are seen as falling within the realm of appropriate discussion (Hill and Ortolano, 1978; Cole and Caputo, 1984; S. Taylor, 1984).

Agency personnel who work most directly with the public construct common perceptions of how to anticipate and "manage" the conflict that frequently develops. Technological controversies have, in their view, well-defined "scripts." These include shorthand calculations to estimate the likely opposition to particular proposals and the response that is typically made to defuse and "channel" the opposition in the manner the agency finds acceptable (see Culhane, 1981; S. Taylor, 1984).

This view of technological decision making thus emphasizes the importance of past organizational perceptions and routines in shaping how individuals make current decisions. Administrators do not fulfill the expansive ideal of "independence" theorists, who believe public officials can carefully examine each complex choice independently and judiciously weigh the particular consequences in light of the most appropriate interests. Instead, administrators tend to look for and apply a standardized response from their past. Their "cut" on the problem takes into account a limited and predictable range of alternatives and impacts, and employs a specific method of assessment structured by their organizational experience.

For example, a state or community that contacted the Corps of Engineers in the early 1960's to solve a flood control problem would typically receive a proposal for a certain type of dam (depending on the geology and topography of the area) that would have been evaluated in terms of its economic impacts using the Corps's standards for estimating the monetary costs and benefits (e.g., the definition of the appropriate discount rate at the time). Even though there were other possible options (e.g., nonstructural changes such as floodplain zoning) and effects to consider (e.g., environmental and social), they would have received little or no serious attention, because they were not identified as important to the members of that agency at that time.

The general value priorities that these procedures reflect can and do change, but it requires considerable political pressure over an extended period. Administrators do not readily abandon methods they believe have served the agency well in the past. To minimize the internal impact, moreover, they seek the least threatening changes that are sufficient to meet external pressures. Thus, the Corps of Engineers adapted to heightened concern for the environment in the 1970's by adding new staff to identify and develop means of mitigating environmental damage that were still consonant with its primary objective of building structural improvements (Mazmanian and Nienaber, 1979; S. Taylor, 1984).

This view of technological decision making by administrators is summarized in Figure 4.1. In making a specific project choice, past organizational perceptions and routines (OPR) play the central role in identifying what substantive effects (SE) are given careful consideration and in structuring how they are weighed (the path from OPR to SE). Commonly held procedural judgments (PJ) about the process that should be followed and the legitimate role that the public ought to play

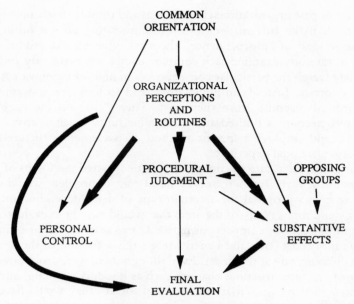

Figure 4.1. Technological decision making by administrators. A factor's relative influence is represented by the width of its arrow.

shape what agency members expect and are willing to "learn" at conferences and hearings with citizens and interest group activists (OPR to PJ).

Although questions of personal control (PC) are not likely to receive a great deal of attention within a government agency, they can arise in debates with outsiders. For example, an agency might be charged with imposing a risk on local citizens without their consent. Organization members tend to see this issue in a manner that is consistent with their agency's mission (OPR to PC). Thus, if their role is to regulate the production of power, they might respond by arguing that all means of generating power involve involuntary risks. The relevant issue, from their perspective, is not the involuntary nature of risk but the differences in the level of hazard from one energy source to the next (see Thomas et al., 1980).

Notice that in Figure 4.1 procedural judgments about a specific project have relatively little influence on administrators' evaluation of its substantive impacts. Because administrators bring well-defined judgments about the technology's consequences (OPR to SE), their assessments of its effects in a given case need not vary, for example, with their perceptions of how well the process of collective decision making has operated. Indeed, since administrators are responsible for managing those deliberations, *their* assessment of the quality of their own decision making should not range very widely.

The certainty and strength of conviction about particular choices is only likely to grow over time. Because of their common background and procedures, agency personnel gather and share information that points to similar conclusions. The weight of the evidence, in their view, becomes increasingly decisive (see Burnstein and Vinokur, 1975; Burnstein and Sentis, 1981). Those most directly involved in an ongoing conflict also tend to reflect on the issues more often, further tightening their arguments (see Tesser, 1978; McGraw and Pinney, 1990).

Organizational predispositions are also much more important than the input of opposing groups (OG) outside the agency (as indicated by the weight of the arrows for OPR to SE and OG to SE). Administrators who bring well-defined views about a given technology to a particular case are unlikely to alter those judgments substantially as a result of criticisms from interest groups (Sabatier, 1978; Jenkins-Smith, 1985). Indeed, the arguments opponents use are usually anticipated as part of how the "script" for technological disputes typically unfolds. As the path model in Figure 4.1 indicates, administrators listen and respond to some of the arguments, but only within the narrow boundaries of what they believe are legitimate areas for citizen input. Larger changes in agency behavior are only brought about by the pressure of significant political power, such as the possibility of a court suit or a serious erosion of public support that threatens funding (see Culhane, Armentano, and Treisema, 1985). Agency procedures, therefore, are not likely to be affected by the dynamics of any particular decision.

Overall, this method of administrative decision making appears to be a defensible strategy for individuals coping with limited cognitive abilities. By distilling their organizational experience into accessible decision-making routines, administrators use and apply their past training and evaluative background in an "efficient" manner for current choices. The method is particularly well suited to technological decisions for which a standardized response can be readily fashioned. Thus, technologies of limited scale, technical complexity, and diversity of effect are easily decomposed into a few, relatively simple tasks for which subroutines can then be developed. Experienced administrators know the limited range of variations for each of the decisions required by such technologies. As a result, their response can be calibrated to the conditions of different contexts (e.g., the construction demands of building a rural highway in mountainous terrain as opposed to flatlands). Over time the reactions and concerns of the public and interest group activists can be incorporated into the value priorities of agency procedures. The orientation, sources of information, and method of analysis that administrators bring to these relatively uncomplicated choices are not likely to miss important impacts or to broadly misperceive the technical or evaluative significance of those impacts. These are the choices for which deference is well earned by the agency.

As the scale, complexity, and qualitative range of effect increase, however, administrators face a much tougher cognitive and organizational task. On technical grounds, a greater number of more complex parameters must be decomposed into separate, manageable problems. In order to ensure effective quality control in the construction and use of the technology, procedures for dealing with the various problems must be designed so that they result in reintegration into a functionally interdependent final product. The technical challenge is far more manageable if this process can be standardized over time, but with particularly large-scale choices, because of varying local conditions, each project is effectively unique, limiting the organization's ability to fashion routines. Technical mistakes are thus more likely to result from poorly developed organizational procedures than from the limits of engineering knowledge. The series of recent failures by NASA with the space shuttle, the Hubble telescope, and planning for a space station, for example, have all been the result of poor management (Marshall, 1990).

Assessing the significance of the impacts from these complex technologies poses even more daunting problems. In any single choice administrators may face a large number of diverse impacts, each affecting a broad spectrum of interests and presenting a potentially wide range of substantive variation. For example, a large structure such as a dam or an urban highway can have geological, ecological, and historical impacts that run from the insignificant in one locale to unique and extraordinarily important effects in another.

Under the National Environmental Policy Act (NEPA), when federal agencies make a choice about a "major action," they are expected to predict and consider all of the outcomes on the "human environment," including economic, environmental, social, and historical among others (Finsterbusch, 1980). In reaching a final decision, an agency is expected to weigh these consequences judiciously for each choice. In interpreting NEPA, for example, the U.S. Fifth Circuit Court of Appeals argued:

NEPA mandates a case-by-case balancing judgment on the part of federal agencies. . . . The particular economic and technical benefits of planned action must be assessed and then weighed against the environmental costs. . . . In some cases, the benefits of the action will be great enough to justify a certain quantum of environmental costs; in other cases, they will not be so great and the proposed action may have to be abandoned or significantly altered. . . . The point of the individualized balancing analysis is to ensure . . . that optimally beneficial action is finally taken. (Calvert Cliffs Coordinating Committee, Inc. v. AEC, Fed 2d., 1123)

The organizational background of administrators, however, does not provide them with the evaluative tools to fulfill these demands. The limits of cognitive abilities and past experience inevitably focus their attention on as few as one or two key effects, strongly biasing their assessment toward a particular outcome. The desire to develop standardized procedures for the "normal" or "average" choice, moreover, constrains how sensitive administrators are to the attributes of particular cases. Calibrating decision-making routines that are responsive to the full range of characteristics of such difficult choices requires facing and assessing a particular type of technology many times. An unavoidable consequence of large scale, however, is that these decisions are made less frequently than simpler technologies, thus limiting the opportunities for administrators to fine-tune their procedures across a wide spectrum of effects.

To their credit, the architects of NEPA recognized that government administrators tend to neglect effects that are not central to their organization's mission. Moreover, they realized that information alone is unlikely to force consideration of impacts that might otherwise be ignored (Dreyfus and Ingram, 1976). As a result, that act requires the views of outside groups to be solicited. Representatives of other government agencies, for example, are encouraged to identify impacts for environmental review and to comment on the final report. In the past such involvement produced alterations in the design of some projects. Under the Reagan administration, the disarray that occurred in the leading environmental agencies, such as the Environmental Protection Agency and the Council on Environmental Quality, has resulted in less aggressive bureaucratic oversight (Andrews and Sansone, 1984; S. Taylor, 1984; Caldwell, 1989).

NEPA also solicits the views of groups who may have an interest in and background with the choice under consideration (see Nelkin and Fallows, 1978; Daneke, 1983). The impact of citizen activists on the process of decision making has been more notable than that of interested agencies and their concern and involvement have not subsided in recent years. In evaluating the contribution of political activists to technological decision making, we should recognize that present decision-making procedures do at least create an opportunity for members of the general public to become involved if they are interested enough to pay the "costs" of participation, including attending and speaking at public hearings. A social-process perspective, however, expects that the individuals who show up and are heard begin, like administrators, with prior predispositions about the type of technology or impacts that are under review. Without such background, citizens have difficulty defining their interests in a complex decision; certainly they are not likely to reach judgments that are sufficiently unequivocal to make the cost of involvement appear worthwhile.

Political Activists

Members of the laypublic clearly have different degrees of experience with particular technologies and varying propensities to become involved in a public debate. Those who are best prepared and most willing to participate are usually members of existing interest groups who have past experience with assessing the issue in question. Their background provides them with a complete hierarchical "system" of schematic judgments to assess both the means and the impacts of a new proposal. At the highest levels of their belief systems, their evaluative framework is structured and informed by a global view of the relationship between technology and society that places them either in broad support of or at odds with a particular agency's mission. For example, they may perceive themselves as being for development or for preservation of particular resources, as committed to the use of large-scale, "hard" energy sources or small-scale, "soft" technologies, or as partisans for structural improvements to limit flood damage or for nonstructural techniques of flood abatement (see Sabatier, 1987).

Members of a particular political organization are likely to have been drawn to a common cause because they see these general issues from a similar viewpoint. By sharing information and assessments in meetings and in newsletters and magazines, they construct more specific group evaluations of the consequences and the value of different kinds of technologies and impacts, such as nuclear power, pesticides, and toxic pollutants (Mazur, 1981; Nelkin, 1984a). Given the range and complexity of issues that are involved, these group positions seek to simplify and "type" technologies by focusing on selective impacts of special concern using only rough estimates of the level of effect and a general assessment of their value. Their substantive interest leads group members to follow controversies that take place elsewhere and to develop broad procedural schemas of the agencies directly responsible for managing or regulating particular technologies.

Then there are individuals who are more strictly impact-oriented. Although these citizens have only a very general background in thinking about and assessing a given type of technology, they have constructed well-defined interpretive structures of a value or package of values that they strongly seek to preserve or promote. As with those who are both means-and-impact-oriented, their specific assessment is usually embedded in and justified by a broader ethos (such as the need to promote economic growth or to protect the character of the local community). The clarity and strength of this predisposition can provide the grounds for evaluating a large-scale project that will bring substantial changes to a particular area. When this perspective is shared by others, it can stimulate the formation of a group or the mobilization of an existing organization to support this goal in the political process. Because of their lack of previous background with technological issues, however, one would expect that these individuals might have less staying power in their willingness to participate than those who bring a broader and more well-defined concern.

Finally, there are citizens who have a diffuse interest in the subject matter and who show up at public hearings or attend a group's meetings on an intermittent basis. Unless they develop the cognitive background and the social network that sustains the activists, their voice is unlikely to be heard in public deliberations.

Once a proposal has been made, those who are means-and-impact-oriented use their past judgments to assess the current case. Since they already share with other group members rough estimates of the level and the evaluation of a type of technology, they quickly reach a preliminary assessment by interpreting the new project as another example of the problems or benefits that they perceive with the generic technology. Their assessment of the effects of a single project can easily cue a concern for global interests, such as the well-being of future generations or the nation (e.g., a hydroelectric dam that is seen as either destroying a scenic river or promoting "energy independence"). Their evaluation of the personal effects, however, often is of equal or greater effect. Since they bring firm convictions about the collective effects of the generic technology, they have few doubts about its personal consequences. Those who believe that a technology is generally unsafe will find it, by definition, threatening to themselves if they live in the neighboring area.

Their procedural predispositions also guide their evaluation of the project and the agency responsible for it. If they judge, for example, that the manner in which an organization has made past decisions represents a pattern of being unresponsive to local concerns and promoting its own interests, this directs their interpretation of its present actions as well as the tactics that they employ in response. For technologies that include some degree of risk, their assessment of potential threats to personal control derives from both their general orientation and their group's prior position on this issue. Critics, for example, might argue that a potentially hazardous technology is not only unwarranted but should be avoided because it imposes a risk on individuals without their consent.

Activists who are just impact-oriented do not have as much substantive knowledge about a particular technology or the agency in charge. Given the clarity and intensity of their orientation toward promoting or protecting a certain value or values, however, they are able to rapidly develop an assessment of a large-scale technology that brings with it a particular type of development (e.g., from the construction of a major highway or a large reservoir). If many local residents visit the countryside for solitude, for example, a proposal for a nearby airport with its accompanying noise and traffic will provoke an immediate negative reaction. On the other hand, a group seeking to keep an economically depressed area from sinking into further decline will greet the same project with a correspondingly positive judgment. For members of each organization, the perceived magnitude of the impact in light of the strength of their predispositions is sufficient for them to reach an unequivocal judgment and to organize to support or oppose the project.

The key role of the group's previous position on these issues is reflected in Figure 4.2. The past heavily structures the gathering and interpretation of information about the current initiative in a manner that is remarkably similar to the approach employed by administrators, as was shown in Figure 4.1. Activists focus on those impacts that are cued

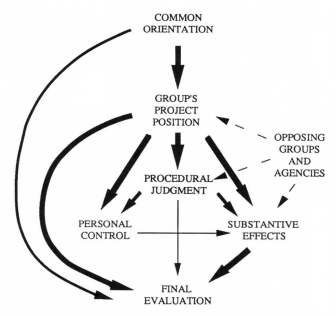

Figure 4.2. Technological decision making by members of interest groups. A factor's relative influence is represented by the width of its arrow.

by their group's shared schemas. Effects that are idiosyncratic or specific to a particular case are incorporated into their public position insofar as they are consistent with the group's broader predispositions. The "weight" that different impacts receive, however, is contingent on more enduring judgments at higher levels in their value and belief system.

Since activists believe that they already know what the general effects of the technology are, an important task is to gather the necessary information about the current proposal so that they can fill in the "specifics" of their argument for the case under review. Just as with administrators, their convictions in a particular case are only strengthened as other members of their organization bring in confirming evidence or construct telling arguments. Confident in their group's project position (GPP) and often distrustful of "government" expertise, activists are unlikely to readily acknowledge the credibility of opposing groups or agencies (OG/A), particularly any conclusions that conflict with their own preconceptions (compare GPP to SE with OG/A to SE). Activists are not much concerned with questions about how competent or credible decision makers are in a specific case, because they do not typically have high expectations in this regard nor are they looking to the agency for guidance (compare the weight of GPP to SE with PJ to SE). Of course, any new information that helps bolster the activists' case with the uncommitted is welcome and publicized. This path model suggests, however, that such information has little effect upon the activists themselves, who begin from more general predispositions about the type of technology.

Activists differ most often from administrators in the impacts they focus on and the factual and evaluative premises they employ to evaluate those consequences. Recent decision-making reforms, designed in part to provide an institutionalized opportunity to air alternative viewpoints, serve a useful purpose. Participation by activists thus increases the number and qualitative range of technological impacts that will be brought out in public deliberations. Moreover, as the debate proceeds there is a strong incentive to gather new information that might advance one's case and further illuminate the consequences of choosing a particular option.

This procedural model is quite similar to the academic analyses of Herbert Simon and Charles Lindblom. Well before such procedural reforms were enacted, Simon and Lindblom argued that efforts to force administrators to be comprehensive and "synoptic" in evaluating complex decisions were doomed to failure. Any such narrowly drawn and selectively trained group of individuals would be unlikely to have the cognitive and evaluative capabilities to effectively judge a large number of diverse consequences. The "intelligence" of democracy, according to Lindblom, is that the policy process allows access by many individuals who approach complex problems from widely divergent backgrounds and interests. The interaction of multiple partisans vying for influence produces far better decisions than any individual reaches acting alone or in a small group (Lindblom, 1965, 1990; see also Monroe and Woodhouse, 1986).

The purpose of the reforms, however, goes beyond simply soliciting additional information and alternative viewpoints. The goal is to provide for the careful weighing of the specific effects of any major governmental action, presumably in terms of the interests of the full range of citizens who will be affected. Participation of political activists represents a step in this direction but does not fully achieve the objective—

an objective that Lindblom's procedural "solution" of simply opening up the process to multiple points of access does not effectively address.

The assessments of political activists merely offer another "cut" on a complex project with multiple impacts. There is no reason to expect, as a result of the interest of different groups of activists in particular outcomes, that *all* of the impacts or affected interests will have a vocal advocate. As has been noted, the assessments of both sides of such a debate are largely defined by past cognitive investment. Present consequences that are unanticipated or that have not been previously visible or controversial many not get the attention they deserve.

Activists also share with administrators limited experience in calibrating the worth of the impacts in which they are interested. As a means of cognitive economy, they too use shorthand characterizations of the generic technology or types of impacts that are not necessarily sensitive to the range of case-specific variation a large project can produce. More importantly, however, interest-group representatives do not provide a means for weighing the wide range of impacts over which they and administrators frequently disagree. Activists only offer another partial assessment of a multifaceted project. As many have pointed out, NEPA does not provide a scale for judging how much weight should be placed on the judgments of different political actors (Caldwell, 1989).

Since each side focuses on particular types of effects for which they have developed very strong predispositions, their overall assessments are heavily weighted, in the abstract, toward a particular conclusion of support or opposition. These final evaluations are unlikely to change when participants are presented with the characteristics of specific choices. Thus, the overall assessment of either side may be a poor barometer of the worth of a particular project.

In the face of conflicting assessments, there is little hope that public deliberations can resolve or narrow the range of issues over which groups disagree. The past predispositions of both sides play such a dominant role in structuring their case-specific assessments that their substantive judgments, and certainly their overall assessments, are not particularly responsive to the evaluative arguments or information offered by opponents. The quality of the debate often suffers, as they "talk past one another" and address only the issues that are of central concern to themselves (e.g., Wildavsky and Tenebaum, 1981; Robinson, 1982).

If differences cannot be accommodated within the range of alterations that administrators are willing and technically able to make in the
design of a particular project, then the prospects for early resolution are
poor. As a controversy develops over time, the distance between sides
is only likely to increase, as each focuses on and retains those arguments
or data that are consistent with their predispositions, strengthening
their resolve (see Rajecki, 1982).

The evaluative limitations of activists, therefore, are virtually the
same as those of administrators. Each makes a prior investment in substantive premises about a technology or set of impacts that produces
contending partial assessments, each representing a selective range of
interests. The degree to which these judgments are well calibrated for
the characteristics of the case at hand or responsive to new information
and evaluative arguments is problematic. Since neither side has a strong
incentive to resolve their differences, the prospect for a long and contentious dispute is great—and the longer the dispute lasts, the more
"evidence" each side is likely to collect that questions the good intentions of the opponents.

The empirical support for these expectations is similar to the pattern
described for the laypublic in Chapter 3. There is substantial evidence
that past experience shapes the preferences and methods that administrators and activists employ through the early stages of public deliberations. What happens after more extended deliberations is not entirely
clear, although some investigations provide at least partial support for
a past-structured perspective (see Mazmanian and Nienaber, 1979; S.
Taylor, 1984). More importantly, however, we do not have a study that
effectively compares the evaluative methods and capabilities of political
veterans and the laypublic after an intensive debate.

The General Public

Let us return then to the model of the laypublic's participation presented in Chapter 3. The model argues that members of the general
public employ a very different approach than administrators and activists in evaluating major projects. When a proposal for a project is first
made, members of the laypublic have very little to offer. Given sufficient time and incentive, however, their "present-driven" method of
assessment exhibits strengths that directly address the past-structured
limitations of the political principals. Indeed, the fit between these two

approaches is remarkably complementary and far more positive than previous analyses reveal.

Most citizens, for example, do not attempt to assess the characteristics of a specific project in terms of a generic assessment of a particular type of technology or impacts. Their evaluative predispositions are not that well defined and provide only the most global orientations toward technology and politics. Lacking extensive background and faced with a potentially large-scale choice, members of the laypublic have a strong incentive to draw on the arguments they hear in public deliberations to overcome their own evaluative deficiencies. Common orientations toward technology give them some initial sense of evaluative direction, focusing their attention to one side of the debate or the other. Without tightly defined "priors," however, they have considerable schematic slack to select the positions and issues important to them. Motivated by the debate about this specific choice, they are likely to focus on its characteristics rather than on arguments or evidence about the technology or the agency's general policies.

Because the laypublic's procedural judgments are likely to be more highly defined than their substantive orientation, most citizens are particularly interested in the credibility and competence of the individuals and organizations who will construct or regulate the project, and they are very sensitive to new information that offers them insights in this regard. How well the principals respond to the objections of their opponents is crucial for determining if they have the interests of a broad range of citizens at heart.

Citizens, furthermore, are hardly provincial when compared to activists. Their broad orientation includes multiple levels of interest that are applicable to any given choice, although their global judgments are not going to be held with the same fervor as an activist's. As the debate progresses, the laypublic constructs a continuum of socially shared positions in response to the structure of public debate, reflecting a judgment of which impacts and interests raised are of central importance to them. Interestingly enough, because members of the general public do not have prior assessments of the level of effects that a certain type of technology is expected to produce, they are unlikely to personalize the outcomes as quickly as political activists and may therefore be less concerned with their personal well-being. Thus, on theoretical grounds, they evoke an image of comparative moderation: their evaluative horizons are neither as broad nor as self-serving as those of political activists. In addition, the judgments of a representative cross-section of the "public" are difficult for the principal actors to ignore, because they carry the weight of social legitimacy. Both sides of any public debate want to claim that the "average person" supports their position.

The characteristics of the general public's method of assessment thus balance and complement the approach of the political veterans. The assessments of a cross-section of the major positions among ordinary citizens could potentially improve the process of public deliberation and the quality of decision making. The laypublic, in this case, is not a jury rendering final assessments. They lack the technical background to make ultimate decisions about the quality of technological projects. Instead, "representatives" of social positions that emerge in response to public debate act as a sounding board to move the process toward a more socially optimal conclusion.[2]

Their case-specific concern, for example, could serve to focus debate on the trade-offs that need to be made for the choice at hand. Their sensitivity to the process of deliberations would provide an added incentive to ensure that new information receives appropriate attention and that the norms of openness and responsiveness are upheld in the conduct of public deliberations. Since citizen "representatives" have listened to both sides, their assessment offers a rough test of the breadth of appeal of the evaluative arguments made by supporters and opponents and can potentially narrow the range of debate to a few key issues.

The ability of particular members of the laypublic to perform this role, however, varies with the degree of attentiveness with which they follow the debate (see Figure 4.3). Those who are less interested and observant are likely to have made little past investment in a common orientation toward politics and technology. Consequently, their evaluative assessments are constructed almost entirely in response to the socially defined perspectives articulated by participants in the public debate and by friends and acquaintances. If there are risks involved or if

[2]Proposals have been made to select a random sample of citizens to judge particular government policies or projects in order to gain, in a cost-effective manner, a more representative view of citizen assessments than present methods can provide (Heberlein, 1976; Crosby, Kelly, and Schaefer, 1986). These suggestions, however, fail to identify who these individuals would actually represent or how they are supposed to contribute. For example, a relatively small number of citizens are typically selected to limit the cost of the procedure and to ensure that it is manageable. Though randomly choosing small numbers of individuals lowers the likelihood of systematic bias, it does not by any means guarantee that these individuals represent the views of the larger population.

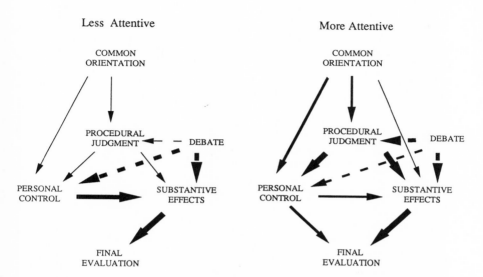

Figure 4.3. Paths of assessment for citizens, less and more attentive. A factor's relative influence is represented by the width of its arrow.

the effects are subject to a great dispute, they use a low-cost strategy for acquiring information by assessing the characteristics of the technology in terms of judgments about personal control. Without a great deal of knowledge, the number of dimensions or attributes that they consider is not likely to be great.

In contrast, those who are highly attentive and interested begin with at least some general orientation concerning technology and politics from which they can reach an early appraisal of the project. By paying closer attention to and reflecting on the events as they unfold, the project-specific schemas for these individuals develop more quickly and become internally consistent at an earlier time than those of their less attentive counterparts. The schematic factor that typically requires the most time and information to play an important role—procedural judgment about collective decision makers—emerges more rapidly for these observant citizens and thus has a more decisive effect on their overall assessment as they try to disentangle the contending claims. By paying closer attention to the debate, they incorporate into their interpretive structures a greater number of substantive dimensions about the technology than do their less interested neighbors. This does not necessarily mean that they are stronger supporters or opponents than others, only that they have considered and weighed a wider range of the technology's effects (see Petty and Cacioppo, 1986).

Those who are more interested and attentive would be best suited to fulfill the "representative" role for the laypublic described above. Spokespersons for major social positions among the laypublic could thus sit at the table with the principals. Early in the deliberations, their role would be to ensure that procedural norms were upheld and that case-specific issues received the attention that they deserved. In the later stages of review, their substantive assessments would identify and weigh the relative importance of the impacts and interests of central concern to the full spectrum of citizens likely to be affected by a project.

A social-process theory thus directly contests the prevailing views of citizen assessment. Cost-benefit analysis and decision techniques typically assume commonality in preparation and method and so deny that experience plays a systematic role in shaping evaluative procedures. Current methods of citizen participation adopt a past-structured approach that acknowledges the cumulative effect of background but, thus far, have gone no further. By taking into account the effects of past and present deliberations, a social-process perspective offers a potentially more complete and valid picture, with significant implications for technological decision making.

CHAPTER FIVE

Measuring the Impact of Public Debate: The Case of the Diablo Canyon Nuclear Power Plant

UNTIL THIS BOOK, there had been no published empirical study that tests the central propositions of the social-process theory. Indeed, the expectation that members of the laypublic can be responsive to public deliberations and effective in their evaluative capabilities pushes well beyond the present boundaries of our theoretical and empirical understanding of citizen assessment. Past studies, for example, which posit an ideal of political sophistication and try to determine how prevalent it is, indicate that most citizens do not adopt conventional ideologies nor do they learn a great deal about most of the specific candidates or policies in question. Compared with political veterans, who bring extensive backgrounds in policy assessment, the laypublic is poorly prepared for evaluating complex political choices, at least at the beginning of public deliberations. According to some arguments, the pattern of empirical findings suggests that most of the general public cannot respond to politics in a more sophisticated manner because they lack the basic "cognitive capabilities" (Campbell et al., 1960; Smith, 1989).

The social-process view of assessment does not contest the view that citizens' backgrounds or views about politics are limited. Because of normal cognitive constraints, we can expect that the majority of citizens will concentrate on the pressing demands of family and career before addressing the more distant problems of politics. The social-process theory does, however, directly dispute the argument that most of the general public is *incapable* of reacting to public deliberations in a responsive and effective manner. Rather, it argues that on theoretical grounds, developing schemas is a *common* human response to new and challenging developments. Thus, given the limitations of the laypublic's past cognitive investments in politics, scholars should investigate, not general orientations, but the *process* by which citizens develop new schemas when presented with particular policy choices.[1] Only those issues that provide strong incentives to pay attention to a well-defined debate, however, are likely to provoke this present-structured response. Choices about major technologies are particularly useful for investigation because they often give citizens both the necessary motivation and a well-developed debate.

Ironically, my study indicates, as we will see, that the system of interpretive structures that members of the laypublic develop about a *particular* technological choice appears to exhibit almost all of the characteristics of sophistication ascribed to *general ideologies*. The choice-specific schemas of citizens include multiple arguments and factual premises that are internally consistent, arrayed on a socially defined continuum running from support to opposition. In other words, they are horizontally constrained. Moreover, substantive positions and final evaluations are vertically constrained by common orientations and procedural schemas developed for this particular project. Where the laypublic fails to match the skills of veterans is in its failure to invest in and use abstract belief systems. Yet the more challenging and unique a choice is, the more likely it is that the choice-specific method of the laypublic will complement the past-structured assessment of political veterans, whose focus on general issues limits their ability to assess effectively the highly variable characteristics of particular projects.

All of this suggests that we can generalize about and study the common processes of schematic specification that develop in response to specific choices. Although the particular issues and the scale of incentive naturally vary from one decision to the next, different actors should follow predictable methods of assessment. The most challenging set of propositions concerns the anticipated reaction of members of the laypublic. After a long controversy over a particularly challenging technological project, their schemas should be well-formed, allowing us to more effectively compare their evaluative procedures with the methods of political veterans who have been exposed to the same issue.

My study examines the processes of assessment employed by the laypublic and political veterans after a well-developed technological dispute. By using a survey instrument that allows each respondent the

---

[1]Robert Huckfeldt and John Sprague reach similar conclusions, but from a theoretical perspective that focuses on the micro process of how individuals share political information with more immediate co-workers, friends, and family (see Huckfeldt, 1983; Huckfeldt and Sprague, 1987).

freedom to construct his or her own schemas, I can measure the impact of public debate on a random sample of the laypublic and compare its effects with the reaction of more experienced political actors. This type of design is limited because it does *not* follow the development of their schemas over time. Yet we can address the most important questions before us: whether the laypublic is responsive to public deliberations and whether it exhibits a pattern of assessment that complements that of political veterans.

The Choice of a Project

To conduct this research we must select a major technological project that provides citizens and political veterans with an intellectual challenge. The project should present difficult choices, posing a wide topical range of impacts that affect many levels of interest. In addition, the potential scale of effect should be large enough that most local residents feel they have an incentive to follow public deliberations. Finally, the debate should be well-defined, with the arguments of each side widely disseminated over an extended period of time so that virtually every individual in the affected area is exposed to them at some time.

I contacted federal agencies and government organizations involved in sponsoring or regulating technologies that might meet these needs. Approximately fifteen projects were identified in the western United States, and from these a short list of three was chosen as having the greatest potential: the proposal for building a high-speed rail link, or "bullet train," between San Diego and Los Angeles; the efforts to clean up the Stringfellow toxic chemical dump near Glen Avon, California; and the decision to finish construction of and start generating power from the Diablo Canyon nuclear power plant in San Luis Obispo County, California. All of these endeavors met my criteria to some degree, but the Diablo Canyon nuclear power plant was selected as the one that appeared to come closest to fulfilling all of them.

The Diablo Canyon Power Plant

The Diablo Canyon plant is located on the California coast, roughly midway between Los Angeles and San Francisco, near the community of San Luis Obispo, and has two nuclear reactors that produce up to 2,200 megawatts of electricity. The specific site was chosen by Pacific Gas and Electric Company (PG&E) in 1966 after another possible location not many miles down the coast, at Nipomo Dunes, was dropped from consideration because of opposition by the Sierra Club on environmental grounds.[2] Although PG&E was granted a construction permit for Unit 1 in 1968 (the permit for Unit 2 was tendered in 1970), the unit did not go to full power and connect to the energy grid until March 1986.

To assess this project, local residents were presented with a wide range of substantive effects, including questions about health and safety, economic gain and loss, and environmental and social impacts that could potentially affect their interests within and beyond the county. The debate about the safety of Diablo Canyon tended to focus—as have the controversies surrounding other nuclear power stations—on the risks to human health from a catastrophic accident and, to a lesser extent, on the possible threat from regular releases of small amounts of low-level radiation. The chance of a very large emission of radioactivity from a major accident attracted a great deal of attention because the plant was inadvertently located within three miles of an earthquake fault. There is also the safety threat from having to store high-level nuclear wastes on the site for a number of years. At some as yet undetermined date those wastes will have to be transported to a national repository that must protect the environment and the health of future generations for thousands of years (*T-T*, Aug. 6, 1985).

The economic costs and benefits, however, are also significant. The construction of the plant brought considerable economic activity to the area. In addition, at the time of the survey PG&E paid substantial property taxes—over $34 million in 1986—to the county (*Davis* [Calif.] *Enterprise*, Feb. 10, 1987). Nevertheless, the price tag for this generating station increased significantly over time, rising from an initial estimate of $365 million in 1968 (*T-T*, Apr. 16, 1984) to a final cost of approximately $5.5 billion in 1987. (*Sacramento Bee*, July 28, 1988).

The economic benefits from construction also brought unintended social costs. Neighboring communities had to absorb substantial numbers of transient workers, sometimes very rapidly. The housing market became congested, and price increases made it difficult at times for longer-term residents to find affordable rental housing. Demand for social services rose as well, and there were charges that the availability and use of drugs increased as the number of workers grew during peak construction periods (*T-T*, Aug. 10, 1985).

[2]A concise but thorough history of the plant can be found in the *San Luis Obispo County Telegram-Tribune* (cited hereafter as *T-T*), Aug. 11, 1984. It serves as the basis for the chronology in Appendix A and is the source for historical information not otherwise cited in the text.

The plant is located on a spectacularly beautiful coastline. Over the history of this dispute, groups expressed concern over coastline preservation and the possible effect of the plant's thermal discharges on sea life and fishing in the area.

These varied and wide-ranging substantive effects are particularly interesting to examine on theoretical grounds because they affect varying levels of interests. The health risks and social costs fall most directly on the people who live in the immediate vicinity of this power station. Much of the city of San Luis Obispo (population 50,000) and several smaller communities, for example, are within the 10-mile evacuation zone from the plant. They face greater risks because of their close proximity, but they also receive the benefits from property taxes and the economic stimulation that constructing this project brought.

The power plant also serves interests and imposes costs that extend far beyond the boundaries of the county and that local residents could presumably take into account in their assessment. Nearly two million PG&E customers in central and northern California receive electricity from the plant (PG&E Information Center, San Luis Obispo). During the time that the plant station was being debated, the United States went through two periods of rapid price escalation from foreign oil producers. The justification for the project was framed by some in terms of the need to make the country energy independent and to ensure that the state and the local area have sufficient energy supplies for future economic development. On the other hand, the production of high-level and long-lived radioactive wastes has directed attention to the possible costs that future generations have to bear.

The History of the Dispute

Local citizens have been exposed to a challenging technological choice with a broad range of substantive issues that affect varying levels of interest. The stakes appear impressive. How local residents judge the impacts, however, depends on their ability to perceive and interpret the significance of these issues. With little background in technological assessment, most citizens are unlikely to immediately understand or have a ready scale for assigning relative weights to low-probability, high-impact accidents or the contribution of a large electric power plant to reducing the nation's dependence on foreign oil.

Political arguments can serve to give citizens those interpretive tools, *if* they pay attention. Given the competing pressures on their attention, large numbers are not going to make this cognitive investment unless they believe that there is a real controversy between cred-ible groups over the level and value of the impacts. Opponents of a technology often suffer in the eyes of the general public because they lack the technical credentials of large corporations or government agen-cies. For their criticisms to be noticed, they typically have to be sup-ported by information from organizations or individuals with accepted credentials or by new developments that appear to give the opponents' case credibility. Throughout its history, the Diablo Canyon plant, like many other major technologies, was buffeted by periodic disclosures about the plant and by outside events that renewed and extended the debate.

When the project was announced in the late 1960's, it won the strong support of local politicians, and a public opinion poll revealed that it also enjoyed the backing of three-quarters of the local residents (*T-T*, Oct. 7, 1975). This was not surprising, for at that time nuclear power was still widely perceived as clean and safe. In addition, the po-litical orientation of most citizens of San Luis Obispo County predis-posed them to be supportive of what was, at the time, a "new" tech-nological development. Their voting patterns for state and national office, for example, are distinctly conservative when compared with the rest of California or the country as a whole, and conservatives tend to support large-scale technologies that stimulate economic development.

The chronology of events given in Appendix A covers the period between PG&E's 1963 announcement of plans to build a nuclear power plant and the granting of full power licenses for both units in 1985. The series of political and technological events during this period could be expected to prompt the public to make a close evaluation of the project and to arrive at conflicting views.

Organized opposition started to develop in 1972, when a local chap-ter of Mothers for Peace, an antiwar group, began to focus attention on the problems of nuclear weapons and nuclear power, particularly Diablo Canyon. In 1973, the group applied for the status of and were authorized to act as active participants, or group intervenors, in the public hearings about the plant. Members raised and publicized a wide range of concerns related to such issues as the release of low-level radia-tion, the possibility of a large-scale accident, problems in transporting nuclear wastes from the plant, and the risk of sabotage. To what extent they enjoyed credibility in these early years of public debate is difficult to assess at this late date. Yet local interest in the plant definitely in-creased when a report from the U.S. Geological Survey was published in 1973 that indicated that an earthquake fault had been discovered three miles offshore of the project site.

Over the next six years, the plant was subjected to increased scrutiny by government officials. After reviewing the project, the Nuclear Regulatory Commission (NRC) ruled that the plant could be made safe from seismic activity with the proper structural reinforcements. While the project was being considered by the appropriate regulatory agencies, it was also debated in the local community and challenged in the courts and administrative hearings by the Mothers for Peace. Simultaneously, another citizens' group, the Abalone Alliance, formed and started to carry out public protests as a means to publicize opposition. With extensive coverage by the local television station and newspaper, each new administrative hearing and public protest provided an opportunity for the utility and the plant's opponents to make their case to local residents.

These events however, were merely a prelude to more dramatic developments. In March 1979 there was an accident at the nuclear power plant at Three Mile Island near Harrisburg, Pennsylvania. The national news media intensively covered events at the crippled plant for over a week. This was followed in September 1981 by the discovery that the plans to increase the capacity of the Diablo Canyon plant to withstand an earthquake were improperly implemented. The blueprints for Unit 1 were used for Unit 2; Unit 2's plans were used for Unit 1. The Nuclear Regulatory Commission voted to suspend the Diablo Canyon's low-power license the following month, the first time it had ever taken this action against a power plant already under construction. By 1982, public support had dropped precipitously. Only 38 percent were in favor of the operation of the power plant, and 55 percent were opposed (George and Southwell, 1985).

In the period following these riveting events, there were charges by "whistleblowers" that quality control was poorly enforced (*T-T*, Feb. 9, 1984) and the NRC criticized PG&E's management of the project (*T-T*, Mar. 3, 1984). As late as 1986 questions were being raised about the plant's evacuation plan and the safety of temporarily storing of high-level nuclear waste on the site.

This series of events often put the utility and its supporters on the defensive. Opponents, on the other hand, engaged in practices that could bring disapprobation by some, particularly in the period after 1979. The project was halted or slowed by numerous court suits. Demonstrators undertook civil disobedience by symbolic occupations or blockades of the site. At particularly large actions of this type, hundreds of arrests were made, and the county's criminal justice system was strained at times to handle the cost of processing this many individuals.

The visibility of opposition groups led many supporters of the plant to form a group called Citizens for Adequate Energy, to show that there was also active support for the project in an important segment of the local community. Although the Citizens never achieved the prominence of the Mothers for Peace and the Abalone Alliance, they still made an impact by running a speaker series and testifying at administrative hearings in support of the project.

In sum, the Diablo Canyon plant offers an excellent first test for a social-process approach. There is a diverse range of challenging technological impacts, and the political and technological events provide potentially strong incentives for citizens to construct project-specific schemas to understand and weigh the well-defined arguments between the supporters and opponents. As a result, by the spring of 1985, I had made my choice. I then wrote and won approval for a grant to conduct a methodological test from the Universitywide Energy Research Group, an organized research unit within the University of California system. At this time, both Unit 1 and Unit 2 had been completed and were undergoing low-power tests. The supporters appeared to have won the battle over Diablo Canyon, but the victory was relatively recent. Even at this late date the plant was subject to litigation. There were also periodic critical reviews by the local media and political activists on a range of issues such as quality control, waste storage, and the adequacy of evacuation plans. The controversy was still alive, and the schemas that I planned to measure should still be intact.

Methods

Testing a social-process explanation is a methodological challenge. After a random sample of the laypublic is drawn, one has to identify the schemas for common orientation and the project-specific factors of procedural judgment, personal control, and substantive effects that are hypothesized to shape an individual's overall assessment. The effect of public debate must then be calculated by discovering what social positions citizens adopt from the arguments they hear and where these fall on the social continuua for each factor. Next, the strength of the relationships among the factors must be gauged to determine which factors have the greatest relative impact in influencing citizens' final assessments (see Appendix B). No methodological road map is readily available for testing these propositions. Only rarely have schemas been directly measured, and no means have yet been developed to test the degree to which these multi-attribute positions are structured by public deliberations (see Conover and Feldman, 1984). Given the complexity of this task, my goal is to address these issues in the most straightforward manner possible.

Q Methodology

The most direct way to measure a schema is to give respondents the full range of stimuli relating to an issue and allow them the freedom to impose their own order on the material. Fortunately, there is a technique—Q methodology—that fulfills this need (Brown, 1980; Feldman and Conover, 1984). This method asks the subject to review a set of statements designed to represent the stimuli from a particular issue and then rank these items along a continuum running from "most agree" ($+3$) to "most disagree" (-3). Since there is a single scale, the respondent reveals which items are relatively important and which are virtually without significance (a score of 0). This property of transitivity is not usually disclosed by traditional survey methods.

The relationship among the statements, or the process of reasoning and assessment in this "Q-sort," can be inferred from the pattern of rankings (i.e., their direction and intensity) for each set of statements. The items that an individual reacts to most strongly provide a structure within which the less provocative statements are understood and judged. In describing one's common orientation toward politics and technology, an environmentalist, for example, might place great emphasis on the general principle that nature should be valued for its own sake and the belief that the present rate of technological development is destructive of environmental values. If these statements are followed by a desire to protect wilderness areas forever, the former provides a reason for the latter. The focus on wilderness also gives further definition to this broad perspective.

This ranking system is particularly useful for the types of research questions that this investigation raises. The importance of different levels of interest (e.g., effects on the individual vs. those to the community) in judging substantive effects, for example, should be immediately apparent from a person's Q-sort for that factor (e.g., is the national interest $+1$ or $+3$?). If consistency is believed to increase the chance that one is a strong supporter or opponent on any particular schema, this can also be inferred from the pattern that emerges (e.g., the perception that the agency in charge is not only trustworthy but also responsive and competent as well should indicate support for the project).

The number of statements a respondent is asked to judge in a Q-sort is typically many times larger than the available points on the scale of agreement to disagreement. This means that several items are likely to fall under each point on that scale. Past experience reveals that directing the respondent to create a normal or quasi-normal curve of distribution (by literally arranging cards, each of which contains one of the statements, under each point on the scale so that there are, for example, 2 statement cards under both +3 and -3, 3 under +2 and -2, 5 under +1 and -1, and 6 under 0), encourages careful distinctions between the relative importance of different statements (Coke and Brown, 1976; Brown, 1980).

To identify the schemas that citizens employed for evaluating the Diablo Canyon plant, Q-sorts were constructed for each of the hypothesized factors: common orientation (CO), procedural judgment (PJ), personal control (PC), and substantive effects (SE). After a careful review of the literature on technological assessment and the public record of this project, I determined that the range of debate for CO, PJ, and SE could be best represented by Q-sorts with 26 statements for each of these factors. Because discussion about personal control was more limited, it required only 16 statements. (A more complete review of the content of the statements and the way in which they were chosen appears in the last section of this chapter.) The seven-point scale indicated above was used for ranking the items of all four Q-sorts (-3, -2, -1, 0, $+1$, $+2$, $+3$) with a requested distribution of 2-3-5-6-5-3-2 for the 26-statement schemas and 1-2-3-4-3-2-1 for the 16-item factor.[3]

Measuring schemas for four separate factors makes the theoretical assumption that these four are distinct, integrated wholes which influence other assessments. No doubt for some individuals, the boundaries between these factors are not so sharply defined. The population as a whole, however, should tend to separate these factors because, as we saw in Chapter 3, each issue focuses on distinct parts of the conceptual problem and each factor is hypothesized to develop at different times

[3]For purposes of logistical simplicity, I attempted in the beginning to include the same number of statements in all of the Q-sorts on the assumption that this would make it easier to explain the process to the respondent and to train interviewers in the proper survey procedure. After conducting the open-ended interviews and the pretests, however, I realized that the cognitive and evaluative structure for personal control was substantially smaller in content than the others.

and change at varying rates during the decision-making process. However, to ensure that this was a reasonable assumption, I conducted open-ended, exploratory interviews with 14 citizens with varying backgrounds. The specific statements I selected and the boundaries I drew between them reflected the responses from this initial set of pretest interviews.

Using a forced distribution for measuring each respondent's schemas might appear to unnecessarily constrain the options that are open to the respondent. The number of possible patterns that remain, however, is enormous: in the 26-item sorts in this study, for example, there are 519,437,318,400 possible permutations from which each subject can choose; the number of permutations for personal control, though substantially smaller, is hardly constricting at 2,822,400.

The Impact of Public Debate

Despite the broad freedom to select different patterns of statements, the social-process theory proposes that individuals draw heavily on the contending positions they hear in public deliberations. As a result, a limited number of clusters or groups of schematic positions should emerge on a socially defined continuum running from support to opposition. Every respondents' set of rankings on a given factor represents a point on that continuum. The theoretical task is to measure the distances between different citizens' multi-attribute positions and then discover how they cluster together. The product-moment correlation coefficient was chosen to measure these distances because it has been shown to be particularly effective in capturing differences in overall pattern or shape that define a multi-attribute position (Cronbach and Gleser, 1953). By transforming the usual scale of the correlation coefficient (-1 to +1) to a purely positive measure of distance (0 to 2), we can gauge how much each citizen agrees with the full set of rankings of his or her neighbors.

Cluster analysis is then used to identify the similarities and dissimilarities among citizens' schemas. As the name suggests, cluster analysis is concerned with finding "groups" or "clusters" among entities that are similar along some theoretically significant dimension (Massart and Kaufman, 1983; Aldenderfer and Blashfield, 1984). The procedure is relatively simple. A clustering algorithm sorts the objects of investigation based on their distance from each other. Each entity—or, in the case of this research, each person—is initially seen as constituting its own cluster. Then the two individuals that are separated by the smallest

distance are merged to form a two-member cluster. With each subsequent step the groups of individuals that are separated by the least distance are combined until the final two clusters are merged into one.
The result is a hierarchical pattern of groups, growing from many small
tightly bound clusters of citizens to fewer, larger, and more disparate
groupings.[4]

Cluster analysis thus serves the theoretical purpose of revealing the
underlying structure of social positions among the individuals
sampled.[5] Because the analysis reveals how much distance or variance
is required to merge any two clusters, we can learn to what extent each
group of individuals agrees among its members compared with the disagreements between groups. This "social structure" of debate can be
graphically portrayed by measuring the average distance toward support or opposition of a cluster's members from the population mean.
Because the distribution of the statements is forced for every respondent, the maximum score or distance from 0 for any cluster of respondents is limited.[6] An analysis of the range of substantive positions
should reveal whether this range makes sense and varies in a theoretically predictable manner from support to opposition. Unlike studies
that test whether people meet *a priori* notions of an ideologically defined
continuum, this method allows the respondents the freedom to order

[4]The choice of the proper algorithm to apply to this matrix of distances is ultimately
a theoretical decision because it is based on the type of clusters that one anticipates (Everitt, 1980). Ward's (1963) method was selected from the available possibilities (e.g., average distance or complete linkage) because it is designed to discover tightly organized
groupings like those produced by a contentious debate. It identifies clusters from the
correlation matrix that minimize the variance, or the error sum of squares (ESS), within
the groups, thereby maximizing the variance between groups. The formula for the error
sum of squares is:

$$ESS = x_i^2 - 1/n(\Sigma x_i)^2$$

where x is the score on the ith case. At the first step, when each individual constitutes his
or her own cluster, ESS = 0. The algorithm then operates by merging those clusters at
each subsequent step that result in the minimum increase in the ESS, or total within-
cluster variance (see Aldenderfer and Blashfield, 1984). To double-check my results, I
also ran every analysis with the average-linkage algorithm to determine if the overall
cluster structure was an artifact of the algorithm. Within plus or minus 4 people in a
sample of 147, the final two-cluster solution was the same.

[5]Because of the nature of the data I could not use the more conventional methods of
exploratory or confirmatory (i.e., LISREL) factor analysis. Factor analysis requires that
the number of cases exceeds the number of variables (Brown, 1980). Here, however, the
statements (a maximum of 26) are the cases and the individuals (45 for the activists and
147 for the general public) are the variables.

[6]The maximum distance from 0 for the 26-item sort is ± 1.31 and for the 16-item
sort is ± 0.77. So that direct comparisons could be made, I standardized the scores for the
16-item sort in terms of the same scale as the other three Q-sorts, ± 1.31, and multiplied
by 10 to simplify the presentation of the scale as ± 13.0.

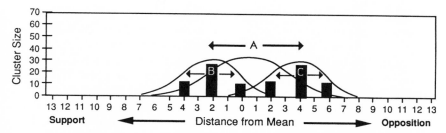

Figure 5.1. The electorate chooses sides: a comparison of cluster distances between and within the final two clusters. *A* measures the average distance separating the members of the final two clusters; *B* and *C* represent the mean distance among the members of the last two clusters. The vertical black bars portray the average distance from the population mean of the groups that make up each of the final clusters.

the issues that are important to them and reveal *their* social patterns of agreement and disagreement.

If, as established theories assume, public debate has little or no impact on the laypublic's evaluative skills, the result should be clearly evident in these measures. When few citizens draw from the arguments of political veterans, the variance within each of the final two clusters of the analysis should be high relative to the differences separating them. In other words, there should not be two distinct positions or "sides" separating the population as a whole. When citizens do not have this choice-specific guidance and they face an enormous range of possible rankings, past research suggests that their response is likely to be highly unstable and arbitrary (Converse, 1964). The distance of the clusters from the population mean under these circumstances should be extremely limited and indistinguishable from randomly sorting their Q-sorts. The continuua of positions should also be poorly defined and have no intelligible logic from one cluster to the next.

On the other hand, if my theoretical expectations are accurate and local citizens do follow the debate, we should see quite different results. As Figure 5.1 illustrates, greater investment in the debate leads to more internal agreement among supporters (distance B) and opponents (distance C) and much more well-defined disagreements between them (distance A). An important threshold—particularly for the general population—occurs when the differences separating the final two clusters are larger than the disagreements within at least *one* camp (A > B *or* A > C). A tightly knit cluster of individuals from common backgrounds, for example, could closely observe the debate and adopt a position opposing a more diffuse group who have given the deliberations only passing attention. The impact is much stronger, however, when the differences between the final two clusters are greater than the disagreements among members of *each* of the two sides (A > B *and* A > C). At this level, the population *as a whole* has invested in the debate and differentiated themselves into distinct camps. Cluster analysis is particularly useful for revealing the overall structure of the debate because it actually measures what proportion of the variance or the differences among all of the respondents separate the last two clusters compared with the differences within each of those clusters.

At these higher levels of attention and cognitive investment, the clusters should become more clearly defined and dispersed toward one side or the other. We should see more differentiation among supporters and opponents as citizens reflect upon and choose *which* arguments from "their side" they believe are the most significant for the case at hand. Rather than just two opposing sides, variants of each camp should emerge, producing perhaps six to eight distinct positions dispersed across the continuum from support to opposition.[7]

The cluster groupings and distances are much more likely to be meaningful if they cannot be reproduced randomly. One of the most devastating critiques of laypublic involvement is that they often choose their positions on public policy issues at random. To test for this possibility, probabilistic cluster distances can be generated by randomly assigning the respondents to clusters and then measuring the distances of these new cluster members from the population mean. Following this procedure several thousand times produces a probability distribution that reveals how likely it is that the actual cluster distances derived from the subjects' rankings of their Q-sort statements can be produced by random assignment.

By graphically portraying the result of this analysis we can clearly see whether the debate is well ordered and nonrandom. Figure 5.2 pro-

---

[7]Relatively few positions emerge because the debate is structured by the arguments of the supporters and opponents and judged in terms of a limited number of broadly shared orientations toward technology and politics. Within a given range of clusters (e.g., 2 to 4 or 5 to 7) diagnostic statistics are available to help one choose "optimal" solutions that minimize the increment of distance or the variance within those groups. When considering where the cut-off point should be, one faces the very real prospect that one or two positions in a multicluster solution might contain such a small number of members that it would be difficult to argue that this represents a distinct social position. Therefore, this study adopts the decision rule that for a cluster solution to be considered, the smallest grouping has to include at least 5 percent of the sample.

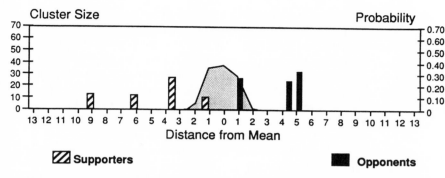

Figure 5.2. Cluster distances from the sample mean and a probability distribution of random assignment.

vides an example that challenges the conventional wisdom. There are seven vertical bars, each representing a different cluster of subjects. The size of each cluster is measured by reading the scale on the left side of the figure. The bottom line reveals how far each cluster is from the population mean. Distance is calculated by subtracting the score of all of the cluster's respondents on each statement from the population average and summing the total.[8] The shaded area in the center shows the probability of achieving these distances by randomly assigning the respondents to clusters. As we can see, the clusters are well dispersed, and five of the seven—a clear majority of the sample—fall outside of the random distribution, suggesting a high level of attentiveness to and reflection on public deliberations.

These measures of statistical dispersion must also be corroborated by a detailed examination of the substantive logic of the positions citizens adopt. Do the cluster positions vary across the continuum for each factor in a manner that is consistent with the expectations of the social process approach and the debate about this project? In a heated and well-defined debate we should see the strongest reaction to the issues held by citizens who reach the most severe judgments about the broadest claims. For common orientation the respondents might forcefully agree or disagree with sweeping arguments about preserving nature for its own sake or ensuring that technological development remains unhindered. There are also theoretical expectations for each factor. For

[8]To ensure that cluster distances accurately represent group members' tendency toward support or opposition, we ran a linear regression on the final two clusters to determine the direction of association between every Q-sort item and particular clusters.

procedural judgment, for example, I argued in Chapter 3 that perceptions of interests are especially significant. If one believes that the other side is driven to pursue its interests at all costs, then nothing its representatives say or do can be trusted. Very strong reactions to global claims about interests thus should signify the strongest reactions on this factor. (The expectations for all factors are laid out more fully later in this chapter, when I review the content of the Q-sort statements.) This analysis of the form and content of citizens' reactions to the debate should give us a good measure of their evaluative capabilities.

In past studies only a relatively small proportion of the laypublic—12–33 percent—has been found to invest in the abstractions of liberal or conservative ideologies (Nie, Verba, and Petrocik, 1979). In effect, I am asking what proportion of local residents, faced with a challenging, high-stakes choice in their own backyard, might adopt similarly well-defined but case-specific evaluative frameworks. In addition, by comparing the cluster distributions for the four factors, we can test whether they fit my theoretical expectations about the impact of experience. A random sample of members of the general public, for example, is unlikely to show a well-defined and highly dispersed set of positions about their general outlook on politics and technology. If they have observed and invested in the arguments from a particular public debate, however, we would expect to see divergent positions emerge, as portrayed in Figure 5.2. By administering the same Q-sorts to political veterans, we can also make direct comparisons between different political actors.

Having identified the range and order of social positions for each of our four schematic factors, we must next estimate the relationships among citizens' broad orientations, project-specific schemas, and final assessments. Every respondent's position is now located on the social continuum of debate for each factor, initially using their cluster memberships and distances from the population mean and double-checked against the theoretical expectations (e.g., imagine that substantive effects might produce seven cluster positions in which the respondents range from strong support—cluster 1—to strong opposition—cluster 7.) The path diagrams in Chapters 3 and 4 provide very specific hypotheses about the relative role of each factor in vertically constraining social positions on project-specific factors and in shaping the final evaluation.

Path analysis was selected to estimate these relationships. This technique calculates the strength, direction, and statistical significance of these hypothesized impacts with multiple regression (Blalock, 1971;

Heise, 1975). The coefficients for each factor reveal the effect that unit changes (in this case, movement from positions of support to opposition) in the explanatory factors have, independent of all other influences, on the factor or final evaluation that we seek to explain. By standardizing our measures of the general and project-specific factors in common numerical terms—standard deviations from their mean values—we can calculate and directly compare their coefficients to determine which factors have the greatest relative success in predicting a given outcome for a particular population. We can learn, for example, whether choice-specific schemas—particularly procedural judgments—have a greater effect in influencing the laypublic's final assessment than does their common orientation. A critical point of comparison would be to examine the effect that common orientation has for political activists, who presumably invest far more time in thinking about their broader views of politics and technology than does the general public. (The actual coefficients for activists and members of the laypublic cannot be *directly* compared because the coefficients will be standardized in terms of the variance of each respective group. Yet we can compare the *relative* role of these factors *within* each group. Does common orientation, for example, have a greater relative impact on final evaluation for activists than it does for the laypublic?)

The methods I have selected thus seek to test each of the components of the social-process view of citizen assessment. After measuring citizens' schemas with Q-sorts, I can identify their social positions and the impact of the structure of public debate through cluster analysis. Calibrating the dispersion of the clusters from the population mean and examining the substantive logic of their positions provides the information to plot their place on the social continuum for each factor and to estimate the relative significance of these schemas with path analysis.

As we have seen, one of the virtues of this approach is that it allows comparisons to be made among different political actors. Given the difficulty of administering such an involved and lengthy survey, I drew only a small random sample from the laypublic.[9] I was fortunate in having the opportunity to measure the judgments of representatives

[9]My target was a sample of 150. A number this small limits the validity of one's generalizations about the larger population. It is large enough, however, to identify respondents from the major social positions. To acquire a more representative sample of 600–1,000 people, however, would be prohibitively expensive because of the time-intensive nature of each interview (an in-person interview that lasts an hour to an hour and a half) and the need to maintain a high level of direct supervision because of the unconventional character of the survey.

from the interest groups who were involved to some degree in the public debate—the Mothers for Peace, the Abalone Alliance, and the Citizens for Adequate Energy. Administrators from PG&E and NRC, however, were not willing to reveal detailed information about individual judgments on such a highly controversial project. Their reaction is understandable. At the time of the survey the plant was still subject to litigation and local feelings were highly charged.

The Survey

To construct the actual survey required a considerable amount of time in developing the most appropriate statements for the Q-sorts. The process of selecting specific statements followed several steps. First, a careful review of the public record was conducted. The local newspaper, the *San Luis Obispo County Telegram-Tribune*, kept a complete file of its stories about the Diablo Canyon plant over the reactor's entire history. In addition, California State Polytechnic University, in the city of San Luis Obispo, holds copies of all official documents about the plant, including many transcripts from public hearings. After examining this material, I conducted a series of open-ended interviews with a cross-section of people from the local community to determine if what appeared to be important from these public sources struck a responsive chord with these individuals. A number of the statements that were ultimately included in the Q-sorts incorporated comments from different individuals who used virtually the same words in describing particular issues in these sessions.

The last step was to put together tentative Q-sorts for each schematic factor and conduct pretests of the full survey, including questions about the respondent's background and summary assessment of the project. The purpose was to learn if all relevant items had been included and phrased in a manner that was clearly understood. In addition, I wanted to ensure that the scale for ranking the statements and the procedures for instructing the respondents on how to perform the multiple Q-sorts worked as anticipated.

Content of the Q-Sorts

The actual statements in each Q-sort provide a wide spectrum of substantive concerns for each factor. These statements vary in terms of their substantive claims, so that we can test whether the structure of the continuua fulfill my theoretical expectations. As I argued earlier, the only hypothesis that applies across all schemas in the survey is that the strongest positions of support and opposition will come from those groups of individuals who reach the most severe judgments about the broadest claims. Thus, there should be variation in the generality of the statements to allow the most forceful judgments to emerge.

Common Orientation

The statements on common orientation tap a person's broad view of politics and technology. Within this outlook, one will also find, as Table 5.1 reveals, general predispositions toward each of the project-specific factors. In addition, several statements are included to measure more traditional ideological predispositions related to questions of government (statements about race and social policy, for example, were excluded). The more general statements for each category are listed at the top of the column; more specific items are located at the lower end. Many of these statements (e.g., numbers 1, 3, 6, 8, 10, and 21) are taken directly from past surveys, in which they have proven to be reliable measures of one's outlook toward these different issue areas. (The statement numbers were chosen at random and have no significance.)

The people most likely to be ardent supporters or opponents of the project should not only fulfill the general criteria just mentioned (e.g., strongly agree with the most sweeping views), but they should also rank substantive statements about technology and the environment ahead of procedural issues. As I maintained in Chapter 3, one would expect that these individuals have developed very strong views about the subject matter itself rather than simply predispositions about how decisions, in general, should be made. As a result, they are likely to reach a firm conclusion about the project rather quickly: if one has very strong views about technology per se or its environmental impacts, one does not have to learn about the process by which the decision will be made, personally or collectively, to come to an initial assessment.

Lacking such strongly held orientations toward technology and the environment, most people should fall toward the center, at least when the project is first proposed, because their judgments are more dependent upon the manner in which a given decision is made. Insofar as procedure is important for the "technological ideologues," however, it should reinforce their substantive predisposition: supporters are more trustful and willing to allow government experts to have control over certain aspects of their life, and opponents are more skeptical of how others might affect them.

TABLE 5.1

Q-sort Statements for Common Orientation

Technology	Political orientation	Procedural judgments	Personal control	Environment
Science and advanced technology have brought us more benefits, through better products and an easier, healthier life, than the problems they may have created. (1)	The government should play an important role in planning for the public good. (21)	You can trust government to do what is right just about all of the time. (8)	Having direct control over the events in my life is extremely important to me. (12)	Nature should be valued for its own sake. (6)
People shouldn't worry about the harmful effects of technology because new inventions will always come along to solve the problems. (4)	Government has become too powerful for the good of the country and the individual citizen. (17)	Government is run by a few big interests for their benefit rather than the benefit of everyone. (10)	People like me can have an impact on what government does. (9)	This country should use its natural resources for the present generation rather than save those resources for future generations. (19)
New technologies are being introduced at a faster rate than they can be evaluated by society. (7)	The national government wastes a lot of money we pay in taxes. (15)	People in business only look out for their own interests. (25)	Government should protect the individual from health risks that are outside his or her control. (24)	There are limits to growth beyond which our industrialized society cannot expand. (3)
The scale and complexity of many new technologies exceeds the ability of experts to judge their worth and control their effects. (5)	Most decisions in society should be left to exchanges between individuals and businesses in the marketplace. (22)	I trust government workers to look out for the welfare of the public. (26)	Our nation should provide more chances for citizens to take part in political decisions. (13)	Our environmental problems can be best solved through more scientific and technological development. (2)
	Business leaders face too many governmental regulations in making decisions about technology. (11)	People who are running the government in Washington are smart people who know what they are doing. (14)	Health risks that the individual does not voluntarily choose are an unavoidable by-product of continued economic growth. (20)	
		The more power is concentrated, the more likely it will be abused. (23)		
		I trust local government more than the national government because I can watch local officials more closely. (16)		
		People should have more say in how things are decided at work and in their community. (18)		

The people of San Luis Obispo County have an interesting political background in this regard. Their overall orientation is perceived as combining a conservative political outlook with strong support for protecting the environment, particularly the beautiful coastline and the local "quality of life." The latter might incline one toward being skeptical of a major new technology with its attendant environmental impacts, but the former, insofar as it is interpreted as being critical of government and supportive of the private sector, provides support for private enterprise (PG&E) and development. If this characterization proves to be accurate, these potentially contradictory tendencies should weaken the overall role of common orientation in giving clear signals for project-specific assessments.

Project-Specific Evaluations

Procedural judgment. As we have seen, one's evaluation of collective decision making for a project like the Diablo Canyon nuclear power plant depends on judgments about several aspects of the political process: the motivations or interests of the actors involved, their truthfulness in revealing accurate information, their ability and expertise in dealing with a highly complex and technical decision, their responsiveness to others who are also participating or who might be affected by their actions, and the overall effectiveness of the political procedures that bring these individuals together to reach a collective choice (see Table 5.2). By their response to the Q-sort statements, individuals can reveal variable grounds and modes of reasoning for making a procedural assessment.

The most extreme conclusions about decision making are likely to come from individuals who believe that the political process is not operating properly because it is being unfairly manipulated by a particular agency, group, or set of individuals for their own "narrow interests." One would expect that a collective entity believed to be solely driven by its own singular goals cannot be trusted to be honest, responsive to the requests of other political actors, or even willing to competently acquire and use the best available information if it does not support the group's position. If such an organization or group is also believed to be politically powerful, then one's distrust might extend to the larger political process as well.

The statements in Table 5.2 offer the opportunity for both supporters and opponents to react in this manner. For example, those who do not want the plant to operate might distrust the motives of PG&E and believe that the hearings are "staged," presumably because of the utili-

TABLE 5.2

Q-sort Statements for Procedural Judgment

Interests of actors	Accuracy of information from actors	Ability of actors	Responsiveness of actors	Effectiveness of procedures
			Present	
PG&E places company profits above the welfare of local residents. (9)	Opponents give a more accurate picture of what is going on than supporters. (10)	Critics of this project lack the technical expertise to challenge the claims of PG&E. (1)	Critics have sought to delay the licensing of this plant because they want to prevent it from ever operating. (2)	Numerous public hearings provided critics ample opportunity to express their concerns about this project. (17)
The Nuclear Regulatory Commission can be trusted to protect the interests of the general public. (7)	We can depend on PG&E to provide accurate information about this plant. (8)	Government regulators have the ability to catch mistakes by PG&E. (4)	Government regulators moved quickly to respond to defects that have been discovered at this plant. (18)	The procedures followed in the licensing of this plant have been administered fairly and impartially. (16)
Critics of the Diablo Canyon facility are looking out for the welfare of this county. (12)	Local residents can count on officials at PG&E to tell them as soon as possible if a serious accident occurs at Diablo Canyon. (14)	The Nuclear Regulatory Commission employs many of the top experts in nuclear power. (3)	PG&E tends to ignore defects that its own employees identify. (25)	Decisions about this plant have been made too quickly. (24)
Demonstrators who oppose the plant do not represent the views of people in this area. (13)		PG&E has hired highly skilled nuclear engineers to work on this power plant. (2)	PG&E has had a great deal of influence on the decisions of government regulators. (11)	Public hearings were "staged" to appear to accept input from the public when, in fact, the decision to license the plant had already been made. (21)
		A person doesn't have to be a nuclear expert to judge		

whether the benefits of this facility outweigh the risks. (5)

The public can draw reasonably accurate conclusions about the quality of this plant by having watched events unfold at this facility over a number of years. (6)

Those who are responsible for making decisions about this plant have been willing to discuss all the issues that concern local residents. (19)

Future

When publicity about the plant dies down, PG&E will be less responsive to local concerns. (23)

I expect that PG&E will have an important impact on political choices made in this county that go well beyond nuclear power energy policy. (26)

The influence of PG&E in this county will grow in coming years. (22)

This project has been studied for such a long time that any serious problem has already been identified. (15)

ty's influence. Supporters can conclude that the project's critics are not looking out for the welfare of the county and that the political process has been unduly delayed by their activities. Each side can be expected to support its assessment by pointing to such things as the accuracy of information, responsiveness, and the like.

A more middle-of-the-road position would not reach such harsh judgments about the motivations of particular groups and would therefore come to less sweeping conclusions that are shaped more by citizens' beliefs in the political system. Even though one might criticize one side or the other for not being as forthcoming as they should be or for failing to hire or consult with the "best" available experts, one could still have faith in the political process: in the ability of rules to govern differences in interests between individuals and to ensure that the "truth" does emerge and is acted upon, albeit slowly or imperfectly.

Personal control. When one faces a risky technological choice, the degree to which it is interpreted as threatening one's sense of personal control is framed by one's sense of whether this type of risk is a commonplace, legitimate risk for government to impose on its citizens. (See Table 5.3). If taking this type of risk is viewed as a necessary and reasonable cost of modern life, then a citizen should be relatively unresponsive to specific attributes. For example, the project's most vocal promoters might believe that the risk from an accident at a nuclear energy facility does not limit their self-determination because they see it as the type of hazard that is relatively common and unavoidable in a "technological" society. In this light, being able to personally verify claims about safety—or economics, for that matter—is not an issue of special concern; as with many other hazards, we must depend upon the expertise of others.

Yet, for those who express reservations about whether a type of risk is a legitimate constraint, being able to personally sense, react to, and voluntarily choose to accept this hazard may become critical in judging a specific case, and their support for the project can be expected to ebb. Indeed, these issues of personal control reflect a continuum of escalating concern. Some individuals may be worried about risks that they cannot sense, but their concerns are limited if they believe that public officials can be counted on to react capably in the event of an accident. Doubting that social response provokes a higher level of concern about one's personal ability to perceive and react to the risk. Those most critical of the plant are likely to perceive that they did not voluntarily choose to expose themselves to a hazard which they consider unusual and for which

TABLE 5.3
Q-sort Statements for Personal Control

Sensibility of hazard	Understanding of hazard	Degree of choice about hazard	Ability to react to hazard
Any negative effects for nuclear power are often delayed and will not be immediately known to those who are affected. (5)	The hazard from this project is no different than the other risks that I face in my daily life. (2)	I voluntarily chose to accept the risk from this power plant. (1)	If a serious accident takes place, I believe that through personal skill I can take actions that would protect me and my family from harm. (3)
I don't think about the things that I can't see, touch, or smell. (10)	This project is so large and complex that it will be difficult for me to determine if I am being charged a fair price for its construction and operation. (7)	Every means of producing energy carries with it involuntary risks. (12)	There would be very little time to react to a serious nuclear accident. (9)
Local residents will be able to detect low-level releases of radiation. (11)	I am skeptical of claims about the safety of this plant that I cannot personally verify. (16)	I wish that I had a direct voice in the decision over licensing this plant. (14)	
What bothers me about radiation is that I can't see it or touch it. (4)	Nuclear power is still new to me. (13)	This project makes me more dependent on the expertise of others. (8)	
	I have a good understanding of the likelihood and the consequences of the risks that this nuclear facility poses. (6)	Renewable energy sources such as solar power can be controlled by people like myself. (15)	

they personally lack the means to detect, comprehend, or react effectively should an accident occur.[10]

Substantive effects. This project presents citizens with a wide range of substantive outcomes—environmental, economic, health, energy supply, and social impacts—that have been subject to evaluative and factual dispute. Statements representing those issues can be found in Table 5.4. Under each topical category, there are statements that reflect the various "levels of interest" raised in this debate. Respondents can thus indicate if an effect is judged purely on individual grounds or in terms of some broader collectivity such as the community or the nation. In addition, several statements on energy supply allow the respondent to indicate how, or if, his or her views about the availability of alternative sources of energy are important in reaching an overall assessment.

At the ends of the social continuum, we should find citizens with strong perceptions of personal impacts combined with and drawn from judgments about the collective consequences of the project. Those who have the firmest convictions are also likely to be more consistent in ranking their evaluations of all of the issues to support their position. Serious questions about safety—at either the personal or the collective level—should rank higher than the other substantive issues because of the high scale of impact (see Hensler and Hensler, 1979). The most vehement opponents are likely to challenge the safety of the plant at all "levels of interest" and maintain that other issues such as the cost of the project and its environmental impacts only provide further reasons to oppose the project. Strong supporters, on the other hand, are likely to dismiss the safety threat and build their case in terms of the need for expanding energy supplies, identifying the economic benefits to the individual and to the local community, and arguing that there are few or no immediate alternatives.

Overall Evaluation

The relative importance of these schemas can be gauged in terms of citizens' summary assessments of the project. Two questions were asked. The first is the most straightforward: "To what degree do you

[10]These attributes for personal control draw heavily from the work of William Lowrance (1976) and the empirical study by Baruch Fischhoff and associates (1978). Unlike their approach, however, I have attempted to keep the procedural and substantive factors separate on theoretical grounds (i.e., they can change at different rates) for the purpose of estimating how the former structures the latter.

TABLE 5.4
Q-sort Statements for Substantive Effects

Environmental effects	Economic effects	Health effects	Energy supply effects	Social effects
Projects like this disrupt the scenery of the coastline and should be built elsewhere. (22)	My electricity bill will increase when I begin to pay for the cost of Diablo Canyon. (3)	I dread thinking about a nuclear accident. (15)	New and more plentiful sources of energy are needed for industrial and agricultural development in California. (6)	The construction and continued operation of this plant has caused a number of problems for residents who live nearby. (24)
Operation of Diablo Canyon will have little or no impact on fishing and sea life in the area. (23)	The payroll for employees at Diablo Canyon directly contributes to the economic well-being of the area. (10)	This project poses a serious health risk to myself and my family. (13)	Few economically feasible alternatives to nuclear power exist to meet the energy needs of this state. (2)	This plant is well protected from sabotage or terrorist attack. (21)
Temporarily storing radioactive wastes at the plant is not a serious hazard. (17)	This county benefits a great deal from the property taxes that PG&E pays for Diablo Canyon. (9)	In the event of a problem at the plant, public safety officials will be able to quickly evacuate those residents who might be in danger. (16)	Government leaders have a responsibility to ensure that the nation is energy independent. (5)	
I am worried that we cannot find a means to safely dispose of the wastes from this power plant over the long term. (18)	Expensive mistakes have been made in the construction of this power plant. (4)	This power plant would not survive a major earthquake without a significant and life-threatening release of radioactivity. (11)	There are safe and economically feasible alternatives to building more nuclear power plants. (8)	
Future generations will have to contend with the wastes from this project. (19)	Without this power plant this area will suffer from a shortage of electricity in the future. (7)	A major accident is highly unlikely. (12)	The scientific knowledge is available to build a safe nuclear power plant. (14)	
	This power plant will reduce the nation's dependence on foreign energy supplies. (1)	The effects of the most serious accident that could occur would last only a short time and extend over an area within a couple of miles of the plant. (26)		
		The chance that low levels of radiation may be released is a significant problem. (20)		
		Exposure to even low levels of radiation likely to be fatal. (25)		

support or oppose the continued operation of the Diablo Canyon nuclear power plant?" (Respondent is given a seven-point scale running from strong support to strong opposition.) Since the power station had recently gone on-line when the survey was conducted, another question was added to see if some portion of those who defended keeping the plant running did so simply because they did not want to write off such a large investment. Thus, the respondents were also asked: "Leaving aside the question of whether the plant should continue to operate or be shut down, what is your overall assessment of this project? Is it very positive, very negative or somewhere in between?" (Again, respondent is given a seven-point scale.)

The Sample

For this study a random sample of the laypublic was drawn from the list of those registered voters in San Luis Obispo County living within 25 miles of the plant. This area includes almost 80,000 voters in six incorporated cities and a number of smaller townships. The boundary for which evacuation plans have been developed in the event of a serious accident is 10 miles. The purpose of going out as far as 25 miles is to capture any potential change in the process of reasoning and evaluation that results from differences in distance from the plant.[11]

A letter was sent to each person drawn in the sample (n = 350) explaining the purpose of the study and the time commitment that would be required. This was followed by a telephone call to determine if that person would be willing to participate. Of those who were directly contacted on the phone (n = 273; many had changed addresses), 54 percent agreed to be interviewed. This response rate is impressive when one recognizes that every individual was told the survey would be conducted in person and would require an hour or more. The most common reason offered among those who declined to participate was the time commitment involved (30 percent). Only a small number (7–8 percent) indicated that they were unwilling to participate because of the subject matter of the survey.

The number of interviews that were properly completed for use in the data analysis was 147, very close to the target figure of 150. Moreover, for such a small sample, the people who were chosen appear to

[11]In past studies of actual technological disputes, such as the controversy about restarting the undamaged reactor at Three Mile Island, distance alone has not had a strong influence on assessment. On theoretical grounds, actual distance is not nearly as important as how that distance is interpreted (see Sorensen et al., 1987).

TABLE 5.5

Party Identification of the General Population in San Luis Obispo County and of the Interview Sample

	General population (1980)[a]	Interview sample (1985)
Democrats	41.8%	49.7%
Republicans	46.2	40.1
Other/declined	12.0	10.2
to state	100%	100%

[a]U.S. Department of Commerce, General Social and Economic Characteristics, *1980 Census of the Population.* Washington, D.C.: U.S. Government Printing Office.

do a reasonably good job of representing the background and general attitudes of the people who live in this area. To the extent that there is a demographic or socioeconomic bias in this sample, the respondents are slightly older and better educated than the norm. The proportion of people over 65, for example, is 5 percentage points higher than in the county as a whole (18.4 percent in the sample versus 13.4 percent for the county). The educational attainment of the respondents is somewhat greater (12.8 years of instruction for the county as a whole; a range of 13 to 15 years for the sample).[12] In terms of financial well-being, however, the median family income of the sample is consistent with the best available estimates for this area.[13]

The partisan identification of county residents and those selected for interviews is shown in Table 5.5. The sample is more Democratic than the county but the margin, 7.9 percent, is not particularly large. Moreover, these people were selected from a section of the county that tends to identify with the Democratic party in slightly greater numbers (approximately 2–3 percentage points) than do those who are beyond the

[12]Countywide statistics are from the 1980 census. When one surveys registered voters, there is likely to be some overrepresentation of citizens who are older and better educated. Research reveals that young people and those who lack a great deal of formal schooling do not register or vote at as high a rate as the population as a whole. The area of the county from which this specific sample was drawn, however, should have a generally high level of educational instruction because it includes the "university town" of San Luis Obispo where California State Polytechnic University is located. In addition, many beach communities, which attract elderly retirees, were included in this sample, but the inland community of Paso Robles, in which one would expect a smaller proportion of the elderly, was outside the 25-mile radius.

[13]The *California Almanac* (1985) reports that the median family income in 1983 for San Luis Obispo County was $24,884; the median for the sample taken in 1985 was in the range of $25,000–$29,999.

25-mile boundary, so the difference in partisan identification is even smaller than it might initially seem.

Interviews

Two different interviews were conducted. The entire sample was surveyed using the Q-sorts and the closed-ended questions that measure summary assessment and background characteristics such as socio-economic status. After the data analysis was completed, a small number of individuals were asked about their views of the plant with open-ended questions to determine if the broader social patterns that had been identified could be reconfirmed at the individual level.

The structured surveys were conducted largely by students from California State Polytechnic University, most of whom were recruited from two classes on quantitative methods. Students were used for the interviewing because it seemed that they would be more likely to appear objective and so to win the agreement of the respondents for a relatively long in-person survey. Even though the decision about the plant had been made at the time of the survey, the community was still deeply divided. I anticipated that many potential respondents would refuse to grant an interview if they had any suspicion that it was not truly independent of the principal actors in this dispute. Because the state university was not seen as having taken sides in this controversy, I hoped that it would be perceived as neutral. The initial letter that was sent to each person was also an effort to allay these fears. The feedback from the interviewers and the in-depth surveys that I personally carried out only reinforced these perceptions. The respondents frequently offered, without prompting, that they would not have been willing to give their time to this study unless they believed that it was sponsored by an outside, "objective" institution.

A total of seventeen interviewers were hired and then trained in a five-hour session by a professional trainer who had experience using Q methodology. Each interviewer was expected to conduct approximately 10 surveys. Since the procedure of using four Q-sorts was unconventional and the interviewers lacked previous experience, equipment was provided to tape *every* interview to ensure that the survey was properly administered. In addition, this provided an opportunity for the respondent to "talk back" and indicate any problems that he or she might have with the statements or the method. After finishing one or at most two sessions, each interviewer was required to allow me to review the tape so that I could provide any necessary feedback on technique.

Although four interviews had to be discarded because they were incorrectly administered, the overall quality of the surveys was very good; in the case of several key interviewers who carried out 15 or more surveys, it was excellent. There is no way to verify that taping these sessions improved the level of performance over what would have otherwise occurred. Yet after listening to more than a hundred hours of interviews, I developed the strong impression that taping these sessions seemed to keep the interviewers "honest" in a way that would not have happened without this recorded transcript. The interviewers would pick their words with what can best be described as a self-conscious care, particularly at those crucial junctures in giving the instructions and responding to questions that had been the focus of the training session. If I made a suggestion to improve a person's technique, almost inevitably in the next session I would hear verbatim that alternative language substituted for the words that had been previously used.

In an earlier grant proposal to carry out this research, several reviewers expressed skepticism about the likelihood that most respondents would agree to have the interview taped. Out of 147 interviews, however, only five individuals refused to be taped. Because of faulty equipment, six additional surveys were not fully recorded. When the interviewer said that taping was a necessary part of the procedure, most people accepted this at face value, particularly when it was pointed out that this gave them the opportunity to respond to structured statements in the survey in a more open-ended manner.[14]

This methodological approach reveals that we can potentially learn a great deal from an in-depth analysis of a particular case (see Appendix B). By measuring the structure and process of citizen assessment after a long debate about a large-scale, controversial technology, we can determine how citizens react when the stakes are high and the arguments for and against are well defined and widely disseminated. Whether members of the laypublic observe and draw from the public arena

[14]On completion of the structured surveys, all respondents were sent a letter thanking them for giving so freely of their time for this study and mentioning that I might ask a few individuals to participate in a follow-up session. After the data analysis was complete, sixteen individuals that the data analysis indicated were particularly good representatives of common patterns of reasoning and assessment were contacted by letter and then telephone, requesting that they grant an open-ended interview that I would conduct. To my surprise, every individual agreed (I had anticipated ten to twelve). These interviews lasted on average about one hour.

should be readily apparent in the social structure of their schemas for the general and project-specific factors. The relationship among these schemas, moreover, reveals the relative influence that procedural and substantive issues carry when citizens are faced with conflicting and highly technical claims. Furthermore, by interviewing both a sample from the laypublic and political activists with the same survey instrument, we can compare whether the pattern of assessment reflects the hypothesized effects of differences in background.

CHAPTER SIX

The Laypublic's Method of Technological Assessment

There are still a lot of people that believe deep down inside that the thing is a ticking time bomb, and I just don't see it that way. I think that it's a too well-developed technology that under the proper safeguards is going to provide essential services to the people that demand it. . . . If you lived in a new condominium in Big Sur and you had to work and live there and raise your family, you'd like to have the power to keep that place cool. You know, if you're in an iron lung in Kern County . . . God bless Diablo . . . keep it running.

Mr. Williams

I think it [an accident] is likely. I would not hazard a guess as to when it might happen. It might not happen for 20 years, but because of the human error element in the operation of the plant and because of the construction problems, and I do think there are some very basic design problems, I think that sooner or later there will be an accident. I don't know what would cause it, whether it will be a give in the earth. We will never know until the fault becomes active, whether in fact the plant is reinforced to the extent that they said it is. None of us know that.

Ms. Todd

THE RESIDENTS OF communities located near the Diablo Canyon nuclear power plant were given ample incentive to pay attention to a long and contentious debate. The stakes were high and the issues multifaceted and complex, raising questions about safety, energy independence, economics, and environmental health. The plant's impact on the individual, the community, the nation, and even future generations were actively debated. Despite such incentives, findings from past studies of national elections suggest, as we have seen, that we ought to lower our expectations about the general public's response. By contrast, the social-process theory argues that we simply have not considered carefully enough how citizens construct their judgments or what conditions motivate them to turn their attention from pressing demands of everyday life—that the polity can, in fact, be quite responsive and able.

My survey of a random sample of registered voters living within 25 miles of the Diablo Canyon plant was designed to capture their schematic forms of reasoning and assessment through their responses to a total of 94 statements. Given the number of possible permutations for each Q-sort of the statements, it is virtually impossible for a subject to "fake" a socially structured position. Only if one has made an investment in the public debate is a continuum of social positions likely to emerge that can then explain a final evaluation.

This chapter presents the results from that survey of the general public, reconstructing the process of citizen assessment in stages. I set the context for understanding these results by reviewing the arguments discussed in Chapter 5, both for and against the power plant, to which citizens were exposed for over twelve years. The data analysis begins by looking at citizens' overall conclusions about the plant and its continued operation. I carefully examine the social structure, content, and interrelationships of their schemas of common orientation, procedural judgment, personal control, and substantive effects to see how well these explain the final assessments. With the results from the survey in mind, I then move to the level of the individual to see if these broader results are reflected in the words and ideas of two representative respondents, whom I will call Mr. Williams and Ms. Todd.

The Debate

From the beginning of active public deliberations in 1972 Pacific Gas and Electric (PG&E) argued that this power plant would provide a reliable and cost-effective source of energy for the state and the nation in a time when domestic and foreign energy supplies were increasingly fragile and the energy future appeared bleak. In addition, the plant would offer people in the county important economic benefits from construction and operation of the facility, with the addition of many new high-paying jobs and a payroll that would stimulate local businesses and contribute a large amount of property taxes to local government.

The health and safety effects from regular low-level releases of radiation were seen as negligible, especially when compared with background sources of radiation. Both PG&E and the Nuclear Regulatory Commission (NRC) maintained that the risk of a more substantial discharge of radioactivity was extremely low because of numerous redundant safety systems incorporated into this plant and all others built and operated in the United States. In looking to the future disposal of the radioactive wastes, the government argued that a process had been established to choose the most appropriate and safe location(s) for a permanent repository, so that the wastes would not remain on site for a long period of time.

This optimistic picture was challenged by a number of citizen activist groups, most notably the Mothers for Peace and the Abalone Alliance. They criticized the development of the nuclear power industry in general, by arguing that the risks from low-level releases of radiation and the probability of a serious accident, in which large amounts of radioactivity would be discharged into the environment, were much higher than PG&E and the government claimed. Moreover, it was very unlikely, in their view, that a repository could ever be found that could safely contain highly toxic radioactive wastes for thousands of years.[1]

In addition to the liabilities associated with the industry as a whole, the Diablo Canyon plant itself was criticized because it was built near an earthquake fault and because there was a history of problems in ensuring quality control in construction (e.g., using the wrong blueprints to install earthquake buttressing, persistent engineering and design problems, and numerous charges made by whistleblowers that construction was shoddy). If an accident should occur, the critics contended, evacuation from this area would be extremely difficult because there were only a few roads leading out and the emergency planning had been inadequate.

In the critics' view, this pattern of problems indicated that PG&E and the NRC lacked credibility and could not be trusted because they consistently promised a power plant that they did not and, perhaps, could not produce. Reinforcing this conclusion was the charge that neither the NRC nor PG&E was responsive to the problems that citizens raised and that the hearings process was "staged" to give the appearance of participation when the decision to license the plant had already been made "behind closed doors." While questions dealing with human and environmental health dominated the agenda of these organizations, the groups also criticized the plant's high cost and maintained that there were economic, feasible alternatives to nuclear power. These issues, however, remained secondary for them.

PG&E and the NRC countered by arguing that the safety record of the industry was excellent and that the primary obstacle to finding a

[1]The planning horizon set by the Environmental Protection Agency to isolate the wastes from the biosphere is approximately 10,000 years.

permanent waste repository was the lack of political agreement rather than a technical solution. With regard to the Diablo Canyon plant, the utility and the government admitted that mistakes had been made but argued that all of the significant problems had been identified and corrected. An observation frequently made to drive this point home was that this was the "most studied plant in the United States." The political process, from the view of PG&E, in particular, provided the intervenors many opportunities to have the NRC carefully consider their criticisms.

Summary Evaluations

Most of the individuals who were interviewed had definite and relatively strong opinions in their overall evaluation of the Diablo Canyon nuclear power plant. In response to the most general and unqualified question about their position on this facility (see Question 1 in Figure 6.1), over one-fifth (22.4 percent) expressed strong support for the continued operation of the plant and virtually the same proportion (23.8 percent) were equally opposed to it. Overall, those who wanted to keep the plant running outweighed those who wanted it stopped by a margin of 51.7 percent to 41.5 percent.

Previous polls had indicated that opposition was more widespread. At the time of those surveys (1981 and 1982), however, the plant was not completed and producing power. Shutting down an expensive, fully operational power plant might seem to be an extreme step for many—even some of those opposed to the project at an earlier period—because the "sunk costs" are so high. The answers to Question 2 in Figure 6.1 support the view that the large investment in the plant appears to temper the judgments of some citizens. When asked to set aside the question of whether or not this power station should be shut down, the proportion of those who negatively evaluate this project increases to 47.6 percent, greater than those who have a favorable assessment 41.5 percent.[2]

The Social Structure of Schemas

To explain how citizens reached these conclusions requires first examining their general and their project-specific schemas. The social

[2]The small sample size (147) could also affect the reliability of these findings.

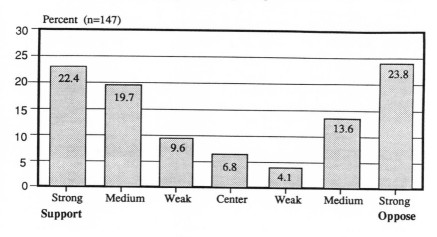

Question 1: To what degree do you support or oppose the continued operation of the Diablo Canyon nuclear power plant?

Percent (n=147)

Strong Support ... Medium ... Weak ... Center ... Weak ... Medium ... Strong Oppose

22.4 — 19.7 — 9.6 — 6.8 — 4.1 — 13.6 — 23.8

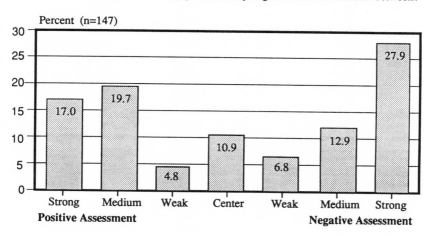

Question 2: Leaving aside the question of whether the plant should continue to operate or be shut down, what is your overall assessment of this project? Is it very positive, very negative or somewhere in-between?

Percent (n=147)

Strong / Medium / Weak / Center / Weak / Medium / Strong
Positive Assessment ... Negative Assessment

17.0 — 19.7 — 4.8 — 10.9 — 6.8 — 12.9 — 27.9

Figure 6.1. Summary evaluations of the Diablo Canyon nuclear power plant, general population.

structures for these factors are hypothesized to be markedly different. Most citizens do not have strong incentives to invest in broad outlooks in politics and technology, but a specific choice that attracts their attention should produce a much higher level of cognitive investment in the arguments of the principals. If the stakes are high and the debate has been long and heated, the population should move into two distinct groups, of supporters and opponents, and then differentiate in terms of the degree to which they support the arguments of "their" side.

Cluster analysis was run on the four Q-sorts. Remember that one of the virtues of this technique is that it measures what proportion of the variance, or the differences among all of the respondents, separates the final two groups compared with the differences among each of those groups. The results from the last stage of that analysis are presented in Table 6.1. What is striking in these results are the deep divisions between the final two clusters for all of the project-specific factors, for which the variance, or distance between clusters, is at least 48.6 percent. The sample variance separating the final clusters for procedural judgment and substantive effects are particularly impressive, ranging as high as 64.7 percent. The disagreements between potential supporters and opponents for all three project-specific factors are thus clearly much larger than the differences among the individuals who fall on one side or the other, more than fulfilling the standard for a strong impact for public debate. It is not surprising that from these project-specific factors, the clusters for procedural and substantive effects are better differentiated than the clusters for personal control: the political process and the outcomes were the central focus of news media reports.

By comparison, citizens' general orientation toward politics and technology is not evenly divided into competing viewpoints. Only a little over 30 percent of the variance separates one very large, disparate group (130 out of 147 members, with 58 percent of the variance) from a much smaller faction. Common orientation thus meets my expectation for a weak, or "threshold," effect for public debate. It appears to be relatively undifferentiated except for the small splinter group that takes exception with the views of most local residents.

Cluster analysis was also used to break down the two final clusters for each of the factors into three to four variants for each side of the debate to determine whether the continuua of social positions are well defined and nonrandom. An analysis of the diagnostic statistics revealed that a seven-cluster solution was the most appropriate for common orientation, procedural judgment, and substantive effects. A four-cluster

TABLE 6.1
*Comparison of the Proportion of the Variance Between and Within
the Final Two Clusters for the Laypublic*

	Proportion of variance separating the final two clusters and the number in each cluster	Proportion of variance explained by the more disparate of the final two clusters	Proportion of variance explained by the more consensual of the final two clusters
Common orientation	30.5% (17/130)	59.5%	10.0%
Project-specific factors			
Procedural judgment	64.7% (66/81)	20.6%	14.7%
Personal control	48.6% (67/80)	30.4%	21.0%
Substantive effects	58.2% (65/82)	25.6%	16.2%

division was adopted for personal control to avoid falling below 5 percent of the total sample in any particular cluster. The distances of the clusters from the sample mean for each factor were plotted and appear in Figure 6.2.

The measure of distance on the bottom of each scale represents how far each cluster is from the mean on all of the items for a particular schema, from 0 to the poles at 13, the highest possible score this structured Q-sort permits. The location of the clusters gives us a measure of the dispersion of this local population. The shaded area in the center of each continuum shows the probability of achieving clusters of this distance from the population mean by random assignment. The size of the cluster is read on the left side of each diagram, and the probability of any point on the center distribution can be found on the righthand scale.

The differences that appeared between project-specific factors and common orientation in the earlier analysis are clearly borne out by the results in Figure 6.2. The most extreme clusters for every choice-specific schema are more widely dispersed than are the clusters for common orientation. Indeed, only a minority of the sample for common orientation—three clusters that represent 39 percent of the respondents—is far enough from the sample mean to be distinguishable from the probability distribution of random assignment at the .05 level.

The project-specific factors, by contrast, *strongly* reflect the expected impact of debate as citizens not only separate into two broad groups of supporters and opponents but clearly differentiate themselves in terms

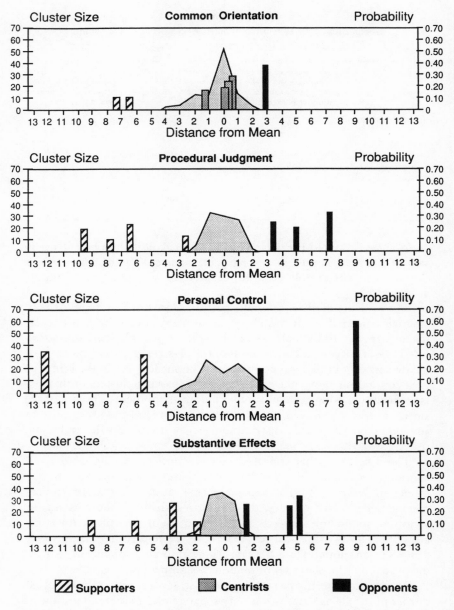

Figure 6.2. Cluster distances from the sample mean and their distribution of random assignment, general population.

of their apparent level of agreement with one side or the other. The clusters are rather evenly spaced across the continuua, except for the obvious breakpoint near the center of each distribution. Most important, an extraordinarily large proportion of the sample adopted positions that could not be reproduced by random assignment at the .05 level of chance. For the two factors that were the focus of public debate—procedural judgment and substantive effects—*100 percent* of the respondents adopted cluster positions that are outside the probability distribution for random assignment. (Point-specific probabilities were calculated for all of the clusters that were close to this random distribution. The two centermost clusters for substantive effects, for example, had a probability of being generated by random assignment of .048 and .034, falling below the .05 level. The only marginal cluster for procedural judgment was .012, also well below the .05 standard.) Predictably, personal control, which received less public attention, did not provoke such a high level of attention among the respondents. Still, 86 percent of the sample identified with a position that could not be reconstructed by random assignment of the respondents, at least at the .05 level.

In terms of the social structure among supporters and opponents and distances for the clusters on the project-specific schemas, the results seem clear. The laypublic groups itself in a manner that strongly supports the expectations of the social-process theory. A random sample of members of the laypublic cannot produce such a striking pattern by chance. They appear to exhibit the cognitive capability to perceive and adopt multi-attribute positions on a social continuum for a very complex public policy choice. To determine whether the patterns make logical sense and conform to my substantive expectations we must look at how the respondents' rankings of statements varies from support to opposition.

The Content of the Schematic Factors

The positions on the social continuua should be ordered in response to issues raised in public debate. As I have argued, there are theoretical expectations specific to the substantive issues for each factor. For all schemas, however, the extremes of favor or disfavor should be held by individuals who agree to the most sweeping and internally consistent positions compared to those in the middle, who are drawn in different directions by less global judgments. Because these schemas are hypothesized to inform subsequent factors in the decision-making process shown by the path diagrams in Chapters 3 and 4, we should also see a consistent pattern of influence as we move from local residents' common orientations to their overall assessment of the power plant.

Common Orientation

The Q-sort for common orientation presents the respondent with very broad statements dealing with technology and the environment, institutional trust, personal control, and ideology. The purpose is to tap commonly held predispositions toward politics and technology as potential cues for each of the project-specific schemas. The substantive premise is that individuals are much more likely to take unequivocal stands if their broad outlook is structured by very general judgments about technology and the environment rather than by procedural concerns, such as one's faith in the government or the desire to have direct control over the events in one's life.

The viewpoints of each cluster for common orientation are identified by first isolating the members of the seven clusters and then averaging the rankings that the individuals in these groups give to each statement (on the scale from -3 to $+3$). A high score for a particular item indicates that most people in that group strongly agree or disagree with that assertion. A profile of the most important statements for each cluster is produced by sorting the absolute value of these average scores from the highest to the lowest.

Owing to the constraints of space, Table 6.2 shows only five of the seven clusters and gives abbreviated versions of the statements. (For the complete statements, see Table 5.1; the numbers in parentheses are the same.) The "A" or "D" beside each item indicates agreement or disagreement. The number following the statement reveals the absolute value of that statement's average ranking among members of the cluster.

These schematic profiles should be read from the top down because the statements that provoke the strongest reaction, the top four or five items, provide the structure for the rest of the material that contributes to that schema. The lesser-ranked statements are important in that they elaborate what this framework "means" to the members of this cluster and how it might be applied in specific cases.

The clusters at either end of the continuum in Table 6.2 were chosen because they reflect the theoretical expectations for people who should have decided tendencies to be favorably or unfavorably disposed toward this power plant. Two out of the three most highly ranked items for cluster 1, for example, indicate a very positive outlook about science and technology, in terms of its past benefits and its capacity to solve today's environmental difficulties. This perspective contrasts with the common orientation of cluster 7, who have very strong and generalized sentiments to preserve nature and are skeptical that the harmful effects of technology will be solved by future inventions.

Insofar as procedural issues are important to the individuals at the poles, they appear to reinforce their substantive predispositions. With regard to potential decision makers, the supporters (cluster 1) express a belief that businesspeople look out for interests other than their own. Government is not perceived as dominated by a few big interests, and the people who serve in it are seen as capable. One can imagine that a utility and a government regulatory agency faced with an important technological decision will receive a favorable hearing, at least initially, from these citizens. At the other extreme, cluster 7, however, there are low expectations that the government can regularly do what is right and doubts about the ability of its employees. Moreover, the desire for having direct control over one's life is ranked highly, suggesting that the willingness of these individuals to defer to others, particularly concerning questions of personal control such as taking risks, is much lower.

As one moves toward the center from each end of this continuum, views moderate slowly but appreciably. The values and beliefs combined in the middle clusters increasingly provide mixed cues for making a decision of this type. Moreover, direct assessments about the worth of technological development and environmental protection progressively weaken in importance and are replaced by concerns about how well individuals or institutions make decisions.

The "moderate supporters" in cluster 2 still express a positive view of government and a belief that science and technology have brought more benefits than problems, but the rank of the latter statement has now dropped from first to third. At the same time, the desire to have direct control over the events in one's life appears as the most highly rated item, and the judgment that nature should be valued for its own sake has taken a place of some importance (ranked fifth). These sentiments are not necessarily inconsistent with being supportive of a major project: citizens could view new technologies as a means to increase control over their life and to better protect nature from the negative consequences of modern life. Yet the importance that such items are given in this cluster does tend to soften what would otherwise be a stronger technological commitment.

TABLE 6.2

Laypublic Cluster Profiles Showing the Ten Highest-Ranked Q-sort Statements for Common Orientation (5 of 7 clusters)

(A: Agree; D: Disagree)

POTENTIAL SUPPORTERS 1	2	4	6	POTENTIAL OPPONENTS 7
A: Science and technology have brought more benefits than problems. (1) 1.556	A: Direct control is extremely important to me. (12) 2.500	A: National government wastes taxes. (15) 2.667	D: Country should use natural resources for the present generation. (19) 2.833	D: Country should use natural resources for the present generation. (19) 2.732
D: Businesspeople look out only for own interests. (25) 1.556	D: Government is too powerful. (17) 2.125	A: You can trust government to do right all the time. (8) 2.381	D: New inventions will solve problems of technology. (4) 2.556	D: New inventions will solve problems of technology. (4) 2.341
A: Environmental problems best solved by more technological development. (2) 1.333	A: Science and technology have brought more benefits than problems. (1) 1.750	A: Direct control is extremely important to me. (12) 2.286	A: Government should protect individual from involuntary health risks. (24) 2.222	A: Nature should be valued for its own sake. (6) 2.244
D: Government run by a few big interests. (10) 1.111	A: I can have impact on government. (9) 1.625	D: Country should use natural resources for the present generation. (19) 2.190	A: Government should plan for public good. (21) 2.111	D: You can trust government to do right all the time. (8) 2.122
A: People in Washington are smart, know what to do. (14) 1.000	A: Nature should be valued for its own sake. (6) 1.250	D: I trust government workers to look out for public welfare. (26) 2.143	A: Nature should be valued for its own sake. (6) 1.556	A: Direct control is extremely important to me. (12) 1.756

D: People in Washington are smart, know what to do. (14) 1.634	A: Direct control is extremely important to me. (12) 1.500	D: People in Washington are smart, know what to do. (14) 1.619	D: New technologies are introduced too fast to evaluate. (7) 1.250	A: National government wastes taxes. (15) 0.889
A: Government should protect individual from involuntary health risks. (24) 1.586	D: We should leave societal decisions to marketplace exchanges. (22) 1.389	D: New inventions will solve problems of technology. (4) 1.523	D: I trust local government more than national government. (16) 1.250	D: I trust local government more than national government. (16) 0.889
D: I trust government to look out for public welfare. (26) 1.512	D: You can trust government to do right all the time. (8) 1.278	D: There are limits to growth. (3) 1.333	A: Government should plan for public good. (21) 1.250	D: There are limits to growth. (3) 0.778
A: New technologies are introduced too fast to evaluate. (7) 1.317	D: Involuntary health risks are an unavoidable by-product of economic growth. (20) 1.167	A: Science and technology have brought more benefits than problems. (1) 1.286	D: Concentration of power leads to its abuse. (23) 1.250	D: New technologies exceed ability of experts to judge. (5) 0.778
D: Involuntary health risks are an unavoidable by-product of economic growth. (20) 1.195	A: National government wastes taxes. (15) 1.057	A: Concentration of power leads to its abuse. (23) 1.190	A: Government should protect individual from involuntary health risks. (24) 1.250	A: You can trust government to do right all the time. (8) 0.778

NOTE: See Table 5.1 for full text of Q-sort statements.

On the side of the potential opponents cluster 6 appears to be similar to cluster 7 because the top two-ranked items are the same. But, as we might expect, the ordering role for support of nature diminishes in importance (statement 6 is third for cluster 7, fifth for cluster 6), while the attitude toward government becomes somewhat more positive in terms of its responsibilities for planning for the public good and protecting the individual from involuntary health risks. Thus, the predisposition to be critical of a project like this is slightly weaker for cluster 6 than cluster 7.

In the "center" position, cluster 4, these trends continue, as procedural and institutional concerns constitute five of the six top-ranked items. Moreover, the substantive inclinations about technology and the environment that follow are much more qualified and equivocal than those at the poles. Members of this group, for example, want to preserve resources for future generations and worry about the harmful side effects of present-day products, but they do not believe that there are limits to growth or that problems of technology outweigh its benefits. Interestingly enough, they are highly critical of the capabilities of government—in particular, indicating doubt about the competence of public officials.

The positions that emerge thus conform to my expectation that there is a predictable pattern to how people differ in the breadth of their concerns, the relative significance placed on substantive as opposed to procedural concerns, and the overall consistency of their views. One's broad outlook on politics, technology, and the environment, however, provides at best limited direction for a project as complex as the Diablo Canyon plant.

Because the general public's common orientation is believed to draw from past experiences and perspectives that have been shared with others, there are likely to be important areas in which individuals have not developed strong predispositions because of a lack of direct experience. In addition, people's outlook may have some relation to a given topic, but its interpretation for a new case might not be altogether straightforward or clear, because of the unique characteristics of that case. The range of perspectives that developed in San Luis Obispo County supports both of these propositions.

The "accepted wisdom" in the community maintains that the general outlook in the county combines elements of political conservatism and a concern for protecting the environment. A large portion of the residents have apparently moved to this area from Los Angeles and San

Francisco to escape the social as well as the environmental problems that plague these larger cities. Whether this is the "correct" explanation for the attitudes of these individuals is open to debate, but their views on politics and technology do appear to integrate certain conservative and environmental ideals. This combination of viewpoints, however, provides no clear-cut guidance for evaluating a project as large and complex as the Diablo Canyon plant.

At one end of the continuum we have clear and unequivocal support for technological development and private industry that is consistent with a conservative outlook and a positive assessment of the power plant. At the other end, however, the desire to protect nature, particularly for future generations, does not suggest automatic opposition to this project. Preserving nature is not equated with being against technological development (e.g., cluster 7 does not agree with the proposition that there are "limits to growth") or with believing that businesspeople only look out for their own interests. Instead, members of clusters 6 and 7 go no further than expressing skepticism that new inventions will always solve today's technological difficulties while the motivations of businesspeople provoke indifference (an average score very close to 0). This is hardly a position of intransigence.

If these individuals are going to become opponents, they require more specific information and evaluative cues that define this plant in their mind as threatening to their environmental and preservationist values. It is not surprising that the Diablo Canyon plant enjoyed substantial support when it was first proposed, because it was not interpreted in this manner and even enjoyed at least the tacit approval of the Sierra Club for a number of years after the present site was substituted for Nipomo Dunes.

The members of the clusters in the middle of the spectrum receive even less guidance from their common orientation because their substantive predispositions are not as well developed. While the procedural judgments that dominate these schemas provide some guidance, they also reveal important omissions and ambiguities. These respondents, for example, are critical of government on several dimensions such as trust and competence—and a government regulatory agency played a significant role in this dispute, particularly in the middle and later stages when a number of problems with the plant were discovered. The most important decision maker, however, has been Pacific Gas and Electric, a representative of private industry, for which the majority of individuals do not have decided, general predispositions. These findings are thus consistent with the belief that experience-based schemas do not always provide clear direction when one faces new and demanding choices.

Project-Specific Schemas

For at least 12 years before the Diablo Canyon plant went on line, the value and severity of its consequences were subject to heated and wide-ranging debate and disagreement. Without formal training and experience with nuclear power, the laypublic was ill equipped to directly evaluate the technical arguments. Yet the public did have a background in judging the credibility of decision makers and the extent to which they themselves were willing to take risks. Developing project-specific judgments about individual or collective decision making could offer a potential first step in addressing their uncertainty about the plant.

Procedural judgment. The most direct way for the layperson to judge the validity of conflicting claims is to determine how much he or she trusts the political principals and the decision-making process. Citizens had ample opportunity to assess the actions as well as the words of the organizations involved. By drawing on past predispositions and cues from those that they trusted in this debate, they could develop relatively well-defined schemas about the credibility of both the decision-making process and the political actors.

The spectrum of viewpoints on procedural judgments is hypothesized to be structured at the extremes by judgments about motivations. "Hard-liners" should believe that the leaders of the organizations on the "other side" are so driven by their narrow interests that they cannot be trusted to act responsibly in providing accurate information, acquiring and using the best technical information, and being responsive to their own members or the community as a whole. To the extent that an organization or group is seen as having political power, it can and will also be viewed as manipulating the political process for its own particular goals. Individuals who take more middle-of-the-road positions, on the other hand, should be critical of one side or the other for much more specific deficiencies. As a result, they reach less global conclusions about motivations and focus instead on the capabilities of the political process to correct the limited problems that they identify.

The schematic profiles in Table 6.3 reveal that residents of San Luis Obispo county reach widely differing views about the decision makers and their critics, views that conform in broad fashion to the expectations just outlined. The members of cluster 1 look more favorably on the claims of the proponents because they believe that the supporters offer a much more accurate picture of this project. Critics of the project are not seen as motivated by this same commitment to the "truth," possibly because of their overriding drive to seek delay after delay in the licensing of the plant in order to prevent it from ever operating.

It is not surprising that members of this group also believe that decisions have been made too slowly, suggesting that they see the opponents as having success in their delaying tactics. In response to the charge that the hearings have been "staged," these individuals strongly disagree and argue, to the contrary, that the process has been fair and impartial and has given the critics more than ample chance to express their concerns. Although PG&E's role does not acquire a place of prominence in this schema, the assessment of the utility is positive, indicating that it does not ignore defects or place its own financial welfare above the interests of local residents.

The potential opponents in cluster 7 counter by arguing that neither PG&E nor the NRC can be trusted to protect the interests of local residents. They support their contention that the utility "places profits over citizens' welfare" by arguing that PG&E does not provide accurate information, ignores defects that its own employees identify, and is unresponsive to local residents. The motivations of the utility are so suspect for this cluster that they doubt the people in the county would be told as soon as possible if there was ever a serious accident. By contrast, critics of the plant are believed to be looking out for the welfare of the county. The political process of hearings and regulatory oversight, which is the responsibility of the NRC, does not overcome the deficiencies perceived by this cluster. Its members think that there was hardly any real deliberation about the licensing of the plant because the decision had already been made. The procedures are thus not seen as fair and impartial, and the process, in their view, has not necessarily identified all of the serious problems at the plant.

Moving toward the middle of the continuum, we discover that the individuals in these clusters have a clear sense of the side that they trust, but their critiques are far less sweeping; matters of process are seen as more important, and they do not go so far as to question the moral integrity of those that they oppose. In cluster 2, for example, the supporters think that decisions about the plant have taken too long and that the hearings have been properly conducted. They believe the plant has been studied for sufficient time to have identified any serious problems.

TABLE 6.3

Laypublic Cluster Profiles Showing the Ten Highest-Ranked Q-sort Statements for Procedural Judgment (5 of 7 clusters)

(A: Agree; D: Disagree)

POTENTIAL SUPPORTERS 1	2	4	6	POTENTIAL OPPONENTS 7
D: Opponents are more accurate than supporters. (10) 2.053	D: Decisions have been made too quickly. (24) 2.111	D: Opponents are more accurate than supporters. (10) 1.643	D: PG&E provides accurate information. (8) 1.955	D: PG&E provides accurate information. (8) 2.500
D: Public hearings "staged," decision already made. (21) 2.053	A: PG&E hired skilled nuclear engineers. (2) 1.214	D: PG&E provides accurate information. (8) 1.214	A: Layperson can judge if benefits outweigh risks. (5) 1.909	A: PG&E places profits above residents' welfare. (9) 2.500
A: Critics sought delays to prevent plant ever operating. (20) 1.947	A: Project studied so long that any serious problems have been identified. (15) 2.000	A: Public hearings provided ample chance to express concerns. (17) 1.071	D: Critics lack expertise to challenge PG&E. (1) 1.546	D: NRC can be trusted to protect interests of public. (7) 2.031
D: Decisions have been made too quickly. (24) 1.842	D: Public hearings "staged," decision already made. (21) 1.778	D: Decision makers were willing to discuss issues that concern local residents. (19) 0.929	D: NRC can be trusted to protect interests of public. (7) 1.500	A: Critics are looking out for welfare of county. (12) 2.031
D: Critics are looking out for welfare of county. (12) 1.790	D: Critics lack expertise to challenge PG&E. (1) 1.556	A: PG&E has had great influence on government regulators. (11) 0.857	A: When publicity dies down, PG&E will be less responsive. (23) 1.455	D: Licensing procedures were fair and impartial. (16) 1.844

D: PG&E ignores defects employees identify. (25) 1.579	A: Public hearings provided ample chance to express concerns. (17) 1.556	A: NRC can be trusted to protect interests of public. (7) 0.643	D: Government regulators moved quickly to respond to defects. (18) 1.409	D: Project studied so long that any serious problems have been identified. (15) 1.656
A: Public hearings provided ample chance to express concerns. (17) 1.474	D: PG&E ignores defects employees identify. (25) 1.556	A: Critics sought delays to prevent plant ever operating. (20) 0.643	A: Critics are looking out for welfare of county. (12) 1.273	D: PG&E will tell residents if serious accident occurs. (14) 1.594
A: Licensing procedures were fair and impartial. (16) 1.421	D: Opponents are more accurate than supporters. (10) 1.333	A: Public hearings "staged," decision already made. (21) 0.571	A: Critics sought delays to prevent plant ever operating. (20) 1.273	A: PG&E ignores defects employees identify. (25) 1.500
D: PG&E places profits above residents' welfare. (9) 1.368	D: When publicity dies down, PG&E will be less responsive. (23) 1.333	A: Influence of PG&E in county will grow. (22) 0.571	D: PG&E will tell residents if serious accident occurs. (14) 1.227	A: Public hearings "staged," decision already made. (21) 1.344
A: Demonstrators don't represent area views. (13) 1.316	A: NRC employs top nuclear experts. (3) 1.333	D: Critics are looking out for welfare of county. (12) 0.571	D: Demonstrators don't represent area views. (13) 1.091	D: Decision makers were willing to discuss issues that concern local residents. (19) 1.281

NOTE: See Table 5.2 for full text of Q-sort statements.

Critics of the plant are thought to lack the expertise to challenge the highly skilled engineers that PG&E employs.

The members of cluster 6, by contrast, disagree about the lack of expertise and support the ability of the layperson to judge whether the benefits outweigh the risks. While this group believes that PG&E has been inaccurate, they do not attribute this, as cluster 7 did, to a single-minded pursuit of profit. The NRC, however, still suffers from serious distrust of its motivations.

The most contradictory position with the least direction appears in cluster 4, at the center. The members of this group conclude that neither the utility nor the critics are particularly accurate or responsive. They believe, for example, that the hearings gave citizens the chance to express their concerns, but they do not think that decision makers are willing to discuss the points that critics raised.

One can see in this range of perspectives the possible influence of general predispositions toward decision makers, which these individuals reveal in their common orientation on politics and technology. At the support end of the continuum, the common orientation is a positive view of the motivations of people who work for government and private industry that is consistent with the conclusions that have been drawn by members of clusters 1 and 2 about the manner in which this specific decision-making process has operated. At the opposite end, government in particular is the focus of broad criticism about its abilities and responsiveness. The Nuclear Regulatory Commission is judged harshly by both clusters 6 and 7.

Personal control. Judging the credibility of collective decision makers, however, is not the only means that citizens can use to choose between the contending claims of proponents and critics. Individuals also have a background in taking risks in their daily lives that can be applied to this choice. Even though residents may lack a technical education in nuclear engineering, they can determine to what extent the characteristics of this hazard conform to or violate their personal norms for decision making. Does an individual believe, for example, that it is necessary for him or her to be able to sense, understand, respond to, or voluntarily make a choice about a risky enterprise such as the release of radiation from a nuclear power plant?

The response to particular characteristics depends on whether involuntary hazards can be seen as legitimate and commonplace and how willing one is to depend on the expertise of others for a choice with these characteristics. Thus, potential supporters are hypothesized to argue that although radiation might be difficult for them to sense or understand, this is not particularly threatening because such risks, in which they must rely on the expertise of others for their safety, are commonplace and warranted in a modern, technologically oriented society. Potential opponents, on the other hand, maintain that the level of restrictions on personal control and the degree of dependence on others in this case is excessive. Therefore, they tend to be more skeptical about positive claims that they cannot confirm, directly or indirectly, in their personal lives. The degree of concern should escalate with increasing perceptions that individual autonomy is limited: beginning with problems of detection, becoming more pronounced with the difficulties in reacting to a threat, and ending with the view that this type of risk has been involuntarily imposed.

The group profiles that emerge from the cluster analysis of this Q-sort generally fulfill these theoretical expectations (see Table 6.4). The characteristics of nuclear risks do not appear to worry the potential supporters of cluster 1 because this hazard is viewed as being no different from the others they face in their daily lives. Even though they perceive that local residents will not be able to detect low-level radiation, they explicitly indicate that it does not bother them. This can be explained by their willingness to depend upon the expertise of others in making judgments about safety and perhaps by their confidence in PG&E and the NRC in this specific choice. Because they believe involuntary risks are unavoidable in energy production, they also see few alternatives.

What is surprising about this group, however, is that they go so far as to maintain that they *voluntarily chose* to accept this risk. Taken at face value this observation is difficult to understand: there has been no mechanism for each individual to express his or her consent other than perhaps one's willingness to stay in the area. Yet, if one believes that the political process has gone to extraordinary lengths to hear the concerns of local residents, as some groups expressed on the dimension of procedural judgment, this provides the grounds for judging that the choice has, in this sense, been voluntary.

This benign view of the individual's need or ability to directly control the risk associated with the plant does not carry over to cluster 2. Members of this group also point out that they will not be able to perceive a release of radioactivity. This characteristic of "insensibility" is something that they think about in this context, perhaps because they believe that any negative effects of nuclear power are often delayed and may not be known to the exposed. Concern about sensing risk is rein-

TABLE 6.4

Laypublic Cluster Profiles Showing the Ten Highest-Ranked Q-sort Statements for Personal Control (4 of 4 clusters)

(A: Agree; D: Disagree)

POTENTIAL SUPPORTERS 1	2	3	POTENTIAL OPPONENTS 4
A: I voluntarily chose to accept the risk from this power plant. (1) 1.412	D: Local residents can detect low-level radiation. (11) 1.939	A: There is very little time to react to a serious nuclear accident. (9) 2.050	D: I voluntarily chose to accept the risk from this power plant. (1) 2.217
A: This hazard is no different than other risks. (2) 1.382	D: I can take actions to protect myself and my family from serious accidents. (3) 1.606	D: Local residents can detect low-level radiation. (11) 1.900	A: There is very little time to react to a serious nuclear accident. (9) 1.983
A: Every means of energy production has involuntary risks. (12) 1.324	A: There is very little time to react to a serious nuclear accident. (9) 1.424	A: The project is so large and complex it's difficult to determine if we are charged a fair price. (7) 1.650	D: I can take actions to protect myself and my family from serious accidents. (3) 1.767
D: Local residents can detect low-level radiation. (11) 1.324	A: This project makes me more dependent on the expertise of others. (8) 1.364	A: Nuclear power's effects are often delayed and not known to those affected. (5) 1.550	D: This hazard is no different than other risks. (2) 1.650
D: I am skeptical of safety claims I can't personally verify. (16) 0.912	D: I don't think about things I can't see, touch, or smell. (10) 1.182	D: I can take actions to protect myself and my family from serious accidents. (3) 1.450	D: Local residents can detect low-level radiation. (11) 1.500

D: I don't think about things I can't see, touch, or smell. (10)
0.765

D: I wish I had a voice in decision on plant licensing. (14)
0.765

A: I understand the likelihood and consequences of risks of this nuclear facility. (6)
0.735

D: Renewable energy sources can be controlled by people like me. (15)
0.676

D: Radiation bothers me because I can't see or touch it. (4)
0.588

A: Nuclear power's effects are often delayed and not known to those affected. (5)
0.879

A: Every means of energy production has involuntary risks. (12)
0.848

D: I wish I had a voice in decision on plant licensing. (14)
0.576

A: The project is so large and complex it's difficult to determine if we are charged a fair price. (7)
0.485

A: I voluntarily chose to accept the risk from this power plant. (1)
0.394

D: This hazard is no different than other risks. (2)
1.350

D: I don't think about things I can't see, touch, or smell. (10)
1.350

D: I voluntarily chose to accept the risk from this power plant. (1)
1.050

A: This project makes me more dependent on the expertise of others. (8)
1.000

A: Radiation bothers me because I can't see or touch it. (4)
0.750

A: Nuclear power's effects are often delayed and not known to those affected. (5)
1.417

A: I wish I had a voice in decision on plant licensing. (14)
1.333

A: I am skeptical of safety claims I can't personally verify. (16)
1.000

D: I don't think about things I can't see, touch, or smell. (10)
0.950

A: This project makes me more dependent on the expertise of others. (8)
0.867

NOTE: See Table 5.3 for full text of Q-sort statements.

forced by contentions that there would be very little time to respond to an accident, should one occur, and little hope that one could take effective actions to protect oneself and one's family. Unlike cluster 1, they do not maintain that this type of hazard is commonplace, yet they also do not indicate that it is unusual or illegitimate in their view.

Cluster 3 builds on similar concerns about the layperson's inability to perceive this hazard and adds to the list of obstacles a concern about understanding the personal financial risk from the plant, because the average citizen cannot determine if he or she is being charged a fair price for the electricity that it produces. Where this outlook most clearly differs from the previous orientation is that the time required to react to an accident is now ranked at the highest level. Limitations in one's ability to respond to this hazard acquire an importance equal to or greater than simply being able to perceive it.

Cluster 4 represents the most complete expression of a perceived loss of individual autonomy associated with this power plant. A hazard that is seen as quite unlike those that they face in their daily lives and to which local residents lack the ability or the time to react effectively in the event of an accident has been imposed on them without their consent.

In the more negative assessments about the loss of personal control, one can see the influence of judgments about collective decision makers. Remember that some individuals believe neither PG&E nor the NRC could be trusted to look out for citizens' welfare or provide accurate information about the plant. Their confidence in PG&E is so low that they do not even think they would be told as soon as possible if a major release of radioactivity took place at the Diablo Canyon plant. As these perceptions develop about the experts who are supposed to protect citizens from harm, it is not surprising that more people begin to think through and worry about how little time or ability they would have to react to the possibility of an accident.

Substantive effects. Judgments about outcomes for this plant require an assessment of the likelihood and the importance of a wide range of impacts for many different levels of interest. Each of the previous schemas should contribute to this determination. Where such internal direction is lacking, one would expect, from a social-process perspective, that the individual should draw directly from the public debate and the people that he or she trusts in it for guidance.

Citizens are hypothesized to reach extreme conclusions of support or opposition if they combine a concern for the widest range of interests with the most severe outcomes. For example, the strongest proponents should take an unequivocal political stand because, in their view, the effects of this power plant, from the personal consequences to the broadest interests (e.g., national energy independence), support the worth of this project in the most clear-cut manner possible. Those who do not see the world in such global, black-and-white terms narrow their range of concern (e.g., to the community) and their estimates and assessments of how much they and other individuals win or lose.

Common orientation can provide cues for these conclusions by revealing the breadth of one's interests. A broad perspective on politics and technology should dictate a correspondingly wide view (e.g., the nation and future generations) while a more qualified outlook should engage less expansive concerns. The severity of effects, on the other hand, should depend to a great extent on which side of the debate appears more credible. Complete confidence in PG&E or the Mothers for Peace in this case ought to produce rather decided judgments of the project's consequences.

A social-process theory also anticipates that the schema for substantive effects reflects the process by which individuals deal with uncertainty about their personal fate. The principal actors in a debate typically provide information in terms of collectivities. It is left then to the individual to judge the credibility of these claims and determine whether this wider set of impacts will have personal consequences. If those who share a particular schema conclude that they individually benefit or suffer from the project, we should also be able to find the collective judgment from which they personalized this individual assessment.

When we examine the rankings in Table 6.5 on substantive effects, there is support for most of these propositions. Cluster 1, potential supporters, is structured by a belief that this project poses virtually no health risk to "myself or my family." The members of this group agree that the knowledge is available to build a safe nuclear power plant. We can assume they believe PG&E's claims that this expertise was used in the construction of the Diablo Canyon plant, because they think the plant will survive a major earthquake without releasing threatening amounts of radioactivity. Even if there is an accident, these individuals argue that residents can be quickly evacuated.

The lack of a threat to personal safety, however, is not their only interest. At the community level, they strongly disagree with the argument that the construction of this plant has caused a number of prob-

TABLE 6.5

Laypublic Cluster Profiles Showing the Ten Highest-Ranked Q-sort Statements for Substantive Effects (5 of 7 clusters)

(A: Agree; D: Disagree)

POTENTIAL SUPPORTERS 1	2	4	6	POTENTIAL OPPONENTS 7
D: Project is a health risk to myself and family. (13) 2.385	D: Most serious accident would last a short time and extend only about 2 miles. (26) 2.143	D: Temporary storage of radioactive wastes is not a serious hazard. (17) 1.667	A: There is no means for safe disposal of wastes. (18) 2.667	A: Plant won't survive major quake without life-threatening radiation. (11) 2.156
D: Exposure to low levels of radiation can be fatal. (25) 1.923	D: Plant won't survive major quake without life-threatening radiation. (11) 1.857	D: Most serious accident would last short time and extend only about 2 miles. (26) 1.444	D: Most serious accident would last a short time and extend only about 2 miles. (26) 2.500	D: Most serious accident would last a short time and extend only about 2 miles. (26) 2.125
A: Knowledge is available to build safe nuclear plant. (14) 1.923	A: Major accident is highly unlikely. (12) 1.714	D: There is little or no impact on sea life. (23) 1.333	D: Temporary storage of radioactive wastes is not a serious hazard. (17) 2.458	D: Temporary storage of radioactive wastes is not a serious hazard. (17) 2.094
D: Plant won't survive major quake without life-threatening radiation. (11) 1.692	A: Payroll increases the area's economic well-being. (10) 1.571	A: I dread thinking about a nuclear accident. (15) 1.222	A: Future generations will have to contend with our wastes. (19) 2.417	D: If problem occurs, we can quickly evacuate residents. (16) 2.063
D: Construction has caused problems for nearby residents. (24) 1.539	D: Construction has caused problems for nearby residents. (24) 1.500	A: Future generations will have to contend with our wastes. (19) 0.889	D: If a problem occurs, we can quickly evacuate residents. (16) 2.000	A: Future generations will have to contend with our wastes. (19) 2.000

A: If a problem occurs, we can quickly evacuate residents. (16) 1.462	D: Project is a health risk to myself and family. (13) 1.429	A: Plant reduces nation's dependence on foreign energy. (1) 0.667	D: Plant is well protected from terrorist attack. (21) 1.833	A: Project is a health risk to myself and family. (13) 1.938
A: Plant reduces nation's dependence on foreign energy. (1) 1.385	A: Government has responsibility to make nation energy independent. (5) 1.429	A: There are few economic alternatives for the state. (2) 0.667	A: Expensive mistakes have been made. (4) 1.833	A: There is no means for safe disposal of wastes. (18) 1.813
A: Major accident is highly unlikely. (12) 1.385	A: More energy is needed for state development. (6) 1.286	A: Expensive mistakes have been made. (4) 0.667	A: I dread thinking about a nuclear accident. (15) 1.375	D: Major accident is highly unlikely. (12) 1.781
A: There are few economic alternatives for the state. (2) 1.308	A: County benefits from property taxes. (9) 1.286	A: More energy is needed for state development. (6) 0.667	D: There is little or no impact on sea life. (23) 1.250	A: Expensive mistakes have been made. (4) 1.469
D: Possible release of low-level radiation is a significant problem. (20) 1.231	D: Exposure to low levels of radiation can be fatal. (25) 1.214	A: If a problem occurs, we can quickly evacuate residents. (16) 0.667	D: Major accident is highly unlikely. (12) 1.167	D: Plant is well protected from terrorist attack. (21) 1.313

NOTE: See Table 5.4 for full text of Q-sort statements.

lems for nearby residents. In terms of benefits, they maintain that the plant reduces the nation's dependence on foreign oil and that the state of California has few economic alternatives to nuclear power. The last two items, in particular, reflect very broad interests that are consistent with the extremely positive view of the institutions of government and science and technology found in the common orientation of supporters. Notice the balance that is drawn between collective and individual levels of concern. Having assured themselves that there are virtually no personal health risks, they are potentially very strong partisans for the project based on benefits to the nation and state that are far removed, in any direct sense, from their individual welfare.[3]

The rankings for the potential opponents provide an even better opportunity to examine the role of collective interests in a citizens' evaluation. One might argue from a very narrow conception of personal well-being that strong opposition is driven primarily by a perceived threat to an individual's own health and the safety of his family. In cluster 7, however, one finds that although personal health risks do play an important role, this concern appears to be complemented and reinforced by wider interests. The two most highly ranked items focus on the risks to the area from a major accident. The plant is seen as unable to withstand a major earthquake, and the effects of the subsequent release of radioactivity, they believe, would last for a very long time and spread much farther than the immediate vicinity of Diablo Canyon.

An issue of almost equal significance in their view is the hazard of keeping radioactive wastes temporarily on site and the question of what to do with them over the long term. They are particularly worried that future generations will have to contend with the wastes from this project. This focus on the future at a relatively high ranking (fifth in the list) is consistent with the strong impulse to preserve the environment for future generations expressed on the scale of common orientation of possible opponents. Only after they express these concerns for larger interests do the members of this cluster indicate that they are worried for their personal safety. Thus, individual welfare appears to be neither the most important factor nor the only one that drives these individuals to become such firm opponents.

In reaching their negative appraisal, they had to contend with the

[3]Indeed, when presented with the Q-sort statement concerning the personal economic effect that including this project in the rate base would have on their own utility bill, this group did not attribute any notable significance to this impact.

uncertainty of very different views about the project and its implications for the individual. It appears that the members of cluster 7 do not find the claims by PG&E and the NRC very credible. Although they reject optimistic expectations, this does not mean they believe that there is an extremely high probability of a major release of radioactivity. They portray the characteristics of an accident, should it take place, as very severe and of the highest rank (first and second). However, when asked to respond to the contention that such an accident is "highly unlikely" their disagreement with this assertion is, relatively speaking, much weaker (eighth). Thus, it appears that they see this as a high-impact but moderate- to low-probability risk. They rate the level of personal health hazard so high because they doubt they would have the ability and time to personally respond to such an accident. This interpretation is reinforced by their judgment that public safety officials will not be able to evacuate local residents quickly in the event of a major accident.

In the middle clusters, the range of interests and severity of consequences tends, for most groups, to diminish in the anticipated manner. In cluster 2, group members still believe that the personal health risks are minimal but their confidence is somewhat weaker than that of cluster 1: the ranking for this statement has dropped from first to sixth. In addition, concerns for collective welfare focus to a greater degree than in cluster 1 on issues within the county. Furthermore, their attention concentrates on impacts—such as the economic benefits from the plant's payroll and the property taxes that PG&E must pay—that are not as dramatic as the issues of potential loss of life and national security that occupy the attention of those on the ends of this continuum.

The individuals in cluster 6 are also less worried about personal health effects. They do not even rank that statement among their top ten. It is surprising, however, that their concern for broader interests appears to be as strong as that of cluster 7 because they attribute a very high priority to the problems associated with short- and long-term storage of radioactive nuclear wastes. Just as with cluster 2, economic issues are more important with this group but are also dealt with at a very general level. They agree, with some conviction, that expensive mistakes have been made at this plant (ranked seventh), but they attribute very little significance to the prospect that their own utility bill might rise as a result of these costs (ranked seventeenth).

Cluster 4 follows the pattern that has appeared in the center of other schemas. Somewhat contradictory elements are brought together to produce a highly contingent assessment. The first five statements suggest that these citizens are potential opponents because they are critical of storing wastes at the plant and of the plant's impact on sea life, among other effects. This negative evaluation, however, is balanced by the views that the project reduces the nation's dependence on foreign energy suppliers and that few economically feasible alternatives are available for the state.

In the schemas for substantive effects, it would be inaccurate and incomplete to reduce citizens' assessments of this project's impacts to narrow judgments of individual gain or loss. These individuals have multiple levels of interests, and they weigh their conclusions, more often than not, in terms of collective rather than strictly personal consequences. This particular use of collective assessments, moreover, is consistent with the manner in which citizens are expected, in the social-process theory, to contend with the political and technological uncertainty that surrounds controversies of this type.

An intelligible and well-differentiated continuum of social positions for and against this project emerges for each of the cognitive and evaluative factors. The imprint of the public debate is apparent in both the structure and the content of these positions. When one examines the substance of different schemas, they appear to be related in a theoretically consistent manner that should provide the necessary means for members of the general public to reach a summary assessment.

The Schematic Paths to a Summary Evaluation

The last step in analyzing the data from these structured interviews is to estimate the strength of the relationships among the general and project-specific factors with path analysis. The role of past and current experiences should be clearly apparent in the weights that different schemas carry in shaping local residents' overall assessments. Because members of the laypublic have limited backgrounds in politics and technology, project-specific factors are believed to have much greater direct and indirect effects on their final evaluations.

As the hypothesized path model in Figure 6.3 suggests, the area in which they have made greater cognitive investments in the past—procedural judgments—should lead citizens to give these factors particularly heavy weight. For example, procedural judgments have a direct effect in helping citizens select between conflicting claims about the project's impacts and an indirect role in stimulating concern about the

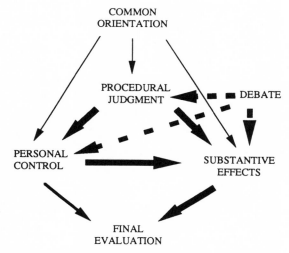

Figure 6.3. Hypothesized path model for the third stage of citizen reaction. A factor's relative influence is represented by the width of its arrow.

potential loss of personal control. Indeed, as personal control is increasingly threatened, individual autonomy becomes an end in itself for some portion of the population, and its influence on one's final evaluation is only somewhat mediated by judgments about the substantive outcomes.

In applying this path model to the data from the Diablo Canyon interviews, the most general and unqualified question about the plant was used as the measure of a person's final evaluation: "To what degree do you support or oppose the continued operation of the Diablo Canyon nuclear power plant?" To ensure that the role of general political predispositions was fully captured, a variable that measures citizens' ideological identification was included in the analysis.[4]

The results from the path analysis for the evaluation of this nuclear power plant are presented in Figure 6.4. Only coefficients that are statistically significant at the .05 level are shown. Remember that the coefficients measure the degree to which unit changes for the explanatory factors (i.e., moving on the continuum of social positions from support

[4] I was persuaded on this by a reviewer of an earlier grant proposal, who argued that a measure of political predisposition other than the result of the Q-sorts and cluster analysis would provide an important check on the validity of these variables.

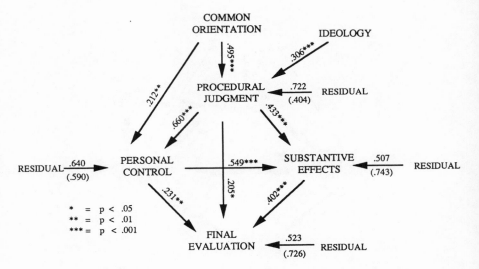

Figure 6.4. Results of path analysis for the general public. The influence of a factor is represented by the standardized regression coefficient of its arrow. The proportion of the variance of each factor explained by the model can be found in parentheses under the path for the residual.

to opposition) produce a corresponding change in the factor or final evaluation we seek to explain. Because every respondent's score is measured in terms of standard deviations from the mean value for each factor, we can compare the coefficients of each explanatory factor within a particular model to determine which ones have the greatest effect. Following the conventions of this methodology, there is a path coefficient for the residual variance for each dependent variable that represents the effect of as yet unspecified causal effects. For the reader used to interpreting the summary impact of a model in terms of how much variance the independent variables explain, the measure of the adjusted R^2 is also included in parentheses below the path coefficient for the residual.[5]

This model testifies that, as anticipated, project-specific schemas

[5]The variables in this path model are measured on what might be best described as an ordinal rather than an interval scale. The use of ordinary least squares estimators in multiple regression techniques, however, has proven to be very robust for handling data of this type. In addition, I should point out that the residuals in this model, and the others that appear in this chapter and Chapter 7, have been carefully reviewed, and there are no distinct patterns that would suggest that they are correlated (see Appendix B).

dominate citizen's assessments when there has been a long and contro-versial debate. The project-specific factors are the only factors having direct effects on one's final evaluation that are statistically significant, and they explain close to three-quarters of the variance (.726) in one's final evaluation of the project.[6] General predispositions have even less influence than expected; the predicted relationship, albeit a weak one, between common orientation (CO) and substantive effects (SE) did not emerge.

Instead, local residents rely on their procedural judgments (PJ) about the credibility of collective decision makers and on their own personal control (PC), or ability to respond to this hazard, to reach their conclusions. The direct influence of each of these variables on SE is close to the same size (.433 for PJ and .549 for PC). Yet citizens' assessments of the principal actors and the decision-making process are very important in evoking the perception that personal control is threatened (the coefficient for the path from PJ to PC is .660 compared with .212 for CO and .640 for the residual). It appears likely that, when citizens believe there is a problem with the integrity or ability of those who are in charge, their sense of individual autonomy is constrained and, as a consequence, they are more skeptical of positive assessments of the project's effects. Thus, the effect of PJ on SE is both immediate and mediated by personal control.

Not only are procedural judgments significant in their influence on residents' evaluation of substantive effects, but they also directly con-tribute, to a surprising degree, to the laypublic's overall final summary evaluation. As anticipated, the evaluation of substantive impacts is the single most important influence on final evaluation (a coefficient of .402), but both PJ and PC have relatively sizable effects (.205 and .231, respectively) as well. The role of personal control in this case is not unexpected on theoretical grounds. If concern about limits on personal decision making is raised to a sufficiently high level in the course of a debate, particularly as doubts about collective decision making grow, it is predictable that the question of autonomy is increasingly seen as an end as well as a means. What was not foreseen, however, was that the judgment about decision makers and the political process would also have a direct effect on one's summary assessment. Given the particularly deep divisions separating the two sides in their views of how well or

[6]There is some multicollinearity, particularly between the project-specific variables. If any of these variables is removed, however, the total amount of explained variance drops by a least 3 percent. In addition, the model is then not properly specified.

how poorly the process operated, the same reasoning could explain this outcome: that is, citizens' support for or opposition to the project varies with their judgments of how well collective decisions have been made over a period of close to fifteen years. This explanation is at best speculative, but it is consistent with the record in this case.

The overall results from this structured survey strongly support the social-process view of the laypublic's method of citizen assessment. In sum, citizens' general orientations are poorly defined by past experience and have only a limited impact in shaping their procedural judgments about this project. The project-specific schemas, on the other hand, appear to be highly structured in response to public debate, producing a well-defined continuum for each factor. Project-specific issues, moreover, explain an impressive portion of the variance in citizens' final assessments, with procedural factors playing a predictably large role.

Although the evidence for a socially defined process appears to be strong on this aggregate level of analysis, we have yet to examine whether individuals echo these larger patterns in their own words. Based upon the strength of these results, local residents should readily use the schemas that were identified for each factor and interrelate them in the manner suggested by the path diagram. Their final assessment should be self-evident in light of the content of their schemas, particularly those that develop in response to the arguments of the activists on each side of the debate.

In Their Own Words

A series of follow-up interviews was conducted among individuals representative of their cluster and of the common patterns of assessment among the clusters. These interviews followed a common format: the respondent was asked a few general questions about the issues in each area covered by the structured survey, such as their general orientation toward politics and technology or their view of the principal actors in this dispute. A series of more specific follow-up questions were also prepared so that I could probe the links a respondent made between factors. In most cases those who were interviewed had thought through their assessment of the various facets of this project well enough that they required only the most general prompting to tell "their story."

The results of two of the sixteen interviews are presented here. The two individuals were chosen, using statistical measures (i.e., correlated with the rankings of their group), as representing two common patterns of judgment—one of support, one of opposition—that emerged from the transcripts of nearly twenty hours of interviews. I have given them pseudonyms to protect their privacy.

The Logic of Support

Mr. Williams works for the state of California as a mid-level supervisor responsible for managing several employees. He is in his fifties, has children, and earns an average income for the area. He completed high school and has taken some college courses. He is a long-term resident of San Luis Obispo County and has been exposed to the debate about the Diablo Canyon nuclear power plant since it was originally proposed in 1966.

A summary version of the social schemas that the cluster analysis identified as "his" positions is shown in Figure 6.5. The correlation of his Q-sorts with each of these group rankings is reasonably high: .75 for common orientation, .76 for procedural judgment, .60 for personal control, and .79 for substantive effects.

His view of the project is reconstructed by following the hypothesized path of assessment, starting with his description of his general outlook on politics and technology and ending with his judgments about the project's impacts and his summary evaluation. At each step in this process, I briefly review the inferences that were drawn earlier about what the rankings of statements appear to show and then allow Mr. Williams to speak for himself.

Common orientation. As we can see in Figure 6.5, the members of this cluster for common orientation are predisposed to support the project because of their positive view of government and of the benefits of science and technology. This is not the strongest position in favor of the plant, however, because of the emphasis placed on maintaining direct control over one's life and on valuing the environment for its own sake. As I have argued, these statements are not incompatible if one believes that technological development and strong government facilitate personal autonomy as well as help protect the environment from future degradation.

Mr. Williams appears to take this position. In his response to a question about the worth of new technologies, he maintains, "I just believe

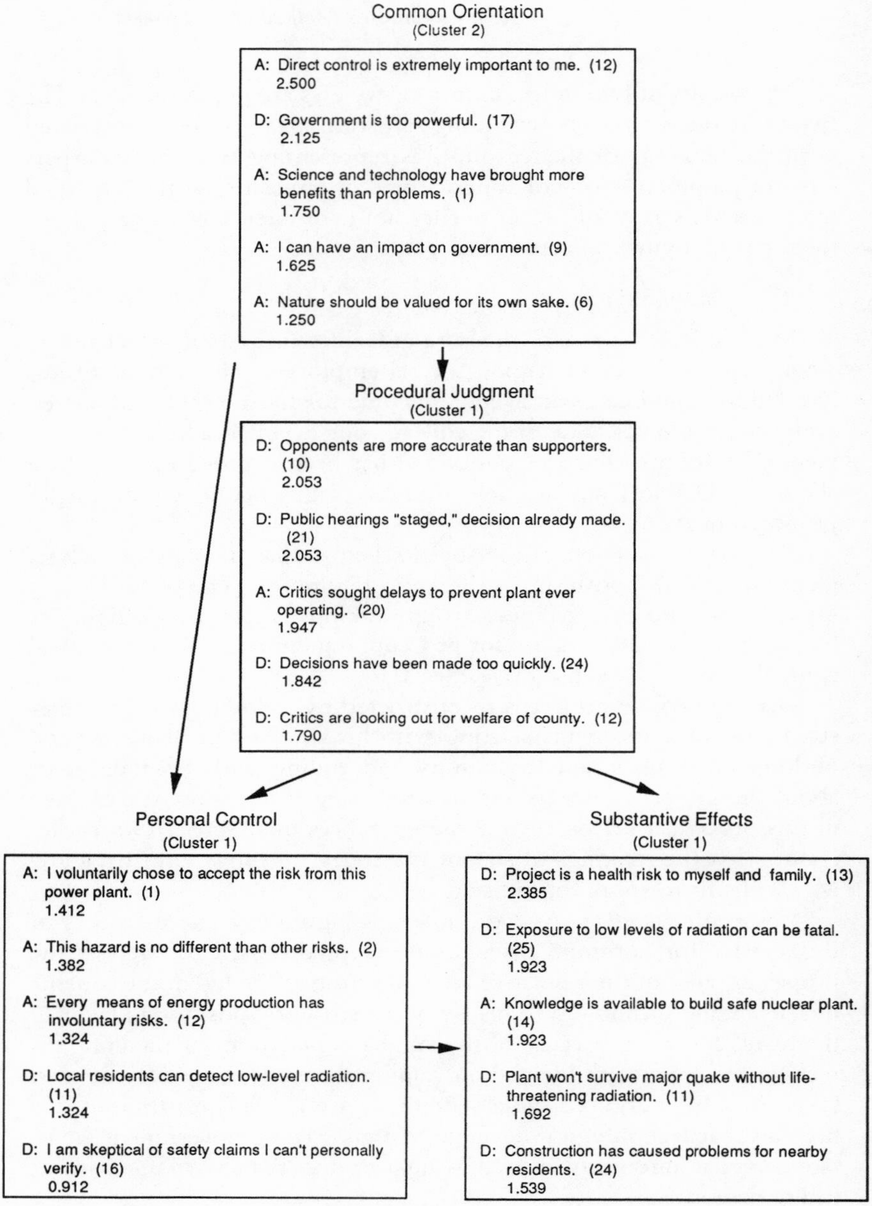

Common Orientation
(Cluster 2)

A: Direct control is extremely important to me. (12)
2.500

D: Government is too powerful. (17)
2.125

A: Science and technology have brought more
benefits than problems. (1)
1.750

A: I can have an impact on government. (9)
1.625

A: Nature should be valued for its own sake. (6)
1.250

Procedural Judgment
(Cluster 1)

D: Opponents are more accurate than supporters.
(10)
2.053

D: Public hearings "staged," decision already made.
(21)
2.053

A: Critics sought delays to prevent plant ever
operating. (20)
1.947

D: Decisions have been made too quickly. (24)
1.842

D: Critics are looking out for welfare of county. (12)
1.790

Personal Control
(Cluster 1)

A: I voluntarily chose to accept the risk from this
power plant. (1)
1.412

A: This hazard is no different than other risks. (2)
1.382

A: Every means of energy production has
involuntary risks. (12)
1.324

D: Local residents can detect low-level radiation.
(11)
1.324

D: I am skeptical of safety claims I can't personally
verify. (16)
0.912

Substantive Effects
(Cluster 1)

D: Project is a health risk to myself and family. (13)
2.385

D: Exposure to low levels of radiation can be fatal.
(25)
1.923

A: Knowledge is available to build safe nuclear plant.
(14)
1.923

D: Plant won't survive major quake without life-
threatening radiation. (11)
1.692

D: Construction has caused problems for nearby
residents. (24)
1.539

Figure 6.5. Summary cluster profile for project supporters. Clusters include the five highest-ranked Q-sort statements.

in . . . progress is going to be inevitable, and our quality of life has been improved." In his view, this is not necessarily at odds with environmental protection:

I think that you can't overlook the importance of the environment. Now we've had some great examples of how it's been spoiled or changed. . . . You see, I've seen this town develop a lot. . . . We're building service facilities for tourists. Well, we need the business that the tourists provide, and if we get a thousand rooms to rent every night, those people come in and spend money that goes into the economy, so I think that it's a trade-off. I think that it's worth it . . . within the boundaries of the controls that we have—the design and location and size and height, and there's a real effort to control the ways it's developed and how it affects people.

In considering the future, however, he adds, "Now, if I am to worry about my grandchildren, if there's going to be any California coast left, I think there is. . . . It's affected, but within reasonable bounds. I don't think we give up nearly as much as we gain."

Broad procedural judgments attracted special attention. Personal control for Mr. Williams is facilitated by relying on technology and the expertise of others:

I think about getting cars. . . . I mean, I would take a new car off the line and take it out and drive it 75, 100 miles an hour because I believe in the technology and the engineers and the people that designed it. If that's reckless, that's reckless, but I just have faith in the professionals. . . . I don't have any death wish.

Despite the frequent criticism it gets, he believes government operates pretty well:

There's always the examples of how the government can be had. That's what people are . . . I think, if that's not too much of a generality. People who are critical of corporate utilities, they're kind of common around here, they're also critical of government, and they're suspicious that the government would be fair and impartial. . . . It's what I see firsthand, you know, occasional abuses, there are always critics, but we have a system of checks and balances that's supposed to keep it under control, and it does very largely a good job.

These general predispositions provide at least some evaluative direction for judging a complex and challenging technology. Mr. Williams self-consciously draws on his past experience to illustrate the lessons he has learned. This orientation, however, is not terribly specific, forcing Mr. Williams to turn to the competing arguments of the supporters and the opponents.

Procedural judgment. Mr. Williams's cluster for procedural judgment reaches definite conclusions about the decision makers and their critics. As Figure 6.5 suggests, the members of this cluster strongly believe that the licensing process for the plant was not "staged." The critics, from their perspective, did not have more accurate information than the supporters, and they delayed the decision far too long by their intervention. Members of this cluster believe that the opponents are simply trying to prevent the plant from ever operating and that they are not looking out for the welfare of the county. As Mr. Williams puts it:

I think that the government has set up controlling factors among the governmental agencies and the Atomic Energy Commission. . . . We'd have a huge list of people that are involved in this research and development, and they continue on doing it. As you know, this plant was built and redesigned and rebuilt, and it went on ad nauseam to get the thing completed, to get it on line, and I just kind of suffered with it . . . because I was always agreeing with the plant.

In reference to the opposition groups, he is explicit, "I don't think the Abalone Alliance and the Mothers for Peace, I don't consider [them] as bad, I mean, but I'm sure not sympathetic with their causes." The influence of his general predispositions as well as his more recent experiences is apparent:

I just think the process is fair, and I never felt like anything was done against my wishes. The length of time involved, and all the avenues of appeal and review, allow those people to have their day in court, and you know, it's not— I don't like to give the impression I think it's the guys in the white hats and the guys in the black hats—but they're outnumbered, and probably that's part of the control of everything that affects us is that it's only a minority voice in objection.

Personal control. An individual's view of the need to exert personal control over a project of this type is also hypothesized to contribute to resolving the uncertainty surrounding a risk that is difficult to sense and control. Mr. Williams's cluster indicates that the risk from nuclear power is no different than the risk from other hazards, even though it involves possible exposure to radiation that cannot be detected by local residents. Interestingly enough, as noted earlier, the members of this cluster believe that they voluntarily chose to take this risk. In his account of the length of the licensing process and its fairness, Mr. Williams has already given an explanation of why he might reach such a conclusion when he said, "I never felt that anything was done against my wishes."

As for the more general concern about individual autonomy, Mr. Williams sees it this way:

A lot of people who object about this plant act like this is the first one in western America. They've never seen one, and they don't, some of them don't know the history of nuclear power, especially in Europe, where they've operated them for a fairly long time. But Chernobyl set everybody off. Everybody hollers, "I told you so." That was a very unfortunate thing. I guess they determined a lot of that was human error, inexperienced operators. The potential is always there, but you know, you can have a nasty fire or a wreck in your car too, if you aren't careful.

Thus, the risk from a car wreck and a nuclear accident are presented as not qualitatively different—both are common risks of a modern technological society.

Substantive effects. These specific judgments about individual and collective decision making should be reflected in the factual and evaluative claims that one accepts about the project's substantive effects. In addition, the range of interests one considers in making that judgment should also be influenced by the debate and by one's broad orientation toward politics and technology. The cluster of rankings for substantive effects in Figure 6.5 indicates that the citizens in Mr. Williams's group do not see a personal danger from the plant. They believe that one can build a safe nuclear power station and that the Diablo Canyon plant apparently has been built well enough to withstand an earthquake. In addition, the plant benefits the state and the nation because there are few economic alternatives that can provide the necessary power (these items are ranked in the range from sixth to tenth in Table 6.5).

Mr. Williams makes the argument in this manner:

There are still a lot of people that believe deep down inside that the thing is a ticking time bomb, and I just don't see it that way. I think that it's a too well-developed technology that under the proper safeguards is going to provide the essential services to the people that demand it. You don't see those people buying kerosene lamps. . . . You know, that's what they're [PG&E] talking about, the whole state is a family.

He further explains:

If you lived in a new condominium in Big Sur and you had to work and live there and raise your family, you'd like to have the power to keep that place cool. You know, if you're in an iron lung in Kern County . . . God bless Diablo . . . keep it running.

In thinking about the future, he adds, "This plant has enormous capacity for the two units. I think the people 20 years from now are going to appreciate the power that's coming from there." And, in summing up his perspective, he observes:

Well, I guess you had to talk to the lunatic fringe on both sides of the story, but I'm sincere, you know, in my opinion of the thing, and I suppose I'm not waving a sign for the majority, but I just think that the process has been fair and the benefits far outweigh the problems.

Mr. Williams also indicated in his final evaluation that he is a strong supporter of the continued operation of the Diablo Canyon plant.

In his statements we find the imprint of past experience and the public deliberations of the previous decade. His general view of the proper balance between economic growth and environmental protection comes, as he says, from watching his town develop. His comments, moreover, reveal a sensitive awareness of both sides of the debate. He constantly refers to the critics and why he did not believe that their arguments were sound. On the other hand, in constructing his own position he draws directly from the case made by PG&E and the NRC.

The Logic of Opposition

Ms. Todd works as an administrative assistant for a professional firm in San Luis Obispo County. She is in her thirties, has children, and has lived in this area for a little more than ten years. Her family income is close to the average, and she has finished high school and taken some college courses. The clusters that the analysis identifies as her perspective are found in Table 6.7. The correlation of her Q-sorts with the group norm is quite high: .81 for common orientation, .90 for procedural judgment, .81 for personal control, and .92 for substantive effects.

Common orientation. In Figure 6.6 we can see that the common orientation for Ms. Todd's cluster places great emphasis on protecting the environment, particularly resources for future generations. Although they do not necessarily distrust technology in general, members of this cluster are skeptical that future developments will always solve today's problems. As far as decision making is concerned, they are deeply distrustful of the government, and direct control over their lives appears to be very important to them.

Common Orientation
(Cluster 7)

D: Country should use natural resources for the present generation. (19)
2.732

D: New inventions will solve problems of technology. (4)
2.341

A: Nature should be valued for its own sake. (6)
2.244

D: You can trust government to do right all the time. (8)
2.122

A: Direct control is extremely important to me. (12)
1.756

Procedural Judgment
(Cluster 7)

D: PG&E provides accurate information. (8)
2.500

A: PG&E places profits above residents' welfare. (9)
2.500

D: NRC can be trusted to protect the interests of public. (7)
2.031

A: Critics are looking out for welfare of county. (12)
2.031

D: Licensing procedures were fair and impartial. (16)
1.844

Personal Control
(Cluster 4)

D: I voluntarily chose to accept the risk from this power plant. (1)
2.217

A: There is very little time to react to a serious nuclear accident. (9)
1.983

D: I can take actions to protect myself and my family from serious accidents. (3)
1.767

D: This hazard is no different than other risks. (2)
1.650

D: Local residents can detect low-level radiation. (11)
1.500

Substantive Effects
(Cluster 7)

A: Plant won't survive major quake without life-threatening radiation. (11)
2.156

D: Most serious accident would last a short time and extend only about 2 miles. (26)
2.125

D: Temporary storage of radioactive wastes is not a serious hazard. (17)
2.094

D: If a problem occurs, we can quickly evacuate residents. (16)
2.063

A: Future generations will have to contend with our wastes. (19)
2.000

Figure 6.6. Summary cluster profile for project opponents. Clusters include the five highest-ranked Q-sort statements.

When asked about the value of technological development, Ms. Todd responds:

Well, generally I think technology benefits all of us. I don't see that many negative aspects other than the pollution issue which is a much larger issue than it seemed to be ten years ago. I am extremely concerned about that, but at this point I don't know exactly how we go about reversing the trend of technology. I think it's impossible, but we do have to do something about the effect of pollution on the environment.

To elaborate about the environmental effects of technology, she argues:

I think it's a real Catch-22. I think technology creates as many problems as it solves. . . . I'm not saying that it's a positive balance; I think it's almost a negative balance because for X number of steps ahead that we take, we leave X number of problems behind us. So I think it's a real ongoing problem.

This has implications for her in considering the future because, she continues:

I try not to only think about my generation but what's going to be left for my grandchildren and their children. I don't know what will be left. It does concern me to think about the state of the environment in 50 or 100 years.

In describing her reaction to the risks of technology, she makes a significant distinction:

Well, I'm probably much more concerned about the things I can't see and I can't smell. They're not anything that I have any way of knowing or judging. Those are the things that I think are much more insidious than something you're going to make a conscious decision about.

Will government respond to the problems that she foresees? Ms. Todd is unequivocal in her judgment. Just as with Mr. Williams, procedural issues even on a general level evoked a strong reaction:

I think government is completely ineffectual in regulating, cleaning up, whatever. I don't think—I think it probably would be better to keep in the private sector, make it something that is competitive. . . . I think that anytime a bureaucracy is left to manage something or oversee something, the purpose gets lost in the bureaucracy, I think there is a problem with civil service people becoming simply civil service people clocking in and clocking out. I know that there are many exceptions, but the problem is that I think that the rule occurs more than the exception does in terms of people don't really care about the quality of their work and when you're talking about monitoring the environment, it's not something where we can afford to have slipups. Certainly, the same thing is going to happen in the private sector, but at least you have a means there to weed those people out. You don't have that option with ease when it's the government we're dealing with.

This was an important point from which she generalized even further:

I think accountability is really important. If the company makes a mistake, if the fireman makes a mistake, if the engineer makes a mistake, I think accountability is important. . . . Progress isn't going to happen without mistakes, and I understand that. But it's probably maybe the real reason that I don't trust the government or big companies is because there is a lack of accountability.

Procedural judgment. After describing her common orientation toward politics and technology, Ms. Todd was asked about her view of the people and the organizations who have been directly involved in making or challenging the decisions about the Diablo Canyon nuclear power plant. Figure 6.6 indicates that the cluster of which she is a part is very distrustful of the motivations of PG&E and of the accuracy of the information that they provide. The government agency responsible for regulating the plant is viewed with almost the same level of skepticism, particularly the manner in which it conducted the licensing procedures. In contrast, critics are believed to be looking out for the welfare of the county.

Ms. Todd started to pay attention to the project when she first arrived in the county in the mid-1970's because of the effect that construction of a project this size was having on the area. There was a definite turning point, however, when her present perspective on this project started to develop. She describes what happened:

Certainly in '82 when it was discovered that the blueprints had been reversed, and the construction was going to stop, and they were going to have to backtrack, and it was going to cost a lot of money. I hadn't been concerned about it up until that point. That was the point at which I stopped believing entirely what I read about PG&E, what efforts they were making, that sort of thing.

Soon after this occurred, she had an opportunity to speak at some length with one of the founding members of the Mothers for Peace, which reinforced her interest in learning more about the plant. She began to follow the public hearings and attended the meetings that were held in the city of San Luis Obispo. Subsequent allegations by whistleblowers regarding quality control and design problems at the plant were also important to her, as she recounts:

Those people are extremely credible because they do have the technological knowledge that I don't have. . . . They can quote book and page what is going on and point at specific examples. There's just been a general unwillingness on the part of PG&E unless they absolutely have to come clean.

The result is that she has reached strong conclusions about the credibility of each side from these experiences. She explains:

Maybe I think they [the Mothers for Peace] have more credibility because their concerns are nearer my concerns. I don't have the same concerns that PG&E has. I don't care if PG&E has any money. I don't care if they show a profit at the end of the year. I don't care about any of that. I care about the environment and the health and safety of my community. Probably because there is absolutely no profit involved with that group that is the watchdog organization. No one there is making any money. Certainly that's not the case with an organization like PG&E.

When asked if the Nuclear Regulatory Commission has properly fulfilled its role in the manner in which the plant has been licensed, she observes:

I think there are major problems in the NRC. I think there probably should be—you could hire a special prosecutor and employ him or her for life to investigate the NRC. I think probably the web of links between the NRC and the utility companies is probably so intricate that it would take years to unravel all of it, but I do think there is a link there, and because of that I don't think they act independently. I don't think they act independently in the best interests of the consumers, and as far as I'm concerned, a government agency is there for the people and for the consumers.

Personal control. A second means to judge the technological and political uncertainty is to determine whether or not the attributes of the choice conform to one's norms of personal decision making. The cluster for this schema in Figure 6.6 suggests that these individuals believe those standards have been violated. The plant is seen as quite different from other choices that they face because it cannot be sensed, there is little time to react to a major accident, and there are few actions that can be taken to protect oneself. Most important to members of this group is that they did not voluntarily choose to take this risk.

In describing her personal ability to understand and respond to the risk of the plant, Ms. Todd drew on her past experience and the more recent judgments that she has developed about the utility and returned to her concern that radiation cannot be detected by an individual:

I am responsible for two children. I feel enormous concern. . . . When PG&E installed the siren system throughout the county, several sirens went up where I live . . . and my older son was about 11 or 12 when they put the sirens up, and he wanted to know what they were. When I found out what they were, I didn't even want to tell him what they were because I thought how frightening to tell him that when these sirens go off—and then after I studied the plan myself and had conversations with lots of people who had attended the hearings and tried to educate myself as I can as a layperson, I pretty much resigned myself to believe that we would not be notified, the sirens would not go off. The sirens did not go off at Three Mile Island as soon as the accident happened. It was three days before anybody knew that there was an accident of the magnitude it was.

When asked why she did not think she would learn more quickly about an accident, she responded,

Because I don't believe that there has been credibility at all with PG&E. I think they've proven that time and again. I think that they would go to any lengths to cover up that sort of mistake until they absolutely had to advise the public. I think that goes directly back to PG&E.

Another factor that reinforced her negative sense of her ability to react effectively in the event of an accident was a conversation she had with a doctor who had helped to organize a group of doctors in opposition to the plant.

There was a lot of discussion here and a lot of everything about the emergency response plan, and what this particular doctor said was something I will never forget. He said that it was beyond him how people would believe that all of the people in the helping professions—policemen, doctors, firemen, hospital personnel—why would we think that all those people would stick around in an emergency. They all have families, and they would want to leave the area as well. He had lots of children and certainly stated very clearly to me, and I don't think it was any secret, that if there were any sort of emergency, his first concern would be his own family.

I asked Ms. Todd if she did not believe that there were a number of risks that society imposed on us as individuals. She countered in this manner:

There's danger wherever you live. There's going to be something. You move some place and then find out that the water is bad. You find out you're living on top of a toxic dump. There's really no way to know that any particular place is safe, but that's probably the price that we pay for technology. I think that the crime of Diablo is that we were not educated, we weren't given an opportunity to voice an opinion as to whether we wanted the plant there.

Substantive effects. In Figure 6.6 it is evident that the prospects of a serious accident dominate the thinking of the members of this cluster because they believe that the plant would not survive an earthquake, the effects would be widespread, and residents would not be quickly evacuated. In addition, they express concern about the problem of storing the wastes on site and protecting future generations from them over the long term.

The conclusions that Ms. Todd reaches are not unexpected in light of her previous judgments about the utility and the Nuclear Regulatory Commission. She focuses a great deal of attention on the possibility of an accident:

I think it's likely. I would not hazard a guess as to whether it might happen. It might not happen for 20 years, but because of the human error element in the operation of the plant and because of the construction problems, and I do think there are some very basic design problems, I think that sooner or later there would be an accident. I don't know what would cause it, whether it will be a give in the earth. We will never know until the fault becomes active, whether the fact the plant is reinforced to the extent that they said it is. None of us know that. But I do think that sooner or later there probably will be some sort of an accident, at least there will be some sort of release of radiation, at what level I don't know.

In considering which issues were most important among economics, energy supply, health, and waste, she reacts in this manner:

I think health and waste are related, and I think those have to be at the top of the list. If there was a power source that was safe and clean, I wouldn't mind paying more for it, but when I know I'm paying more for something that is not safe and potentially devastating to the environment as well, I think those things sort of add injury to insult or insult to injury, if you see what I mean.

What stands out in Ms. Todd's statements is the level of specificity and the well-defined organization of her reasoning and assessment. She has invested a great deal of time in thinking through her position. With very little prompting, her evaluations came tumbling out in well-organized packages of values and beliefs that all have an internal logic. Moreover, these judgments appear to be strongly related to one another in a manner consistent with the basic propositions of the model. While

Ms. Todd's reliance on others and the arguments of the opponents is unmistakable, she appears to have shaped these judgments in light of her own predisposition.

Overall, I was impressed with the degree to which the open-ended interviews for Ms. Todd and Mr. Williams conform to the items found in their social clusters. I conducted as many as sixteen of these interviews (over 10 percent of the sample) because I wanted to double-check the validity of the Q-sort procedure and the findings. The level of consistency between the structured and unstructured surveys for these two individuals was replicated to a surprising extent for all the others who were interviewed.

The broad outlines of the findings for the laypublic are clear. As expected, most citizens have not made substantial investments in general orientations toward politics and technology. Instead, they focus their attention on the immediate arguments they hear about the specific choice before them during public deliberations. The coherent, multi-attribute positions they adopt reflect a level of political sophistication that heretofore has been judged extremely unlikely or even, in the view of some, impossible.

CHAPTER SEVEN

The Costs and Benefits of Political Experience

I know that our whole industrial society, all societies, are based on energy. It has to be reliable, reasonably cheap, and reasonably safe. It has to meet these three tests. Coal is part of it. Hydro is part. Nuclear is a part of it. Nuclear in my judgment is the most benign source. . . . We have to rethink, we as a society, our position on nuclear power and develop a different charter with a different set of assumptions if we're going to have nuclear power. The set of assumptions we are working on now are unworkable. Demonstrable beyond anybody's foggiest vision. Anyone can see that. Otherwise we'll be at the tender mercies of the Arabs in ten years. I'm sure that some of the manipulators in these movements, that's exactly where they want us. I don't mean to say there's a communist under every bed either. But there are people who would restructure this society, and they are well funded through tax exempt foundations. Your tax dollars. Our tax dollars. And I don't like it.

A member of Citizens for Adequate Energy

We were told that it [nuclear power] was clean, safe, and economical. The federal government badgered the utilities to get into it by saying if you don't, we're going to put you out of business. The federal government clearly knew the risks. They had the studies from Hiroshima and Nagasaki and from our own service people. So they knew the risks. They had all the evidence and they went ahead with it anyway. And all the time the people have to file with the Freedom of Information Act to get the true information of what really went on. The Vietnam War—I mean it goes on and on.

A member of Abalone Alliance

[The Mothers for Peace became involved] because of the radiation. The routine release of radiation and the effects it would have on our children. That was and is the overriding issue of this whole thing. Radiation that routinely is emitted in gas form into the air, into the water, into our food chain, and we know that children with their rapidly growing cells are the most vulnerable. . . . We were against the plant whether there was a fault or not because of the emission, because of the radioactivity that is produced out there.

A member of Mothers for Peace

THE EVIDENCE FROM Chapter 6 suggests that contrary to the conventional wisdom, the lack of extensive background in thinking about politics and technology does not stop most citizens from investing in the arguments about particular decisions that provoke intense concern. Whether we should reconsider the role of the laypublic in technological decision making now requires weighing these new-found capabilities against the methods of those political actors who currently dominate the policymaking process.

From a social-process perspective, the experience that political activists bring to technological assessment leads them to respond to public debate in a quite different manner than the case-specific, present-structured approach of average citizens. Through direct experience or speaking with others, activists have typically invested in more general perspectives about politics and technology as well as particular types of technologies and impacts. This background enables them to frame a new choice in terms of the key issues and evaluative arguments that have proven to be significant in the past. Their strength and clarity of conviction motivates them to build their case by gathering and interpreting detailed information about the choice at hand in terms of these more general predispositions. This is especially important in the choosing of sites for large, complex technologies where the level and evaluative worth of the impacts can vary greatly depending on which choice is made. As the mandate of the National Environmental Policy Act argues, we need to assemble this information so that the pros and cons of *each* major action can be carefully considered.

While political activists have strong incentives to identify information about the full range of impacts, their investment in the past, predictably enough, focuses their attention on the impacts and arguments that originally drew them to this issue. The actual process of public debate and deliberation is far more likely to reinforce than to change these predispositions. The arguments of their opponents, for example, are anticipated as part of the "script" for a particular choice. Case-specific information about a particular decision is not presented in a manner that challenges their conclusions because it is typically interpreted by those from their organization who share their general orientation. Indeed, their conclusions about a particular choice only grow more extreme in the process of sharing information about it with those of a like mind.

If these expectations about the role of the past and the response to public deliberations are true, we should discover in the case of the Diablo Canyon nuclear power plant a very different pattern of assessment

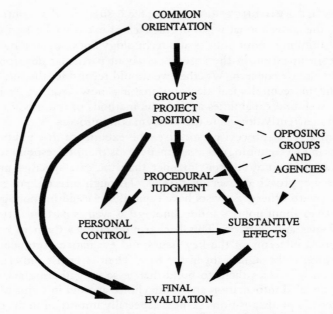

Figure 7.1. Technological decision making by members of interest groups. A factor's relative influence is represented by the width of its arrow.

among political activists than among members of the laypublic. Figure 7.1 graphically portrays this model of assessment. Based on their well-defined orientation toward politics and technology political veterans reach assessments of a specific case that are far more extreme than those of the general public. Because their substantive and procedural assessments are ordered by the past, case-specific issues play a far weaker role, and procedural judgments have little impact on their substantive conclusions.

This chapter tests these expectations based on interviews with the three activist organizations that played the most prominent and lasting role in the Diablo Canyon controversy: the Mothers for Peace, the Abalone Alliance, and Citizens for Adequate Energy. The analysis begins by describing the history of each group and its likely role in shaping the group's common orientation toward nuclear power in general and this project in particular. Their methods of evaluation are revealed using the same type of interview employed with the general public. The results are reviewed by following the hypothesized pattern of assessment, from common orientation to project-specific judgments. The findings are compared at each stage with those from the general public. I then review how ordinary citizens differ among themselves in background and in level of interest and attentiveness to the public debate and suggest the type of individuals who would make the most appropriate "representatives" of members of the general public.

Organizational Histories

The survey that was carried out to test these expectations was conducted in March 1986, approximately four months after the interviews with the random sample of residents of San Luis Obispo County. The groups were chosen because of their long and often prominent involvement in the debate over this nuclear power plant. We can see from each organization's history how the background of the individuals who joined might shape a distinct framework that would guide their evaluation of this particular project.

Mothers for Peace

The interest group with the most enduring participation in public discussions about the Diablo Canyon power plant is a local chapter of Mothers for Peace, an organization originally formed in the late 1960's to oppose American involvement in the war in Vietnam. By the early 1970's, however, many of the Mothers for Peace were turning their attention to the danger from the continued escalation of the nuclear arms race. This interest in nuclear arms soon widened to a critical consideration of the problems that might exist with the civilian use of nuclear power. One member made the link in this manner: "It became increasingly clear that it didn't matter what the source of the radiation was, one ought to be skeptical of it."

In the fall of 1973, the Mothers petitioned to intervene in the licensing hearings for the Diablo Canyon nuclear power plant. Although this was before the earthquake fault had been discovered, the reason for seeking to play an active role was perfectly consistent with their past. As the quote at the beginning of this chapter suggests, the "overriding issue" for the Mothers for Peace was "the routine release of radiation and the effects it would have on our children."

Within three weeks after they were accepted as intervenors, however, PG&E disclosed that an earthquake fault had been discovered approximately three miles offshore of the plant site. This only reinforced their concern, and for the next two years the Mothers represented themselves in the hearings without benefit of legal counsel or the financial ability to hire outside experts such as geologists and nuclear engineers. After seeking help from a number of foundations, they convinced the Center for Law and the Public Interest, a public-interest law firm, to take their case in 1975; the Center has represented the organization since that time in its many legal challenges to the plant.

The actual number of members has varied widely as local attention on the plant has fluctuated in reaction to events such as the accident at Three Mile Island and disclosures by whistle-blowers of problems at the plant. There has been a durable core of 15–20 individuals, however, who have committed from 10 to 30 hours of work a week to support their activities. As late as 1986 their mailing list included approximately 5,000 individuals and organizations.

Since they have legal representation, most of the work by the Mothers themselves is political. One person summed it up this way:

You work for legislation, you work for stronger oversight in Congress, you work for public education, and you do speakers and films and petitions, and you go with resolutions to all the public bodies in your county, and you do everything you can to keep the issue alive in people's minds to keep them willing to work even when they think it's a lost cause.

Although they did not win their battle with PG&E and the NRC to prevent the plant from receiving a license, they have had a significant impact on the political process. For example, they were able to secure four separate Congressional hearings on the Diablo Canyon project. In 1978 they even persuaded the governor of California, Jerry Brown, to join them as an intervenor until the end of his term in office in 1981. This group has thus pursued its goals by working in a conventional manner within the political process to try to stop the Diablo Canyon plant from operating.

Abalone Alliance

A different approach to opposing the plant has been taken by a broad and loose coalition of activist groups called the Abalone Alliance. In 1976, an initiative was put on the ballot in California that sought to severely limit or halt the construction of new nuclear power plants in the state. Although the initiative failed, the debate that it generated led a number of people in San Luis Obispo to consider forming an organization that would complement the efforts of the Mothers for Peace in its intervention in the hearings process.

The Abalone Alliance initially began on the state level in 1977, combining a disparate collection of "peace" organizations such as the American Friends Service Committee, the Modesto Peace Life Center, the Research Center for Nonviolence in Santa Cruz, the Mothers for Peace, and the Abalone Nonviolent Direct Action group from San Luis Obispo. The broad goal was to educate the public about the dangers of nuclear power. The Diablo Canyon power plant, however, soon became the focus of their efforts and the symbol of what they believed was wrong with using nuclear fission as a source of energy.

To publicize their concerns in the community of San Luis Obispo, the Alliance held a number of forums in which outside people such as physicians or representatives of labor unions were brought in to testify about the health and safety issues of nuclear power plants. In addition, from 1977 until 1985, supporters leafleted workers at the gate to the construction site to "educate" them about the problems of nuclear power and the job alternatives to working on this particular project. The activity for which the Abalone Alliance is perhaps best known, however, is the large protests (or "actions," as members prefer to call them) that they organized.

Although the Alliance shared almost exactly the same concerns about the safety of nuclear power as the Mothers for Peace, this desire to take "direct action" represents an important difference in strategy about how to accomplish political change. Those who formed this coalition felt that the hearings process was far too distant and esoteric to be an effective means of public education. Protests and nonviolent civil disobedience, on the other hand, were seen as a way to potentially reach more people. Their largest rally attracted approximately 40,000 people to the city of San Luis Obispo in 1979. In 1981 they carried out a symbolic blockade of the plant for two weeks, during which more than 2,000 people were arrested.

Citizens for Adequate Energy

The most visible proponent of this power plant has always been the utility, Pacific Gas and Electric. Yet there have also been several local organizations of citizens who actively supported finishing the plant. One group called the Diablo 400 was directly organized by PG&E to keep sympathetic community leaders apprised of the project's progress.

This organization, however, did not actively participate in the local debate. The largest support group that has played a public role has been the Citizens for Adequate Energy.

In 1979, a number of energy-related corporations in California (e.g., major oil companies and electric utilities) contributed money to help finance local groups of citizens who would support projects to reduce the nation's and the state's dependence on foreign energy supplies. The chapter of the Citizens for Adequate Energy in San Luis Obispo was the first of 22 created in the state, and it continues to be the largest, with over 400 members.

The avowed goal of the Citizens is to publicize the need for the further development of all forms of energy including nuclear, fossil fuels (e.g., offshore oil), solar, and others. Individuals who were attracted to the Citizens reflect this broad concern for the energy future of the country. One member described his perspective this way:

I feel very strongly that we have the finest country in the world, and I feel that it's up to us citizens to keep it that way, and in doing that I feel we should concentrate on making it as strong as we possibly can in all its phases, economically and in terms of energy. . . . Cheap or inexpensive energy is one of the means by which it can attain that goal. I feel that nuclear power presents at the present time the cheapest, the safest, and the source that has the most plentiful supply of energy that we have.

Support for the Diablo Canyon plant is seen as a direct extension of this goal and as an effort to respond to what the Citizens believe are the distortions of antinuclear critics. This member continued: "I—what got me concerned was the fact that the arguments put up by the antinukes had no scientific basis. And I felt that it was very bad that the public should only see this one side of this project."

Consequently, the Citizens have set their primary task as educating the public. For example, they run a speaker's series, bringing in outside experts to provide information about issues concerned with energy production. The press is invited to cover the meetings and report what was said and by whom. Before the Diablo Canyon plant went on line, the topics were usually related to nuclear power (e.g., plant safety, waste disposal, and the like), but now the organization has turned its attention to the development of offshore oil supplies. Members of the Citizens have also testified in local hearings concerned with this particular power plant. At one time they ran small newspaper ads, but these proved to be ineffective and were dropped.

The Survey

A total of 49 individuals were surveyed with the same technique used to interview the random sample from the general public. Four interviews could not be used: one was incorrectly administered, and three individuals who were interviewed did not appreciably differ in their level of involvement from the typical profile of members of the general public. The data analysis was thus made on a total sample size of 45: 20 from the Citizens for Adequate Energy, 14 from the Mothers for Peace, and 11 from the Abalone Alliance.

The summary assessments of the Diablo Canyon plant by the political activists are presented in Figure 7.2. Their overall assessments are unequivocal and far more polarized than the laypublic, with the sample clustering toward the extremes of support and opposition. These activists differentiate themselves most clearly on the first and most global question about the project's worth. All but one individual indicated either strong support or strong opposition to the power plant. (By comparison, slightly less than half—48 percent—of the sample of members of the general public reached such extreme conclusions.) There is some weakening of these polarized positions, particularly among the supporters, when the respondent is asked to set aside whether the project should continue to operate or be shut down. From the more extended comments that these activists offered, however, it appears that those who express moderately positive or negative assessments do not substantially diverge from the other members of their organization. They qualify their conclusions because of the actions of the "other side." Supporters who reached only a moderately positive assessment in response to question 2, for example, maintain that the only reason the project was not as successful as it might have been is that it was unduly slowed by the legal challenges of the Mothers for Peace.

The Structure and Impact of the Past

On theoretical grounds, the disagreement among political activists should be well-defined in terms of their abstract schemas, the framework within which they develop their case-specific judgments. The history of these particular groups reinforces these expectations, as local activists appear to have invested in the broader arguments about technology and politics, including the worth of the "nuclear option."

The division in their global view of politics and technology is stark

Question 1: To what degree do you support or oppose the continued operation of the Diablo Canyon nuclear power plant?

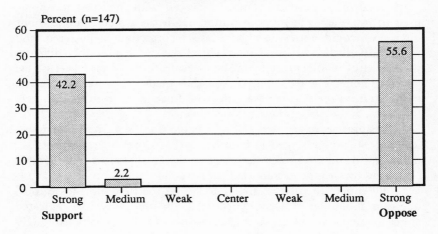

Question 2: Leaving aside the question of whether the plant should continue to operate or be shut down, what is your overall assessment of this project? Is it very positive, very negative or somewhere in-between?

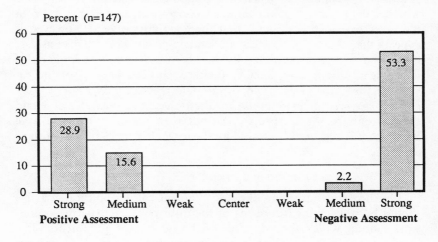

Figure 7.2. Summary evaluations of the Diablo Canyon nuclear power plant, interest groups.

TABLE 7.1

*Comparison of the Proportion of the Variance Between and Within
the Final Two Clusters for Political Activists*

	Proportion of variance separating the final two clusters and the number in each cluster	Proportion of variance explained by the more disparate of the final two clusters	Proportion of variance explained by the more consensual of the final two clusters
Common orientation	58.4% (19/26)	29.0%	12.6%
Project-specific factors			
Procedural judgment	95.5% (20/25)	2.4%	2.1%
Personal control	87.0% (20/25)	7.5%	5.5%
Substantive effects	95.1% (20/25)	3.2%	1.7%

(see Table 7.1). Over 58 percent of the variance divides the final two clusters. With the exception of one individual, all of the members of the Citizens for Adequate Energy are found in one of these two clusters, and all those from the Mothers for Peace and the Abalone Alliance are in the other. By contrast, 30.5 percent of the variance separated one small splinter group (11 percent) of the laypublic from the vast majority (89 percent; see Table 6.1). When the activists' positions are plotted on a continuum for common orientation, every cluster except for a small two-member group, or 4 percent of those interviewed, is well outside the distances generated by chance (see Figure 7.3).[1] This compares rather decidedly with the 61 percent of laypublic whose distance from the population mean was indistinguishable from a random assignment (Figure 6.2).

If the social process of debate has only served to reinforce these broader expectations, we should see clear evidence of this in the cluster structure of the project-specific schemas. The divisions among the political activists for these factors are indeed dramatic, as Table 7.1 shows. Virtually all of the differences in this population of activists separates them into two competing positions. The amount of the variance divid-

[1]Because the vast majority of the variance among the activists separated the last two clusters, the diagnostic statistics did not identify particularly large changes or "cut points" that clearly differentiated between a 4-, 5-, 6-, or 7-cluster solution. I settled on six clusters because this number was large enough to distinguish at least two groups on each side of the debate while not falling below the minimum of 5 percent of the sample for any particular cluster.

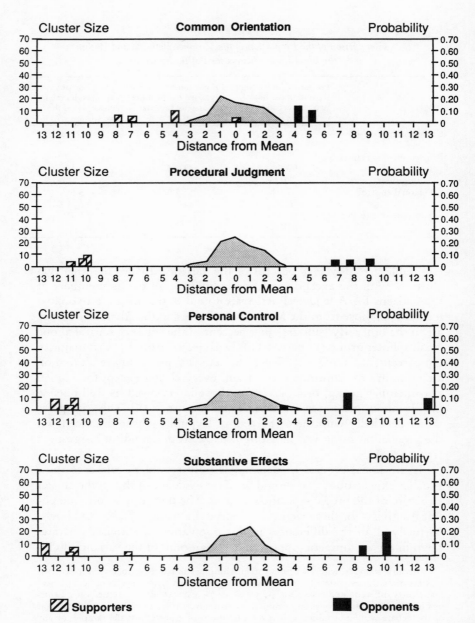

Figure 7.3. Cluster distances from the sample mean and their distribution of random assignment, interest groups.

ing supporters from opponents overwhelms any disagreements within each camp by a factor of more than 10 to 1. Thus, 87.0 percent of the total variance for personal control separates the final two groups compared with 7.5 percent within the most disparate cluster and 5.5 percent within the most consensual grouping. The schemas for procedural judgment and substantive effects are even more distinct, with 95.1 percent of the variance dividing the extremes of supporters and opponents.

When these distances are plotted on a continuum for each factor, the degree of polarization can be seen even more clearly. In Figure 7.3, *none* of the cluster distances for the choice-specific factors falls within a random sort, except for one small three-member cluster for personal control. Even more striking is how widely dispersed these clusters are. Remember the poles of the scale represent the greatest possible distance allowed by the structure of the Q-sort. Clusters on all of the project-specific factors approach this theoretical maximum.

The activists are far more divided and extreme in their judgments than are members of the laypublic. Figure 7.4 overlays the clusters for the laypublic (Fig. 6.2) on the distribution of the clusters for the activists (Fig. 7.3). For *every* factor, the activists define the poles of the continuua while the laypublic chooses gradations between these extremes. Average citizens, with rather evenly spaced positions across the center of the distribution, thus appear to be measured and judicious compared to those who have been carrying the political battle from one administrative hearing to the next.

The results of the path analysis for the survey data are found in Figure 7.5. Because the activists broke down into essentially two groups on their overall assessment, it was not statistically meaningful to estimate the impact of their schemas on their final evaluation (hence the dashed arrows). Based upon their scores for any of the project-specific judgments, one can explain virtually 100 percent of the variance in this summary measure. Nevertheless, we can still evaluate the relationships among their schemas.[2]

The measures for general predispositions—ideology and common orientation—are powerful predictors of the positions that activists adopt for the project-specific factors. One can explain close to 80 percent of the variance for procedural judgment and personal control and over 85 percent of the differences on substantive effects. As expected, common orientation directly shapes the activists' judgments about the

[2]The only variance left to explain is the one activist who did not reach a conclusion of strong support or opposition. Conducting the analysis for this one person would not yield meaningful results.

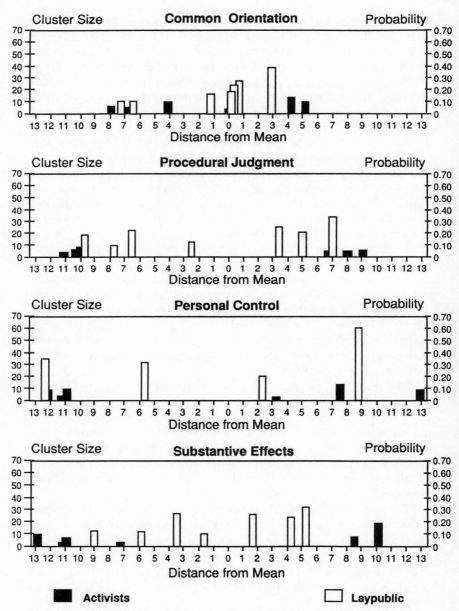

Figure 7.4. Cluster distances for political activists and the laypublic.

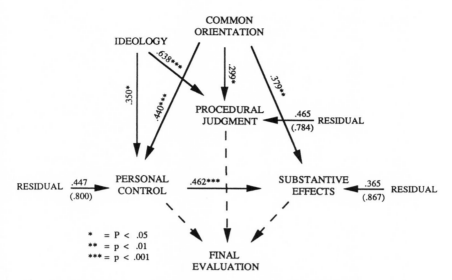

Figure 7.5. Results of path analysis for political activists. The influence of a factor is represented by the standardized regression coefficient of its arrow. The proportion of the variance of each factor explained by the model can be found in parentheses under the path for the residual. Dashed arrows are used where analysis was not statistically meaningful.

plant's substantive impacts. In addition, their general predispositions have an indirect effect on the evaluation of substantive effects through personal control. This relative degree of influence was somewhat unexpected; I did not foresee that any of the procedural schemas would have a strong impact on the substantive judgment about a particular case.

Many of the activists, however, joined these organizations *after* the accident at Three Mile Island and the major disclosures and protests about this plant. One possible explanation for such a sizable influence of personal control on substantive effects is that the newer group members were prompted to join as a result of this particular factor, rather than due to the strength of their global view of technology and politics or their concern about nuclear power.

To test this proposition, I selected a subsample of activists who were members of these organizations before the Three Mile Island incident and the subsequent revelations about Diablo Canyon. General predis-

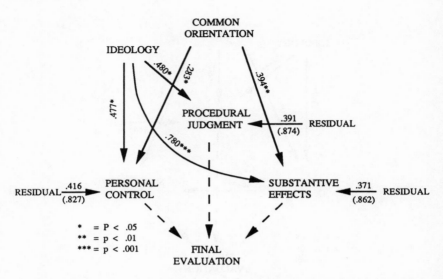

Figure 7.6. Results of path analysis for political veterans of more than five years. The influence of a factor is represented by the standardized regression coefficient of its arrow. The proportion of the variance of each factor explained by the model can be found in parentheses under the path for the residual. Dashed arrows are used where analysis was not statistically meaningful.

positions should play a relatively larger role for these long-term veterans because they became involved at least in part because of their general convictions rather than being attracted to this specific controversy. The paths for the more seasoned activists found in Figure 7.6 support this expectation. Only common orientation and ideology explain this group's stand on the substantive effects. Neither schema for procedural assessment has a direct impact that is statistically significant.

When compared with the pattern of assessment for the general public (see Figure 7.7, which essentially reproduces Figure 6.4), the differences are marked. The relative role of past predispositions for average citizens is much weaker, and to the extent that it does have an effect, it is mediated through procedural evaluations. The laypublic is far more responsive to the case-specific events that shape their judgments of collective decision makers and personal autonomy and control.

An additional measure of the importance of the past predispositions for political activists can be seen in their actual rankings of the substantive impacts and interests. Judging the project from a global orientation

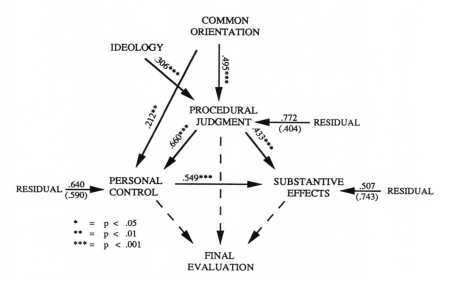

Figure 7.7. Results of path analysis for the laypublic. The influence of a factor is represented by the standardized regression coefficient of its arrow. The proportion of the variance of each factor explained by the model can be found in parentheses under the path for the residual. Dashed arrows are used where analysis was not statistically meaningful.

should lead these individuals to be very concerned about the widest possible interests that relate to a particular proposal and to be confident enough to personalize their assessment of a project's consequences to a much greater degree than does the typical layperson. This more general, past-structured perspective also focuses attention on the impacts that are of enduring significance for the technology of nuclear power rather than the specific issues associated with this plant. By examining the type of issues the activists rank more highly, we can learn what impact their past has had.

The range of judgments revealed by the activists is found in Table 7.2. For substantive effects, the most important issue for those who hold the most extreme views is hypothesized to be safety. The level of concern about safety among the opponents in cluster 6 is so strong that the top four items reflect a preoccupation with this effect. The risk is also seen as a very real personal threat. The statement with which they express the most forceful agreement is the perception that the project

TABLE 7.2
Interest-Group Cluster Profiles Showing the Ten Highest-Ranked Q-sort Statements for Substantive Effects (4 of 6 clusters)
(A: Agree; D: Disagree)

POTENTIAL SUPPORTERS 1	2	5	POTENTIAL OPPONENTS 6
D: Project is a health risk to myself and family. (13) 2.667	D: Plant won't survive major quake without life-threatening radiation. (11) 2.500	A: Future generations will have to contend with our wastes. (19) 2.571	A: Project is a health risk to myself and family. (13) 2.722
D: Exposure to low levels of radiation can be fatal. (25) 2.556	A: Knowledge is available to build a safe nuclear plant. (14) 2.500	A: Expensive mistakes have been made. (4) 2.286	D: Most serious accident would last a short time and extend only about 2 miles. (26) 2.444
A: Plant reduces nation's dependence on foreign energy. (1) 2.222	D: Possible release of low-level radiation is a significant problem. (20) 2.000	A: There is no means for safe disposal of wastes. (18) 2.286	D: Major accident is highly unlikely. (12) 2.111
A: Major accident is highly unlikely. (12) 2.111	D: Project is a health risk to myself and family. (13) 1.833	D: If a problem occurs, we can quickly evacuate residents. (16) 2.286	D: If a problem occurs, we can quickly evacuate residents. (16) 2.056
A: County benefits from property taxes. (9) 1.889	D: Exposure to low levels of radiation can be fatal. (25) 1.833	D: Plant is well protected from terrorist attack. (21) 2.143	A: Future generations will have to contend with our wastes. (19) 2.056

A: Knowledge is available to build a safe nuclear plant. (14) 1.889	A: Plant reduces nation's dependence on foreign energy. (1) 1.667	D: Most serious accident would last a short time and extend only about 2 miles. (26) 2.143	A: There is no means for safe disposal of wastes. (18) 2.000
D: Plant won't survive major quake without life-threatening radiation. (11) 1.667	A: Major accident is highly unlikely. (12) 1.667	D: Without this power plant, area will suffer shortage of electricity in future. (7) 1.713	A: Plant won't survive major quake without life-threatening radiation. (11) 1.722
D: Possible release of low-level radiation is a significant problem. (20) 1.667	A: Construction has caused problems for nearby residents. (24) 1.667	A: Possible release of low-level radiation is a significant problem. (20) 1.571	D: Plant is well protected from terrorist attack. (21) 1.611
D: Construction has caused problems for nearby residents. (24) 1.556	A: Expensive mistakes have been made. (4) 1.500	D: Knowledge is available to build a safe nuclear plant. (14) 1.571	A: Expensive mistakes have been made. (4) 1.556
A: More energy is needed for state development. (6) 1.445	A: Payroll increases the area's economic well-being. (10) 1.500	D: Temporary storage of radioactive wastes is not a serious hazard. (17) 1.571	D: Temporary storage of radioactive wastes is not a serious hazard. (17) 1.556

NOTE: See Table 5.4 for full text of statements.

represents a health risk to "myself and my family." The most committed supporters, on the other hand, start by denying that the project presents any hazard to them at all. Their concern for national energy independence, however, evokes the third highest ranking and reflects the importance that they attribute to the avowed goal of the Citizens for Adequate Energy.

The type of impacts that attracted the greatest attention is summarized in Table 7.3. I identified among the Q-sort statements five issues that have dominated the national debate about nuclear power and another five statements that have been the focal point for the discussion about the Diablo Canyon plant. Whether the knowledge is available to build a safe nuclear power plant or whether there are economical alternatives are examples of generic concerns, while a focus on earthquake safety or the mistakes due to lax quality control are characteristics of this particular project's history.[3] The numbers in Table 7.3 represent the percentage of the samples that rank these technology- or plant-specific statements at the highest levels—as their number one concern or as the top three or top five. The differences in orientation are evident at all levels, as most political activists focus their attention on the technology-specific issues while the laypublic identifies plant-specific concerns as critically important. An even 50 percent of political activists, for example, chose technology-specific statements for the top rank compared with only 13 percent of the laypublic. By contrast, 60 percent of the sample of the local residents identified one of the five project-specific items as the most important issue compared with 24 percent of the political activists.

Procedural Polarization

If general predispositions and organizational involvement produce such distinct viewpoints for substantive effects, we should see a similar intensity in conclusions about the actors who are directly involved and

---

[3]The technology-specific statements are: (1) there are safe and economically feasible alternatives to building more nuclear power plants; (2) the scientific knowledge is available to build a safe nuclear power plant; (3) I am worried that we cannot find a means to safely dispose of the wastes from this power plant over the long term; (4) the chance that low levels of radiation may be released is a significant problem; (5) this project poses a serious health risk to myself and my family. The project-specific statements are: (1) expensive mistakes have been made in the construction of this power plant; (2) in the event of a problem at the plant, public safety officials will be able to quickly evacuate those residents who might be in danger; (3) the construction and continued operation of this plant has caused a number of problems for residents who live nearby; (4) temporarily storing radioactive wastes at the plant is not a serious hazard; (5) this power plant would not survive a major earthquake without a significant and life-threatening release of radioactivity.

TABLE 7.3

Percentage of Political Activists and Members of the Laypublic Ranking Technology-Specific and Project-Specific Statements at the Highest Levels

	Technology-specific Cluster rank			Project-specific Cluster rank		
	1	1–3	1–5	1	1–3	1–5
Political activists	50%	33%	26%	24%	13%	21%
Laypublic	13%	8%	14%	60%	23%	40%

about the operation of the political process itself. Even though procedural judgments do not shape stands on the issues, they are potentially important in influencing the willingness of activists to bargain with those on the other side. The clusters for procedural judgment are displayed in Table 7.4. The rankings are entirely consistent with what we have predicted. The top-rated statement for every cluster, for example, focuses on questions of motivation. Activists critique the "other" side for their perceived inadequacies and reaffirm their belief in their own good intentions.

When asked open-ended questions about their views of the licensing procedures and the role of their adversaries, political activists typically expressed much stronger sentiments than did the general public. Moreover, the key role of past predispositions was evident in the manner in which they reached those conclusions. From members of the Citizens for Adequate Energy, we frequently heard a comment like this:

I think PG&E people, they're just generating power. I think that there have been, in a project of that magnitude, there have probably been some mistakes made. I think these mistakes have been distorted and blown out of proportion by the opponents who are—well, they're liberal Democrats and they're liars. Their agenda is—they couldn't care less. I think the real manipulators there, behind this, behind the scenes, they couldn't care less what kind of power is out there. This is merely a chink to increase the cost of energy for this society. These people coalesce into an antinuclear movement. It's almost as good as Vietnam, the same players there again. I have no sympathy for them because they lie and distort and play upon emotionalism and use emotionalism to play upon the fear of people.

This individual's rather decided views about the intentions of the other side and their willingness to play fairly by the rules of the administrative process draw on observations made over a number of years, but also appear to be framed by strong ideological commitments (i.e., the

TABLE 7.4

Interest-Group Cluster Profiles Showing the Ten Highest-Ranked Q-sort Statements for Procedural Judgment

(A: Agree; D: Disagree)

| POTENTIAL SUPPORTERS | | POTENTIAL OPPONENTS | |
1	2	5	6
D: PG&E places profits above residents' welfare. (9) 2.500	A: Public hearings provided ample chance to express concerns. (17) 2.429	D: NRC can be trusted to protect interests of public. (7) 3.000	D: NRC can be trusted to protect interests of public. (7) 2.500
A: Licensing procedures were fair and impartial. (16) 2.250	D: Opponents are more accurate than supporters. (10) 2.143	A: Critics sought delay to prevent plant ever operating. (20) 2.800	A: PG&E places profits above residents' welfare. (9) 2.438
A: Critics sought delays to prevent plant ever operating. (20) 2.250	D: Public hearings "staged," decision already made. (21) 2.143	D: PG&E provides accurate information. (8) 2.600	A: Critics are looking out for welfare of county. (12) 2.250
D: Opponents are more accurate than supporters. (10) 2.000	D: PG&E places profits above residents' welfare. (9) 1.714	D: PG&E will tell residents if serious accident occurs. (14) 2.400	D: PG&E will tell residents if serious accident occurs. (14) 2.063
D: Critics are looking out for welfare of county. (12) 2.000	A: Decision makers were willing to discuss issues that concern local residents. (19) 1.714	A: Layperson can judge if benefits outweigh risks. (5) 2.000	D: Licensing procedures were fair and impartial. (16) 2.063

D: Public hearings "staged," decision already made. (21) 2.000	A: Critics sought delays to prevent plant ever operating. (20) 1.714	D: Licensing procedures were fair and impartial. (16) 1.800	D: PG&E provides accurate information. (8) 1.938
D: PG&E has had great influence on government regulators. (11) 1.750	D: Decisions were made too quickly. (24) 1.714	A: Critics are looking out for welfare of county. (12) 1.800	A: PG&E ignores defects employees identify. (25) 1.875
A: Project studied so long that any serious problems have been identified. (15) 1.750	A: PG&E will tell residents if serious accident occurs. (14) 1.429	A: PG&E places profits above residents' welfare. (9) 1.600	A: Public hearings "staged," decision already made. (21) 1.625
D: Decisions have been made too quickly. (24) 1.750	A: Project studied so long that any serious problems have been identified. (15) 1.429	A: PG&E has had great influence on government regulators. (11) 1.400	A: PG&E has had great influence on government regulators. (11) 1.500
A: NRC can be trusted to protect interests of public. (7) 1.500	A: Government regulators moved quickly to respond to defects. (18) 1.429	A: Public can judge quality of plant from having watched events unfold. (6) 1.200	A: Decisions have been made too quickly. (24) 1.500

NOTE: See Table 5.2 for full text of statements.

reference to "liberal Democrats") and a well-defined perspective about technology and the need for energy to fuel its development.

The Mothers for Peace and the Abalone Alliance are just as firm in their convictions about the lack of credibility of the other side based on the most general indictment of their motivations. One member of the Mothers put it this way:

> I think it goes back to the dollar. PG&E is in there—I mean the reason they are doing this is for the money. Everybody on the NRC—it's real hard because they can't cut their own throats, which is what they would be doing if they shut down a plant because all the people who work at the NRC, the appeals board, the licensing board, all those people have all come out of the nuclear industry. If they start shutting down plants . . . they won't have their jobs to go back to. So it's essentially like Mothers for Peace, it's all volunteer and all just donations, so actually there's no money at all involved. It's a lot of time and hard work. I think that there is probably more to it than that. It seems that every time that Mothers for Peace comes up with any kind of contention on something that we think is really wrong that the NRC will change the rules, which is really aggravating. That's probably the biggest difference.

Individuals who view their adversaries in such an unequivocal manner are not likely to be willing to readily negotiate their differences. Procedural norms of openness and responsiveness inevitably suffer as well.

Representatives from the Laypublic?

Given the past-structured focus of political activists on broader, technology-specific issues, the method of reasoning and assessment by members of the laypublic appears to be a useful and even necessary corrective. The laypublic's concern with case-specific characteristics balances the preoccupation of activists with generic issues. Moreover, their explicit focus on procedural issues could have an ameliorative effect on the process of decision making by emphasizing procedural standards of competence, credibility, and responsiveness that may eventually produce positive outcomes.

If we are to select representatives to fulfill this role, however, we must recognize how differences in background can clearly affect the ability of particular individuals to meet these positive expectations. Individuals no doubt vary in terms of their level of interest in and attentiveness to the public debate. As I argued earlier, those who watch these deliberations closely are likely to have at least some background in thinking about the issues. Moreover, they probably spend considerable time discussing and reflecting upon the controversy. Those who are not as interested and attentive can be expected to make fewer connections from their common orientation in interpreting this choice. In addition, if they have in fact reasoned to a position, it will reflect a lower-cost strategy, relying on schemas that do not require a great deal of information, such as the schema for personal control (compare the path diagrams in Chapter 3).

I broke my sample of general citizens in two groups based on their level of interest in and attentiveness to public debate. Those who are less concerned and observant reported that they had never become involved in community deliberations in any way (e.g., attend a meeting, sign a petition, etc.) and they only discussed this issue with their friends and family about once a month. The more interested individuals chose to debate the issue more regularly and expressed their interest in a more concrete fashion.

The results of path-model analysis for each group can be found in Figure 7.8. The common orientation for those who are less interested plays, as expected, a very weak role. Their procedural judgment (PJ), in turn, has much less influence on personal control (PC) and substantive effects (SE) than the path coefficients for the residual variables. The major factor that shapes their judgments of the substantive impacts is the degree to which they believe that the project either conforms to or violates their conception of personal control (the path from PC to SE is .646, and from PJ to SE the coefficient is a much weaker .296). This is, in fact, a relatively economical way to reach their conclusions.

Citizens who have shown real interest in this decision, by contrast, have much tighter and presumably more instructive social constructs. Their past predispositions play a comparatively larger role in shaping their evaluations about how well decisions have been made about this particular power plant. The effect of their involvement and interest is most noticeable, however, where they rely very heavily on the judgments that they have developed about the decision-making process and its major participants. Individuals who are this responsive to new information and to the dynamics of how the process is being run would be the most suitable choice to represent the major social positions among the laypublic. They have a sensitivity to the political process, as well as general evaluative standards to apply to a specific case. As a result, they are much more likely to modify their overall assessment based on what happens during public deliberations.[4]

[4] A global interaction test revealed that these path models were significantly different at the .05 level.

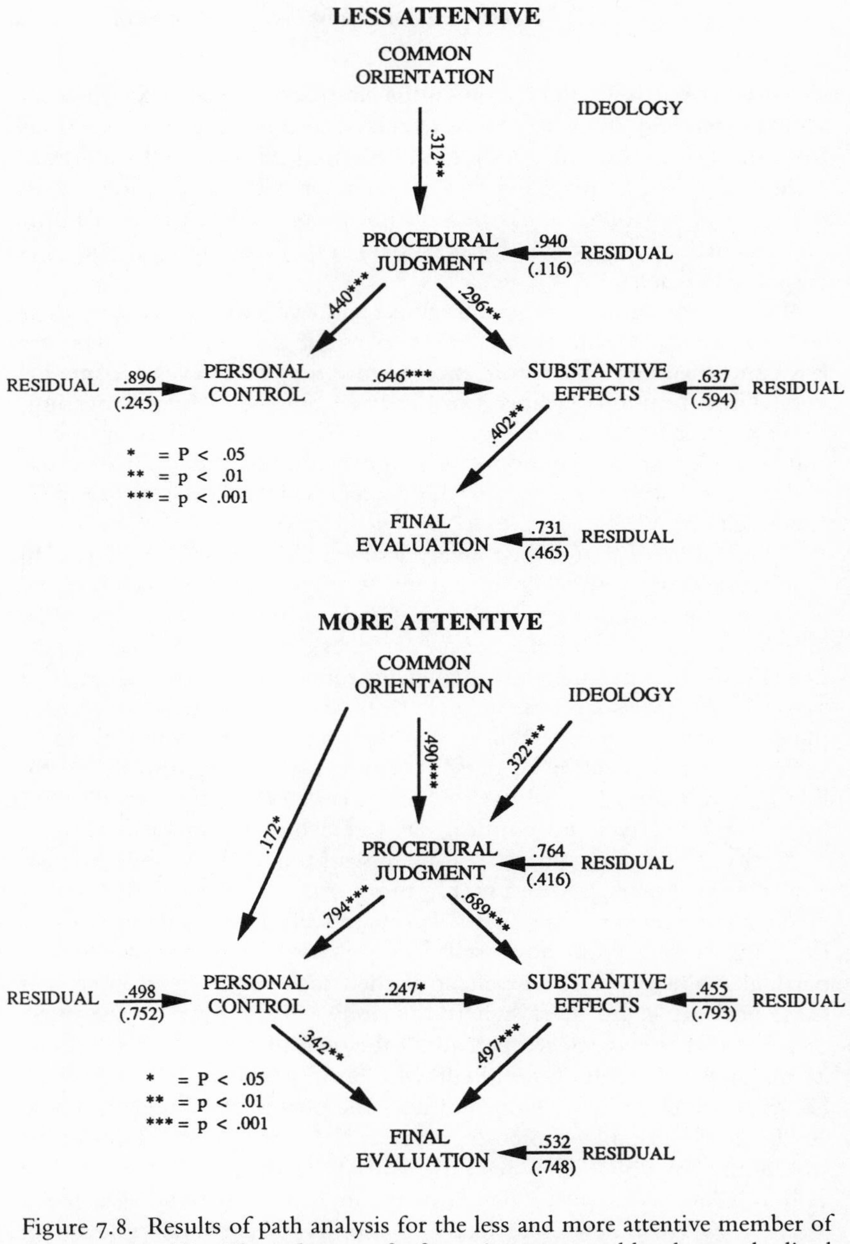

Figure 7.8. Results of path analysis for the less and more attentive member of the general public. The influence of a factor is represented by the standardized regression coefficient of its arrow. The proportion of the variance of each factor explained by the model can be found in parentheses under the path for the residual.

I encountered an interesting example of an individual for whom this had happened immediately prior to our scheduled interview. Mr. Jackson, as I will call him, had participated in the original structured survey and had been selected for a follow-up interview because his final conclusion and responses to the project-specific statements indicated that he was being pulled in different directions. His position on social continuua for substantive effects and personal control were moderately supportive (clusters 3 and 2, respectively) of the plant. However, his assessment of the collective decision makers was somewhat critical (cluster 5 for procedural judgment). His final assessment, before the interview, indicated only weak support for the continued operation of the power plant.

As a manager of a medium-sized business, Mr. Jackson followed the debate about how the plant had been constructed and regulated with some interest. Over time he had become increasingly critical of this operation. When I asked him which side of this dispute had more credibility in his view, he responded:

Probably a little suspect on both. Once again, from their [PG&E's] perspective they're attempting to sell, and PG&E is the rosiest picture in the world. You wouldn't need rose-colored glasses, everything was going fine, and yet instance after instance, it was not going fine. The Mothers for Peace, if you believe them, you'd better pack up or cut your throat, because the world is coming to an end in a couple of days. And then the groups that made a party out of it.

What changed Mr. Jackson from an unenthusiastic supporter to a vocal critic was a news article that indicated PG&E had been cited for a second time for failure to follow "established procedures" when dealing with an issue of some importance concerned with the safety of the plant. This event pushed Mr. Jackson over the edge. When he was asked why this was so significant, he explained:

Because PG&E is deviating from established procedures. That concerns the hell out of me, because as I say, we're getting back into this rut of nobody cared how long it took, what it cost, and who was paid to build the damn thing. Now somebody is not viewing this in the true light that, if not run correctly, becomes a weapon. . . . It was not acts of God at Chernobyl or [Three Mile Island]—it was man screwing up!

It is this characteristic of responsiveness to the specific events of this case that make the Mr. Jacksons of the world potentially so valuable for the conduct of technological decision making.

CHAPTER EIGHT

Taking Stock

THE ACTIVISTS AND MEMBERS of the laypublic interviewed in this study are examples of the raw material from which democratic institutions are formed. The characteristics of their desires and of their methods of assessment determine what options are available for designing institutional procedures that are responsive to citizen interests in making technological decisions. Thus, I have argued, only by being clearheaded and realistic about citizen assessment can we properly judge proposals that seek to structure and improve the process of public deliberation for making complex, controversial choices. By developing and testing a new model of citizen assessment, this study seeks to achieve that goal.

Although this study proposed and investigated selective hypotheses, I believe my method of analysis holds the potential to substantially improve how we evaluate procedures for ensuring that government choices about technology are responsive to citizen interests. Indeed, if we are going to properly evaluate the implications of the social-process theory I have developed and tested, we should start by identifying the manner in which current efforts at assessing prescriptive methods might be reformed and then judging to what degree this project moves us down that road.

The premise of this study—that we should critically evaluate the empirical premises of our prescriptive methods—is certainly not new, especially to those who have enjoyed success in constructing political institutions. The leading architect of the American Constitution, for example, was quite explicit and sober in his assessment of human nature and made clear how this perspective shaped his proposals. James Madison argued that the desire for a free and democratic society is constantly threatened by the desires of one faction to use political power to oppress members of other groups. His solution—to "pit ambition against ambition" by dividing power and creating checks and balances among the various branches of government—serves as a hallmark of lucid institutional reasoning. His assumptions about citizen assessment played a critical role throughout his recommendations for structuring institutional procedures to protect individual freedom and ensure a responsive government (see Dahl, 1956).

More recently the methods of social science have tested some of the most enduring hopes of a democratic society, such as the expectation that average citizens are well informed or that they have clearly defined and defensible judgments of most government policies. During the early years of the behavioral revolution in political science of the 1950's and early 1960's, investigating whether there is empirical support for these propositions was touted as a logical step in developing an empirically grounded theory of democracy (Berelson, Lazarsfeld, and Mc-Phee, 1954). Unfortunately, the crude methodological assumptions and spartan concepts that guided many of these early studies limited the breadth of appeal for the enterprise as a whole (see King, 1990). In response to critics major improvements were made in the quality of the data and methods. Designing empirical studies that have significant procedural implications is now well established in political science and policy studies.

Today there is a growing need to develop a systematic variant of this method of analysis specifically for judging prescriptive methods of technological assessment. Technological decision making has become a virtual laboratory of constructing or modifying methods of policy analysis and citizen participation. As we have seen, the stakes in modern technological choices are large, and the evaluative issues are numerous and diverse. Judging these choices has become more difficult over time as activists and the laypublic have come to identify a wider range of issues and impacts that should be considered and to argue that the views of more citizens should be taken into account. Many politicians and scholars of the policy process also acknowledge that more work needs to be done.

In looking to the future, there is no indication that the pressure for procedural innovation will abate. Government agencies continue to face traditional technological choices: existing legislative mandates for mitigating the effects of pollutants are far from fulfilled, and major sections of the industrial infrastructure have to be rebuilt (Vig and Kraft, 1990). Novel evaluative issues are being raised in new areas of development such as biotechnology (Blank, 1988). Moreover, increasing political concern over the interdependency of ecological systems is widening the scope of analysis to include a long list of impacts that affect other nations and even the biosphere as a whole. I believe the method of analysis presented in this book can provide a defensible means for carefully assessing how well different prescriptive methods serve specific procedural objectives—a means that enables us to judge both the accumulation of past innovations in procedures and specific new initiatives.

Clearly, as I have argued, the choice of a method and an evaluative framework indicates a policy analyst's implicit or explicit expectations about the strengths and weaknesses of citizen assessment. Whose judgment is sought out and how that judgment is handled reveals an assessment of the capabilities of different political actors and the best approach for measuring those judgments. Such empirical premises constrain, in some cases very tightly, the range of evaluative issues and prescriptive means that will be considered and so may indirectly affect the outcome. Judging the plausibility of the assumptions underlying a particular method or set of prescriptive approaches thus offers potentially great leverage in determining its worth, for what is at stake is the entire fabric of reasoning about the specific means and ends under review.

The method for generating such a broad-reaching assessment is, in concept, simple. A particular prescriptive method and its associated model of assessment lay out a definable pattern of characteristics for citizen preferences and methods. The model will propose either commonality or variation in the manner in which different individuals face a range of choices, contexts, and interests over time. The most important question for judging an evaluative framework is determining what is necessary to produce and maintain this configuration of characteristics over time. By identifying a process that yields this result, or a specific set of conditions that would be necessary to preserve it, we focus debate on a limited set of issues that can differentiate among current methods and test the validity of their assumptions.

Examining the available evidence for these ordering conditions will give us an initial reading on a particular model of assessment. An important question is how well these conditions in fact apply across the full range of issues prescriptive methods must confront—or at least the issues that are most important to the operation of the particular prescriptive technique. Failure on one issue might suggest larger, systemic problems. In addition, by identifying the ordering conditions that support an entire model of citizen assessment, we may more easily see the possibility of a quite different approach if these conditions ultimately prove to be problematic. This degree of theoretical power offers very creative analytic possibilities.

After we have defined the assumptions and conditions that differentiate the models of assessment the next logical step is to establish an ongoing research program on citizen assessment. Once the debate is engaged at the highest levels and key propositions that separate different models are tested, subsequent research should focus on developing the models for those approaches that appear to hold the greatest promise. Our expectations, however, should not be unduly inflated. Conducting this type of research is not going to produce consensus among those who are now strong partisans of different methods. Identifying the model of assessment that underlies a particular technique is imprecise and subject to uncertainty and disagreement. In judging the most general models of assessment, a clean and unequivocal verdict is unlikely. Weighing a model's theoretical power and level of empirical support by comparing it against the case for an alternative offers too many points of comparison and areas of discretionary judgment to produce unanimity. In addition, our explanatory efforts will never be complete. They only offer limited theoretical cuts on a complex process that can at best expand the realm of our understanding rather than master it (see Brunner, 1991).

Although a high degree of precision and consensus is unlikely, this exercise should nonetheless increase the level of self-reflection and the quality of debate among prescriptive analysts as they revise old techniques and develop new approaches. We will understand more clearly how the range of evaluative means and ends is structured by an underlying model of assessment that is highly contingent on key ordering premises. Through the give and take of a wider debate, partisans of different approaches will be forced to face up to hidden empirical assumptions and explicitly identify the values their methods support for improving the process of assessment. Even though current advocates are unlikely to shift their sentiments, providing a wider analysis of the grounds and methods of particular approaches gives politicians and new generations of analysts a much better idea of the strengths and weaknesses of these procedures.

Current prescriptive methods are not now analyzed at such a global level. The most common approach is to develop a response within a particular set of empirical assumptions to meet a pressing political demand. Every decade raises new issues that call for a response—identifying wasteful "pork barrel" projects in the 1950's, implementing maximum feasible participation in the 1960's, developing measures of environmental, social, and risk impacts in the 1970's, and mediating resolutions to long-term disputes in the 1980's. Few prescriptive analysts ask whether the framework they operate within is empirically defensible. Instead, they accept those assumptions as given and move to address new political demands, to resolve inconsistencies across impacts and people, or to make improvements within this set of expectations.

Specific questions about how citizens actually judge technology are often raised in discussions of prescriptive methods. Yet the scope of the analysis is typically limited to understanding the manner in which a given set of political actors responds to particular impacts or an analysis of the effect that a prescriptive technique has on the political process (e.g., Mazmanian and Nienaber, 1979; Culhane, 1981; Taylor, 1984). Over 30 years ago much broader questions were raised by the seminal work of Herbert Simon (March and Simon, 1958) and Charles Lindblom (1959). They constructed a descriptive model of rationality that was used to critically evaluate a rational-comprehensive approach to decision making—what I have called preference-driven methods. By arguing that assessment is structured by past experience and constrained by our limited abilities to process information, Simon and Lindblom challenged whether the expectations of the rational model were accurate. Because real individuals cannot consider or carefully assess the full range of impacts and options for complex choices, promoting that ideal, they argued, might produce worse results than would otherwise occur. This theory of bounded rationality has had an enormous impact on our efforts to explain policy making and has been fruitfully applied to a large number of topics from budgeting and organizational change to environmental policy-making. In particular, their contention that government agencies were limited by past methods of solving problems was used to justify providing greater access for opposing viewpoints in technological decision making.

In my view, however, the most important and valuable change that this work represented—a change in how we think about and conduct research on prescriptive methods—has had far less impact. The work of Simon and Lindblom spoke directly to the need of continually developing a better and broader understanding of citizen assessment as the basis for making sound prescriptive recommendations. Yet today analysts do not judge how well their underlying models of assessment cope with the complex circumstances of technological decision making. There has been no effort to identify and critically evaluate the ordering conditions for the most general evaluative frameworks. Finally, there is no ongoing research program that seeks to develop and test the defining propositions for the prevailing approaches, much less to construct alternative models.

In this context, my study is a first cut at what would be a long and complex process of identifying the ordering conditions for the most global models of assessment and then constructing and testing the theoretical propositions that can discriminate between existing approaches and possible alternatives. My justification for focusing on the impact of experience on assessment is simple: it offers the most powerful set of ordering conditions for differentiating between prevailing models of assessment. We can see, for example, that virtually all of the expectations of commonality in preference-driven approaches are contingent on the belief that experience has no systematic impact on the characteristics of preferences or the methods of assessment. And yet the varying levels of influence actually wielded in participatory techniques by administrators, activists, and members of the laypublic in fact presuppose a quite different expectation: that direct experience has slow, cumulative, and largely beneficial effects. The views of those with greater experience thus are given greater weight.

Identifying the importance of the impact of experience, of course, is not new. As I mentioned earlier, proponents of bounded rationality have argued that it is critical. Yet as the name "bounded rationality" suggests, proponents of this approach placed the greatest emphasis on the limited ability of individuals to process information in a comprehensive and rational manner. This focus on cognitive limits, however, may have unnecessarily weakened the distinctions between various models. It is not surprising, for example, that proponents of rational-comprehensive methods see the failure of decision makers to carefully consider all relevant options and impacts as nothing more than a way of coping with an obvious constraint of costly information, a constraint that can never be overcome but should be met by determined and clever efforts to mitigate its worst effects. The traditional ideal of rationality thus has remained intact. By focusing our attention on what we cannot do or cannot do well, this effort to develop a better descriptive understanding of citizen assessment was seen by some as undercutting our commitment to discover more effective ways of prescribing improvements in decision making (Archibald, 1970).

What receives less attention from theorists of bounded rationality are the effects of experience that I emphasize: the expectation that differences in background produce wide variation among political actors in the specificity of their wants and their methods of analysis. The critical difference between the rational-comprehensive model or the preference-driven approach and this past-structured model is that political actors must differ greatly at any particular moment in the precision of their wants and their methods, irrespective of how much information they are given at that time. This change in analytic focus has the advantage of being supported by a vast amount of evidence from studies of public opinion and voting behavior. The ideal of comprehensive rationality is now at stake, at least for members of the general public, because their preferences and methods have not been calibrated for many of the impacts that are at issue.

This empirical insight, however, does not undermine our efforts to improve technological decisions. It suggests, instead, that by determining the manner in which this process of specification operates, we can develop a better idea of how to use different political actors more effectively. Lindblom spoke to this possibility when he argued that individuals from diverse backgrounds can improve the social rationality of the process of policy-making by evaluating complex choices from different perspectives. Unfortunately, he rarely went beyond applauding the virtues of an open system that would provide access to as many viewpoints as possible. If we can develop an understanding of how those skills are specified, however, a theory of citizen assessment can begin to offer more detailed and effective prescriptive advice about procedural reform. By examining the process of specification, we can see the strengths and weaknesses of different political actors based on the length and depth of their experience.

I selected schema theory to address these questions because it offers the basic elements of a general explanation of the impact of experience. Indeed, it is the only theoretical approach that is general enough to deduce the response of such a broad range of political actors to the varied and complex attributes of technological choices over time. It is particularly useful because it challenges us to think about the role of experience in a new way. We do not begin by asking whether the vast majority of individuals have the capability to form a coherent set of ideas or an evaluative position about a particular phenomenon. Rather, schema theory starts from the premise that the vast majority *can* form these cognitive structures, and it focuses, instead, on how variations in past and present experience produce different patterns of reasoning and assessment (compare with Sniderman, Brody, and Tetlock, 1991). Thus we would expect that the judgments of political veterans are shaped by general, substantively oriented perspectives from the past and that the laypublic will develop complementary skills by constructing case-specific, procedurally informed schemas from current debate.

One might argue that politics is qualitatively different from other areas of our lives, that it presents a cognitive challenge most cannot meet. I disagree. The vocabulary of politics can be, at times, difficult to understand initially, but I have yet to see a convincing case that, once this hurdle is overcome, comprehending and evaluating the basic elements of a political argument is inherently more complex than what the average person accomplishes on a daily basis in negotiating interpersonal relations or managing to perform a job at a minimal level of competency.

The test of citizen assessment in the case of the Diablo Canyon nuclear power plant certainly supports that conclusion. The issue was far more complex than the norm. The random sample of subjects was asked to respond to a very large number of statements, many more than has typically been presented to subjects in past studies. Virtually the entire sample revealed the capacity to form coherent positions in response to public debate on these issues. As expected, those who were more interested in the project revealed a tighter chain of reasoning and assessment. The different weights that members of the laypublic and political activists gave particular factors—from general orientations to procedural and substantive judgments about the project—strongly supported the expectation that cognitive structures are shaped by the accumulation of past and current experience. What is especially telling are the differences in the relative weights and the overall pattern of assessment one finds within the samples of the laypublic and of political veterans and in a comparison of the two.

Because this investigation measured citizen assessment at one point in time, we cannot discover which schemas emerged first and then structured subsequent assessments. The particular events of this case no doubt also influenced the weight that respondents placed on specific factors. The consistent differences in the *relative* weights that activists and members of the laypublic gave to general and substantive factors compared to project-specific and procedural ones, however, cannot be explained away by the characteristics of this case or by the limitations of a cross-sectional study. Those are precisely the differences in weight that experience is expected to produce. These results are particularly instructive because, as Eric Smith (1989) has pointed out, there have been few direct comparisons of the general public with political veterans on the same issues using the same survey instrument (see Appendix B).

Moving to the next step of constructing prescriptive methods requires pushing our theoretical propositions and empirical work far beyond what we learned here. Some may be disappointed that I have not proposed more than general outlines of what those methods should look like. I have not gone further because my theory of citizen assessment is not sufficiently developed at this time to offer or support detailed recommendations.[1] For example, if the laypublic has something to contribute, decision makers obviously cannot wait for many years of debate to unfold in order to select representatives from the positions that emerge among the laypublic. Subsequent work needs to investigate whether the pace of this process can be accelerated under more artificial conditions in which, for example, advocates present a case to a jury of individuals who approach an issue from the available spectrum of general orientations toward a particular technological issue. We need to learn whether a more contrived setting limits or aids the process of deliberation: How many times would the jury have to meet to allow reflection and discussion with others? Would the dynamics of having laypublic "representatives" directly confront and question partisans of each side facilitate or impede the social rationality of the process?

I do not know the answers to these questions. At this stage of development, all I can say with confidence is that making this investment appears to be worthwhile.

[1]Methods that seek to intensively measure the technological assessments of a few members of the laypublic are now attracting more attention from prescriptive analysts (see Renn et al., 1984; Kenney, von Winterfeldt, and Eppel, 1990). The problem with these approaches is that proponents have yet to lay out and substantiate a theory that tells us specifically what the laypublic will contribute. Why should we take the time to learn what they want in such exhausting detail? Selecting a relatively small number of individuals for intensive scrutiny, moreover, does not ensure that the individuals who are selected in any way represent the general population. The social-process theory that I have proposed begins to answer these questions. We learn what the laypublic's comparative skills are. Because the response of the laypublic to public debate forms a continuum of social positions, we can also, in theory, identify a few citizens who represent the full range of judgment. At the present time, however, we do not know how they should participate to take advantage of these potential skills.

Appendixes

Chronology of Events, 1963–1985

1963		Pacific Gas and Electric (PG&E) announces plans for a nuclear power plant in San Luis Obispo County at Nipomo Dunes. Site opposed by Sierra Club on environmental grounds.
1966		Diablo Canyon site, near the city of San Luis Obispo, is formally chosen.
1968		Unit 1 is granted a construction permit.
1970		Unit 2 is granted a construction permit.
1972		Mothers for Peace, a group that organized to oppose the Vietnam War, turns its attention to nuclear weapons and nuclear power.
1973	*October*:	PG&E applies for an operating license for Units 1 and 2, and Mothers for Peace intervenes, based on concerns related to low-level radiation releases, large-scale accidents, problems in transporting nuclear wastes from the plant, evacuation plans, and the risk of sabotage.
	November:	U.S. Geological Survey reports the discovery of an earthquake fault (Hosgri fault) three miles offshore from the Diablo Canyon site.
1975		Nuclear power debate at California State Polytechnic University in San Luis Obispo attracts 4,000 people to a two-day forum.
1976	*January*:	Nuclear Regulatory Commission (NRC) staff officials state that PG&E will have to prove the

plant can withstand an earthquake of magnitude 7–7.5 on the Richter scale from the offshore earthquake fault. NRC believes the plant can eventually operate.

February: Eight people are arrested at the gates of Diablo Canyon for trespassing during a protest against the plant.

March: Hearings are held on security precautions. Mothers for Peace intervenes.

1977 *February*:   The Abalone Alliance, a network of antinuclear groups, is formed and holds its first major "action" by attempting to occupy the plant site; 46 are arrested. Protests in support of those arrested draw 1,000.

October: Hearings are held on emergency evacuation plans. Mothers for Peace intervenes.

December: NRC licensing hearings are held on earthquake safety. Mothers for Peace intervenes.

1978 *August*:   An attempt to blockade Diablo Canyon results in the arrests of 487 on trespass charges, and more than 3,000 people attend a rally against the plant.

November: NRC staff report concludes that Diablo Canyon meets or can be made to meet all NRC earthquake safety criteria.

1979 *March*:   Accident occurs at the Three Mile Island nuclear power plant near Harrisburg, Pennsylvania.

May: NRC places a moratorium on licensing new plants.

September: NRC ends moratorium.

October: Federal Licensing Board declares that Diablo Canyon is earthquake safe.

1980 *June*:   Earthquake issue is reopened in light of a larger than anticipated earthquake in the Imperial Valley.

July: PG&E applies for a low-power test license.

1981   *May*:   Hearings are held on low-power test license.

       September 15:   Abalone Alliance begins blockade of the plant over two weeks which results in nearly 2,000 arrests.

       September 21:   NRC issues low-power test license to PG&E.

       September 28:   PG&E announces that plans to make the plant seismically safe have been incorrectly implemented. The blueprint for Unit 1 was used for Unit 2, and Unit 2's plans were used for Unit 1.

       October: NRC officials ask for extensive review, citing a number of seismic design problems at the plant.

       November: NRC votes to suspend Diablo Canyon's low-power license.

1982   *February*:   NRC votes to chastise PG&E for making false statements on seismic design work.

       May: PG&E admits some problems with quality-control efforts for welds but says steps have been taken to overcome these deficiencies.

1983   *June*:   Construction workers arrive in large numbers for the "retrofit" work on seismic design.

       November: NRC authorizes loading of fuel at Diablo Canyon, and PG&E begins the process.

       November 30:   Current and former employees at the plant charge that there are serious quality-control problems. These complaints are the first of hundreds of allegations that are brought to the attention of the NRC, leading to a new review.

1984   *January–April*:   Abalone Alliance stages protests at the plant over four months. Demonstrations attract thousands of protesters and result in the arrest of 537 people.

       April: NRC removes its 2½-year suspension of the low-power operating license. Circuit Court of Appeals rejects requests by Mothers for Peace to prevent low-power testing. Unit 1 is started for the first time.

	June:	PG&E asks the California Public Utilities Commission for a rate increase that, if granted, would mean that the average electricity bill would go up by 7.5 percent.
1985	*March*:	Unit 1 goes to full power.
	May:	Unit 2 goes to full power.

Justification for This Research Design

THE SOCIAL-PROCESS theory that I have developed ranges broadly: it offers hypotheses about how citizens from different backgrounds judge diverse impacts in response to a contentious public debate. The empirical test that I propose, however, may strike some as being comparatively narrow: measuring the schemas of a relatively small number of respondents from the general public as well as political activists, in a single case and at a single point in time. Let me be clear that I do not claim I am testing all or even most of the hypotheses laid out in the earlier chapters of this book. Yet I believe that my research design does function to establish the plausibility of those propositions in which my theory diverges *most significantly* from the current literature.

The first important point of difference is my hypothesis that, given sufficient incentive and information in a public debate, a majority of the laypublic can construct coherent, multi-attribute positions about a specific policy choice and that those positions form an intelligible social continuum, running from support to opposition. Obviously, this proposition contradicts both those who deny outright that most members of the laypublic have such an ability and those who believe it is severely circumscribed (see the literature review in Chapter 1). A spate of new works has found that the general public is more rational and capable than previously thought, but even these retain a pessimism about the laypublic's ability to form relatively complex policy positions. Samuel Popkin (1991), for example, argues that the general public is at best capable of low-information reasoning or "gut" rationality. Paul Snider-

man, Richard Brody, and Philip Tetlock (1991) believe that most individuals use only simple heuristics to reason to their policy positions.
Benjamin Page and Robert Shapiro (1992) maintain that although there
is rationality in the judgments of the collective, a large majority of individuals is probably not fully rational.

I do not disagree with these broad conclusions. Under typical conditions of political debate, the vast majority of the laypublic has not
thus far exhibited impressive levels of political sophistication. But the
problem with these findings is that we do not know if they result from
limited capabilities among laypublic or from lack of sufficient motivation and/or of easy access to relevant information. Discovering in just
one case that a clear majority of the citizenry in a local community can
respond in a far more sophisticated manner would lend considerable
support to the plausibility of my hypothesis.

For such a test to carry much weight, it should be both theoretically
meaningful and conservative. The Q-sort is an appropriate methodology for discovering the laypublic's positions because it requires that we
lay out the full range of relevant stimuli for each respondent and allow
that individual to rank their relative importance. As a result, the findings are not limited by the subject's own ability to recall this material,
nor are the rankings an artifact of the statistical procedure that is employed. Moreover, the number of items that the subject is asked to
sort—16 or 26—is far larger than the number of items typically correlated in national election studies to determine horizontal constraint.
The number of ways each set of items can be sorted is so enormous
(more than 2 million for 16 items or 500 billion for 26 items) that the
respondent cannot hope to fake a position that others consistently
adopt. Comparing actual distributions of group positions against those
generated by random assignment provides an effective way to validate
this conclusion. Most important, the actual pattern of each group's
rankings reveals whether there is a substantive logic to the spectrum of
positions as we move from support to opposition.

Some may question whether the sample of 147 is large enough to
generalize to the local population. Even with a sample this small the
margin of error for a one-tailed test at 95 percent confidence is less than
6 percent. Therefore, to support my hypothesis, we have to discover
that at least 56 percent of the sample exhibits the ability to reason to
coherent multi-attribute positions on this complex project. If my theoretical premises under the conditions of this case are as strong as I have
proposed, the results should easily exceed this threshold.

I do not wish to overstate my claim. This type of test is limited. We cannot learn to what precise degree these results are generalizable to other contexts, and a cross-sectional study does not allow us to track exactly how the cognitive investment of the laypublic develops over time. For example, we do not have evidence to determine whether the factors actually followed the hypothesized directions shown in the path diagrams. Yet these deficiencies are not critical at *this stage* of theoretical development. *First* we must learn if a random sample of the general public can in fact exceed our current, pessimistic expectations about their capabilities.

Discovering that the laypublic can construct a sophisticated array of social positions naturally invites comparisons with the capabilities of political activists. My second major proposition is that we should see quite different but complementary patterns, reflecting the distinct backgrounds of each set of actors and their roles in this dispute. Specifically, activists should be governed predominantly by their past, emphasizing general, substantive factors in contrast to the laypublic's more immediate concern for case-specific and procedural issues.

The schema concept, from which these expectations were deduced, has been criticized by some political scientists for its lack of specificity (Wildavsky, 1987; Kuklinski, Luskin, and Bolland, 1991). I agree with this general reaction to "schema theory": I have been frustrated in my own work at times with its lack of clear direction. Yet, for this particular proposition, I think my expectations of its usefulness are well founded. As Pamela Conover, Stanley Feldman, and Arthur Miller (1991) have pointed out, the relative strength of the schema concept is the key link that it draws between the hierarchical organization of schemas—from general to specific or, in this case, from past to present—and the role these structures play in information processing. The distinct patterns that I anticipate among the laypublic and activists represent a direct application of this principle to the context of technological decision making.

The critical test for my hypothesis lies in comparing the levels of development and the interrelationship of the four sets of factors—common orientation, procedural judgment, personal control, and substantive effects—to determine if they conform to the *relative* patterns that I have hypothesized. I emphasize relative because the premise that experience structures both the characteristics and the method of assessment leads us to expect consistent differences among these factors for political actors who bring dissimilar backgrounds to a long, contentious dispute. Indeed, I believe that we can *only* see these differences at full maturity *after* such a dispute. To repeat, then, we are looking for broad contrasts: members of the laypublic should reflect greater development in and give more weight to project-specific factors, particularly procedures, than to common orientation, while political activists should reveal relatively more development in and reliance on common orientation in reaching their final evaluations. These same patterns should also emerge when we examine subpopulations of each group: activists who were involved at the earliest stages of the dispute should give particular weight to common orientation while the members of the laypublic who have been most attentive and involved should rely most heavily on the information-intensive judgments about procedure. The more consistent the hypothesized relationships between background and evaluative approach for *different* individuals, the more plausible the experience-structured hypothesis becomes.

Consistent success in predicting this relationship for different political actors also serves as an important means to check whether these findings reflect the idiosyncratic characteristics of the specific case rather than our theoretical expectations about evaluation. Because the development and role of every factor is hypothesized to vary with background, discovering that a particularly prominent factor in this case has roughly the same effect across the range of political actors would indicate that the findings could well be case-specific. By contrast, a pattern in which the factors varied consistently with the background of the individual would support the theoretical interpretation.

Being able to compare how different actors developed and weighed the *same* factors is thus an important part of this research design. To ensure that I did not misrepresent how the respondents structured this material, I conducted extensive pretest interviews, reviewed the transcripts of the structured surveys, and double-checked the boundaries of these factors in the unstructured interviews. I have already argued in the text that I could not use traditional data-reduction techniques like confirmatory factor analysis or LISREL to test how the respondents divided the stimuli into one or more factors (the large number of variables—147—and the relatively small number of cases—26 or 16—for any particular factor prohibits convergence on a single solution). Even though this problem could be circumvented to some degree (one can, by running LISREL several thousand times, construct a probability distribution that reveals the likelihood of particular solutions), conducting a confirmatory factor analysis to test these divisions was not the purpose of this investigation.

Finally, I used standardized ordinary least-squares estimators (OLS) to calculate the regression coefficients for these factors because of the ease of presenting and interpreting these coefficients for the widest range of readers. The ordinal character of the independent and many dependent factors in this design, however, violates the restrictive assumptions of OLS and path analysis. Before presenting these results, I therefore double-checked my findings by carefully examining the unstandardized coefficients. I then ran the same models with ordinal probit (Maddala, 1983)[1] and introduced dummy variables when there were large jumps on the ordinal scales for the independent factors. The results of this analysis either support the OLS conclusions or reveal slight adjustments that actually move in a direction that is *more* consistent with my theoretical expectations. (For example, in the ordinal probit for the laypublic, procedural judgment did not have a direct, statistically significant impact on final evaluation but its effect on substantive effects remained quite strong.)

This investigation thus has much greater potential than we normally associate with a cross-sectional case study. Learning whether the laypublic has relatively sophisticated evaluative capabilities that complement the methods of political activists could represent an important advance in our current understanding of citizen assessment.

[1] The results of this analysis can be obtained by writing the author. In addition, I will soon be submitting for review a paper that lays out this analysis in great detail to directly challenge the low expectations found in public-opinion and voting-behavior literature regarding the capabilities of the laypublic.

Reference Matter

Bibliography

Aberbach, Joel, Robert Putnam, and Bert Rockman. 1981. *Bureaucrats and Politicians in Western Democracies.* Cambridge, Mass.: Harvard University Press.

Aberbach, Joel, and Bert Rockman. 1976. "Clashing Beliefs Within the Executive Branch: The Nixon Administration." *American Political Science Review* 70: 456–68.

Achen, Christopher. 1975. "Mass Political Attitudes and the Survey Response." *American Political Science Review* 69: 1218–31.

Ackerman, Bruce, Susan Rose-Ackerman, James Sawyer, and Dale Henderson. 1974. *The Uncertain Search for Environmental Quality.* New York: Free Press.

Adelman, Leonard, Thomas Stewart, and Kenneth Hammond. 1975. "A Case History of the Application of Social Judgment Theory to Policy Formulation." *Policy Sciences* 6: 137–59.

Ahearne, John. 1987. "Nuclear Power After Chernobyl." *Science* 236: 673–79.

Ajzen, Icek, and Martin Fishbein. 1980. *Understanding Attitudes and Predicting Behavior.* Englewood Cliffs, N.J.: Prentice-Hall.

Albrecht, Stan, and H. Reed Geertsen. 1978. "Land Use Planning: Attitudes and Behavior of Elected Officials and Their Constituents." *Social Science Quarterly* 59: 20–36.

Aldenderfer, Mark, and Roger Blashfield. 1984. *Cluster Analysis.* Beverly Hills, Calif.: Sage.

Allison, Graham. 1971. *Essence of Decision: Explaining the Cuban Missile Crisis.* Boston: Little, Brown.

Amy, Douglas. 1983. "Environmental Mediation: An Alternative Approach to Policy Stalemates." *Policy Sciences* 15: 345–65.

Andrews, Barbara, and Marie Sansone. 1984. *Who Runs The Rivers? Dams and Decisions in the New West.* Stanford, Calif.: Stanford Environmental Law Society.

Andrews, Richard. 1976. *Environmental Policy and Administrative Change: Implementation of the National Environmental Policy Act.* Lexington, Mass.: D. C. Heath.

Archibald, K. A. 1970. "The Views of the Expert's Role in Policy Making: Systems Analysis, Incrementalism, and the Clinical Approach." *Policy Sciences* 1: 73–86.

Arnstein, Sherry. 1969. "A Ladder of Citizen Participation." *Journal of the American Institute of Planners* 35: 216–24.

Arrow, Kenneth J. 1966. "Discounting and Public Investment Criteria." In A. V. Kneese and S. C. Smith, eds. *Water Resources Research*. Baltimore, Md.: Johns Hopkins University Press.

Ascher, William. 1978. *Forecasting: An Appraisal for Policy Makers and Planners*. Baltimore, Md.: Johns Hopkins University Press.

Bacow, Lawrence, and Michael Wheeler. 1984. *Environmental Dispute Resolution*. New York: Plenum.

Baram, Michael. 1980. "Cost-Benefit Analysis: An Inadequate Basis for Health, Safety, and Environmental Regulatory Decisionmaking." *Ecology Law Quarterly* 8: 473–531.

Barber, Benjamin. 1984. *Strong Democracy: Participatory Politics for a New Age*. Berkeley: University of California Press.

Barke, Richard. 1986. *Science, Technology, and Policy*. Washington, D.C.: Congressional Quarterly Press.

Becker, Gary. 1976. *The Economic Approach to Human Behavior*. Chicago: University of Chicago Press.

Bendor, Jonathon, Serge Taylor, and Roland Van Gaalen. 1987. "Stacking the Deck: Bureaucratic Missions and Policy Design." *American Political Science Review* 81: 873–96.

Bennett, W. Lance. 1977. "The Growth of Knowledge in Mass Belief Studies: An Epistemological Critique." *American Journal of Political Science* 21: 465–500.

Berelson, Bernard, Paul Lazarsfeld, and William McPhee. 1954. *Voting*. Chicago: University of Chicago Press.

Berger, Peter, and Thomas Luckemann. 1966. *Social Construction of Reality*. Garden City, N.Y.: Doubleday.

Bernstein, Theodore. 1975. *The Careful Writer*. New York: Atheneum.

Bingham, Gail. 1987. "Resolving Environmental Disputes: A Decade of Experience." In David J. Brower and Daniel S. Carol, eds., *Managing Land-Use Conflicts*. Durham, N.C.: Duke University Press.

Birch, A. H. 1971. *Representation*. New York: Praeger.

Bish, Robert, Robert Warren, Louis Weschler, James Crutchfield, and Peter Harrison. 1980. *Coastal Resource Use*. Seattle: University of Washington Press.

Bishop, Richard, and Thomas Heberlein. 1979. "Measuring Values of Extra-Market Goods: Are Indirect Measures Biased?" *American Journal of Agricultural Economics* 61: 926–30.

Blackwood, Larry, and Edwin Carpenter. 1978. "The Importance of Anti-Urbanism in Determining Residential Preferences and Migration Patterns." *Rural Sociology* 43: 31–47.

Blalock, Hubert, ed. 1971. *Causal Models in the Social Sciences.* Chicago: Aldine.

Blank, Robert. 1988. "Ethics and Policy: Issues in Biomedical Technology." In Michael E. Kraft and Norman Vig, eds., *Technology and Politics.* Durham, N.C.: Duke University Press.

Bohm, Peter. 1973. *Social Efficiency: A Concise Introduction to Welfare Economics.* New York: John Wiley.

Boland, Laurence. 1979. "A Criticism of Friedman's Critics." *Journal of Economic Literature* 27: 503–22.

Borgmann, Albert. 1988. "Technology and Democracy." In Michael E. Kraft and Norman Vig, eds., *Technology and Politics.* Durham, N.C.: Duke University Press.

Brady, Henry, and Paul Sniderman. 1985. "Attitude Attribution: A Group Basis for Political Reasoning." *American Political Science Review* 79: 1061–78.

Braybrooke, David, and Charles Lindblom. 1963. *A Strategy for Decision.* New York: Free Press of Glencoe.

Brewer, Garry, and Peter deLeon. 1983. *The Foundations of Policy Analysis.* Homewood, Ill.: Dorsey Press.

Brower, David J. and Daniel S. Carol, eds. 1987. *Managing Land-Use Conflicts.* Durham, N.C.: Duke University Press.

Brown, Steven. 1980. *Political Subjectivity.* New Haven, Conn.: Yale University Press.

———. 1986. "Q Technique and Method: Principles and Procedures." In William Berry and Michael Lewis-Beck, eds., *New Tools for Social Scientists.* Beverly Hills, Calif.: Sage.

Brunner, Ronald. 1982. "The Policy Sciences as Science." *Policy Sciences* 15: 115–35.

———. 1991. "The Policy Movement as a Policy Problem." *Policy Sciences* 24: 65–98.

Brunner, Ronald, and Vivian Westan. 1980. "Citizen Viewpoints on Energy Policy." *Policy Sciences* 12: 147–74.

Burke, Edmund. 1969. "The Representative as Trustee." In Hannah Pitkin, ed., *Representation.* New York: Atherton Press.

Burke, John. 1989. "Reconciling Public Administration and Democracy: The Role of the Responsible Administrator." *Public Administration Review* 49: 180–85.

Burnstein, Eugene, and Keith Sentis. 1981. "Attitude Polarization in Groups." In Richard Petty, Thomas Ostron, and Timothy Brock, eds., *Cognitive Responses in Persuasion.* Hillsdale, N.J.: Lawrence Erlbaum.

Burnstein, Eugene, and Amiram Vinokur. 1975. "What a Person Thinks upon Learning He Has Chosen Differently from Others: Nice Evidence for the Persuasive-Arguments Explanation of Choice Shifts." *Journal of Experimental Social Psychology* 11: 412–16.

———. 1977. "Persuasive Argumentation and Social Comparison as Determinants of Attitude Polarization." *Journal of Experimental Social Psychology* 13: 315–32.

Burt, Barbara, and Max Neiman. 1987. "Elite Belief Consistency and the Effect of Position in the Policy-Making Process." *Western Political Quarterly* 40: 121–36.

Byrd, Daniel, and Lester Lave. 1987. "A Framework for Risk Regulators." *Issues in Science and Technology* 3 (Summer): 92–100.

Caldwell, Lynton. 1982. *Science and the National Environmental Policy Act.* University: University of Alabama Press.

———. 1989. "A Constitutional Law for the Environment: 20 Years with NEPA Indicates the Need." *Environment* 31: 6–11, 25–28.

Calvert, Randall, Matthew McCubbins, and Barry Weingast. 1989. "A Theory of Political Control and Agency Discretion." *American Journal of Political Science* 33: 588–611.

Campbell, Angus. 1981. *The Sense of Well-Being in America.* New York: McGraw-Hill.

Campbell, Angus, Philip Converse, Warren Miller, and Donald Stokes. 1960. *The American Voter.* New York: John Wiley.

Campbell, John L. 1988. *Collapse of an Industry: Nuclear Power and the Contradictions of U.S. Policy.* Ithaca, N.Y.: Cornell University Press.

Campbell, Rex, and Lorraine Garkovich. 1984. "Turnaround Migration as an Episode of Collective Behavior." *Rural Sociology* 49: 89–105.

Carmines, Edward, and James Stimson. 1980. "The Two Faces of Issue Voting." *American Political Science Review* 74: 78–91.

Casper, Barry, and Paul Wellstone. 1981. *Powerline.* Amherst: University of Massachusetts Press.

Checkoway, Barry. 1981. "The Politics of Public Hearings." *Journal of Applied Behavioral Science* 17: 566–82.

Chen, Kan, J. C. Mathes, Kewan Jarboe, and Janet Wolfe. 1979. "Value-Oriented Social Decision Analysis: Enhancing Mutual Understanding to Resolve Public Policy Issues." *IEEE Transactions on Systems, Man, and Cybernetics* 9: 567–80.

Cheng, P. W., and K. J. Holyoak. 1985. "Pragmatic Reasoning Schemas." *Cognitive Psychology* 17: 391–416.

Cherfas, Jeremy. 1990. "Peer Review: Software for Hard Choices." *Science* 250: 367–68.

Cnudde, C. F., and D. J. McCrane. 1966. "The Linkage Between Constituency Attitudes and Congressional Voting Behavior: A Causal Model." *American Political Science Review* 60: 66–72.

Coke, James, and Steven Brown. 1976. "Public Attitudes About Land-Use Policy and Their Impact on State Policy Makers." *Publius* 6: 97–134.

Cole, Richard, and David Caputo. 1984. "The Public Hearing as an Effective Citizen Participation Mechanism: A Case Study of the General Revenue Sharing Program." *American Political Science Review* 78: 404–16.

Coleman, Richard P. 1978. "Attitudes Toward Neighborhoods: How Americans Choose to Live." Working Paper 49. Joint Center for Urban Studies of MIT and Harvard University.

Conover, Pamela. 1984. "The Influence of Group Identifications on Political Perception and Evaluation." *Journal of Politics* 46: 760–85.

———. 1985. "The Impact of Group Economic Interests on Political Evaluations." *American Politics Quarterly* 13: 139–66.

Conover, Pamela, and Stanley Feldman. 1981. "The Origins and Meaning of Liberal/Conservative Self-Identifications." *American Journal of Political Science* 25: 617–45.

———. 1984. "How People Organize the Political World." *American Journal of Political Science* 28: 95–126.

Conover, Pamela, Stanley Feldman, and Arthur Miller. 1991. "Where Is the Schema? Critiques." *American Political Science Review* 85: 1357–80.

Converse, Philip E. 1964. "The Nature of Belief Systems in Mass Politics." In David Apter, ed., *Ideology and Discontent*. New York: Free Press.

———. 1975. "Public Opinion and Voting Behavior." In Fred Greenstein and Nelson Polsby, eds., *Handbook of Political Science*. Reading, Mass.: Addison-Wesley.

Cook, Brian, and B. Dan Wood. 1989. "Principal-Agent Models of Political Control of Bureaucracy." *American Political Science Review* 83: 965–78.

Coombs, C. H. 1975. "Portfolio Theory and the Measurement of Risk." In M. F. Kaplan and S. Schwartz, eds., *Human Judgment and Decision Processes*. New York: Academic.

Coombs, C. H., and G. Avrunin. 1977. "Single-Peaked Functions and the Theory of Preference." *Psychological Review* 84: 216–30.

Craik, Kenneth, and Ervin Zube. 1976. *Perceiving Environmental Quality*. New York: Free Press.

Crandall, Robert, and Lester Lave, eds. 1981. *The Scientific Basis of Health and Safety Regulation*. Washington, D.C.: The Brookings Institution.

Crocker, Jennifer, Susan Fiske, and Shelley Taylor. 1984. "Schematic Bases of Belief Changes." In J. Richard Eiser, ed., *Attitudinal Judgment*. New York: Springer-Verlag.

Cronbach, L., and G. Gleser. 1953. "Assessing Similarities Between Profiles." *Psychological Bulletin* 50: 456–73.

Crosby, Ned, Janet Kelly, and Paul Schaefer. 1986. "Citizen Panels: A New Approach to Citizen Participation." *Public Administration Review* 46: 170–83.

Culhane, Paul. 1981. *Public Lands Politics*. Baltimore, Md.: Johns Hopkins University Press.

Culhane, Paul, Thomas Armentano, and H. Paul Friesema. 1985. "State-of-the-Art Science and Environmental Assessments: The Case of Acid Deposition." *Environmental Management* 9: 365–78.

Culhane, Paul, H. Paul Friesema, and Janice Beecher. 1987. *Forecasts and Environmental Decision Making: The Content and Accuracy of Environmental Impact Statements*. Boulder, Colo.: Westview Press.

Dahl, Robert. 1956. *A Preface to Democratic Theory*. Chicago: University of Chicago Press.

———. 1985. *Controlling Nuclear Weapons*. Syracuse, N.Y.: Syracuse University Press.

Daneke, Gregory. 1983. "Public Involvement: What, Why, How." In Gregory Daneke, Margot Garcia, and Jerome Priscoli, eds., *Public Involvement and Social Impact Assessment*. Boulder, Colo.: Westview Press.

Davis, Kenneth Culp. 1969. *Discretionary Justice*. Baton Rouge: Louisiana State University Press.

Day, Richard B., Ronald Beiner, and Joseph Masciulli. 1988. *Democratic Theory and Technological Society*. Armonk, N.Y.: M. E. Sharpe.

Desvogues, W. H., and Kerry Smith. 1988. "Focus Groups and Risk Communication: The 'Science' of Listening to Data." *Risk Analysis* 8: 479–84.

Devine, Donald. 1972. *The Political Culture of the United States*. Boston: Little, Brown.

Doniger, David. 1978. "Federal Regulation of Vinyl Chloride: A Short Course in the Law and Policy of Toxic Substances Control." *Ecology Law Quarterly* 7: 500–677.

Douglas, Mary, and Aaron Wildavsky. 1982. *Risk and Culture*. Berkeley: University of California Press.

Downs, Anthony. 1957. *An Economic Theory of Democracy*. New York: Harper and Row.

Dreyfus, Daniel, and Helen Ingram. 1976. "The National Environmental Policy Act: A View of Intent and Practice." *Natural Resources Journal* 16: 243–62.

Dunlap, R., and M. Allen. 1976. "Partisan Differences on Environmental Issues: A Congressional Role-Call Analysis." *Western Political Quarterly* 29: 384–97.

Dunlap, R., and R. Gale. 1974. "Party Membership and Environmental Politics: A Legislative Roll-Call Analysis." *Social Science Quarterly* 55:670–90.

Dunn, William, ed. 1986. *Policy Analysis: Perspectives, Concepts, and Methods*. Greenwich, Conn.: JAI Press.

Edwards, Ward. 1977. "How to Use Multi-Attribute Utility Measurement for Social Decision Making." *IEEE Transactions on Systems, Man, and Cybernetics* 7: 326–40.

Eisenstadt, S. N. 1954. "Studies in Reference Group Behavior." *Human Relations* 7: 191–213.

Entman, Robert. 1989. "How the Media Affect What People Think: An Information-Processing Approach." *Journal of Politics* 51: 347–70.

Erikson, Robert. 1979. "The SRC Panel Data and Mass Political Attitudes." *British Journal of Political Science* 9: 89–114.

Etzioni, Amitai. 1986. "The Case for a Multiple-Utility Conception." *Economics and Philosophy* 2: 159–83.

Everitt, Brian. 1980. *Cluster Analysis*. New York: Halstead.

Fairfax, Sally. 1978. "A Disaster in the Environmental Movement." *Science* 199: 743–48.

Fandel, Gunter, and Jaap Spronk, eds. 1985. *Multiple-Criteria Decision Methods and Applications*. New York: Springer-Verlag.

Feldman, Stanley. 1988. "Structure and Consistency in Public Opinion: The Role of Core Beliefs and Values." *American Journal of Political Science* 32: 416–40.

Feldman, Stanley, and Pamela Conover. 1984. "The Structure of Issue Positions: Beyond Liberal-Conservative Constraint." *Micropolitics* 3: 281–303.

Ferejohn, John. 1974. *Pork Barrel Politics: Rivers and Harbors Legislation, 1947–1968*. Stanford, Calif.: Stanford University Press.

Festinger, Leon, ed. 1964. *Conflict, Decision, and Dissonance*. Stanford, Calif.: Stanford University Press.

Finsterbusch, Kurt. 1980. *Understanding Social Impacts: Assessing the Effects of Public Projects*. Beverly Hills, Calif.: Sage.

Fiorino, Daniel. 1988. "Regulatory Negotiation as a Policy Process." *Public Administration Review* 48: 764–72.

———. 1989. "Technical and Democratic Values in Risk Analysis." *Risk Analysis* 9: 293–99.

———. 1990. "Citizen Participation and Environmental Risk: A Survey of Institutional Mechanisms." *Science, Technology, and Human Values* 15: 226–43.

Fischhoff, Baruch, Paul Slovic, Sarah Lichtenstein, Stephen Read, and Barbara Combs. 1978. "How Safe Is Safe Enough?" *Policy Sciences* 9: 127–52.

Fischhoff, Baruch, Paul Slovic, and Sarah Lichtenstein. 1983. "'The Public' vs. 'The Experts': Perceived vs. Actual Disagreements About Risks." In Vincent Covello, G. Flamm, J. Rodericks, and R. Tardiff, eds., *The Analysis of Actual Versus Perceived Risks*. New York: Plenum.

Fischhoff, Baruch, S. Watson, and P. Hope. 1984. "Defining Risk." *Policy Sciences* 17: 128–40.

Fishbein, Martin, and Icek Ajzen. 1975. *Belief, Attitude, Intention, and Behavior*. Reading, Mass.: Addison-Wesley.

Fiske, Susan T. 1981. "Social Cognition and Affect." In John Harvey, ed., *Cognition, Social Behavior, and the Environment*. Hillsdale, N.J.: Lawrence Erlbaum.

———. 1982. "Schema-Triggered Affect: Applications to Social Perception." In Margaret Clark and Susan Fiske, eds., *Affect and Cognition*. Hillsdale, N.J.: Lawrence Erlbaum.

Fiske, Susan T., and Donald Kinder. 1981. "Involvement, Expertise, and Schema Use: Evidence from Political Cognition." In Nancy Cantor and John Kihlstrom, eds., *Personality, Cognition, and Social Interaction*. Hillsdale, N.J.: Lawrence Erlbaum.

Fiske, Susan T., Donald Kinder, and W. Michael Carter. 1983. "The Novice and the Expert: Knowledge-Based Strategies in Political Cognition." *Journal of Experimental Social Psychology* 19: 381–400.

Fiske, Susan T., and Patricia W. Linville. 1980. "What Does the Schema Concept Buy Us?" *Personality and Social Psychology Bulletin* 6: 543–57.

Fiske, Susan T., and Mark Pavelchak. 1986. "Category-Based versus Piecemeal-Based Affective Responses: Developments in Schema-Triggered Affect." In Richard Sorrentino and E. Tory Higgins, *Handbook of Motivation and Cognition*. New York: Guilford Press.

Fiske, Susan T., and Shelley E. Taylor. 1984. *Social Cognition*. Reading, Mass.: Addison-Wesley.

Friedman, Milton. 1953. "The Methodology of Positive Economics." In M. Friedman, *Essays in Positive Economics*. Chicago: University of Chicago Press.

Friedrich, Carl. 1948. "Representation and Constitutional Reform in Europe." *Western Political Quarterly* 1: 124–30.

Fritschler, A. Lee. 1983. *Smoking and Politics: Policy Making and the Federal Bureaucracy*. Englewood Cliffs, N.J.: Prentice-Hall.

George, David L., and Priscilla Southwell. 1985. "Opinion on the Diablo Canyon Nuclear Power Plant: The Effects of Situation and Socialization." Unpublished paper (available from authors).

Georgescu-Roegen, Nicolas. 1971. *The Entropy Law and the Economic Process*. Cambridge, Mass.: Harvard University Press.

Gilbert, Richard. 1991. *Regulatory Choices*. Berkeley: University of California Press.

Glazer, Amihai, and Bernard Grofman. 1989. "Why Representatives Are Ideologists Though Voters Are Not." *Public Choice* 61: 29–39.

Gormley, William. 1989. *Taming the Bureaucracy*. Princeton, N.J.: Princeton University Press.

Goudy, Willis J. 1982. "Further Consideration of Indicators of Community Attachment." *Social Indicators Research* 11: 181–92.

Gregory, Robert. 1989. "Political Rationality or 'Incrementalism'? Charles E. Lindblom's Enduring Contribution to Public Policy Making Theory." *Policy and Politics* 17: 139–53.

Griggs, R. A., and J. R. Cox. 1982. "The Elusive Thematic-Materials Effect in Wason's Selection Task." *British Journal of Psychology* 73: 407–20.

Haefele, Edwin. 1973. *Representative Government and Environmental Management*. Baltimore, Md.: Johns Hopkins University Press.

Hagner, Paul, and John McIver. 1980. "Attitude Stability and Change in the 1976 Election: A Panel Study." In John Pierce and John Sullivan, eds., *The Electorate Reconsidered*. Beverly Hills, Calif.: Sage.

Haimes, Yacov, and Vira Chankong, eds. 1985. *Decision Making with Multiple Objectives*. Berlin: Springer-Verlag.

Halperin, Morton. 1974. *Bureaucratic Politics and Foreign Policy*. Princeton, N.J.: Princeton University Press.

Halperin, Morton, and Arnold Kanter, eds. 1973. *Readings in American Foreign Policy.* Boston: Little, Brown.

Hamill, Ruth, and Milton Lodge. 1986. "Cognitive Consequences of Political Sophistication." In Richard Lau and David O. Sears, eds., *Political Cognition.* Hillsdale, N.J.: Lawrence Erlbaum.

Hammond, Kenneth R., Jeryl Mumpower, Robin L. Dennis, Samuel Fitch, and Wilson Crumpacker. 1983. "Fundamental Obstacles to the Use of Scientific Information in Public Policy Making." *Technological Forecasting and Social Change* 24: 287–97.

Hannan, Edward. 1984. "Goal Programming: Methodological Advances in 1972–1983 and Prospects for the Future." In Milan Zeleny, ed., *MCDM: Past Decade and Future Trends.* Greenwich, Conn.: JAI Press.

Harberger, Arnold. 1983. "Basic Needs versus Distributional Weights in Social Cost-Benefit Analysis." In Robert Haveman and Julius Margolis, eds., *Public Expenditure and Policy Analysis.* 3rd ed. Boston: Houghton Mifflin.

Hastie, R. 1981. "Schematic Principles in Human Memory." In E. Troy Higgins, C. Peter Herman, and Mark Zarma, eds., *Social Cognition.* Hillsdale, N.J.: Lawrence Erlbaum.

———. 1986. "A Primer of Information-Processing Theory for the Political Scientist." In Richard Lau and David O. Sears, eds., *Political Cognition.* Hillsdale, N.J.: Lawrence Erlbaum.

Haveman, Robert. 1965. *Water Resource Investment and the Public Interest.* Nashville, Tenn.: Vanderbilt University Press.

———. 1972. *The Economic Performance of Public Investments.* Baltimore, Md.: Johns Hopkins University Press.

Haveman, Robert, and Julius Margolis, eds. 1983. *Public Expenditure and Policy Analysis.* 3rd ed. Boston: Houghton Mifflin.

Haveman, Robert, and Burton A. Weisbrod. 1983. "Defining Benefits of Public Programs: Some Guidance for Policy Analysis." In Robert Haveman and Julius Margolis, eds., *Public Expenditure and Policy Analysis.* 3rd ed. Boston: Houghton Mifflin.

Heberlein, Thomas. 1976. "Some Observations on Alternative Mechanisms for Public Involvement: The Hearing, the Public Opinion Poll, the Workshop, and the Quasi-Experiment." *Natural Resources Journal* 16: 197–212.

Heise, David. 1975. *Causal Analysis.* New York: John Wiley.

Hensler, D. R., and C. P. Hensler. 1979. *Evaluating Nuclear Power: Voter Choice on the California Energy Initiative.* Santa Monica, Calif.: Rand Corporation.

Higgins, E. Tory, and Gillian King. 1981. "Accessibility of Social Constructs: Information-Processing Consequences of Individual and Contextual Variability." In Nancy Cantor and John Kihlstrom, eds., *Personality, Cognition, and Social Interaction.* Hillsdale, N.J.: Lawrence Erlbaum.

Higgins, E. Tory, and N. S. Rholes. 1976. "Impression Formation and Role Fulfillment: A Holistic Reference Approach." *Journal of Experimental Social Psychology* 12: 422–35.

Hill, Stuart. 1985. "Political Culture and the Evaluation of Nuclear Power: A Comparative Analysis of France and the United Sates." In A. Groth and L. Wade, eds., *Public Policy Across Nations*. Greenwich, Conn.: JAI Press.

———. 1986. "Lumpy Preference Structures." *Policy Sciences* 19: 5–32.

Hill, William, and Leonard Ortolano. 1978. "NEPA's Effect on the Consideration of Alternatives: A Crucial Test." *Natural Resources Journal* 18: 285–311.

Hilsman, Roger. 1987. *The Politics of Policy Making in Defense and Foreign Affairs*. Englewood Cliffs, N.J.: Prentice-Hall.

Hirsch, Fred. 1976. *Social Limits to Growth*. Cambridge, Mass.: Harvard University Press.

Hirschleifer, Jack, and David Shapiro. 1983. "The Treatment of Risk and Uncertainty." In Robert Haveman and Julius Margolis, eds., *Public Expenditure and Policy Analysis*. 3rd ed. Boston: Houghton Mifflin.

Hochman, H. M., and J. D. Rodgers. 1969. "Pareto Optimal Redistribution." *American Economic Review* 59: 542–56.

Hoos, Ida. 1972. *Systems Analysis in Public Policy*. Berkeley: University of California Press.

Huckfeldt, Robert. 1983. "The Social Context of Political Change: Durability, Volatility, and Social Influence." *American Political Science Review* 77: 929–44.

Huckfeldt, Robert, and John Sprague. 1987. "Networks in Context: The Social Flow of Political Information." *American Political Science Review* 81: 1197–1216.

Hufschmidt, Maynard M., David James, Anton Meister, Blair Bower, and John Dixon. 1983. *Environment, Natural Systems, and Development: An Economic Valuation Guide*. Baltimore, Md.: Johns Hopkins University Press.

Huntington, Samuel P. 1981. *American Politics: The Promise of Disharmony*. Cambridge, Mass.: Belknap Press.

Hurwitz, Jon, and Mark Peffley. 1987. "How Are Foreign Policy Attitudes Structured? A Hierarchical Model." *American Political Science Review* 81: 1099–1120.

Inglehart, Ronald. 1977. *The Silent Revolution: Changing Values and Political Styles Among Western Publics*. Princeton, N.J.: Princeton University Press.

———. 1981. "Post-Materialism in an Environment of Insecurity." *American Political Science Review* 75: 880–900.

Iyengar, Shanto. 1989. "How Citizens Think About National Issues: A Matter of Responsibility." *American Journal of Political Science* 33: 878–900.

Jackson, John E. 1983. "The Systematic Beliefs of the Mass Public: Estimating Policy Preferences with Survey Data." *Journal of Politics* 45: 840–65.

Jacoby, William. 1986. "Levels of Conceptualization and Reliance on the Liberal-Conservative Continuum." *Journal of Politics* 48: 423–32.

———. 1988. "The Impact of Party Identification on Issue Attitudes." *American Journal of Political Science* 32: 643–61.

———. 1990. "Variability in Issue Alternatives and American Public Opinion." *American Journal of Political Science* 52: 579–606.

Janis, Irving, and Leon Mann. 1977. *Decision Making*. New York: Free Press.

Jenkins-Smith, Hank. 1985. "Adversarial Analysis in the Bureaucratic Context." In Peter Brown, ed., *Advocacy Analysis*. Baltimore: University of Maryland Press.

Kahneman, Daniel, Paul Slovic, and Amos Tversky. 1982. *Judgment Under Uncertainty: Heuristics and Biases*. Cambridge, Eng.: Cambridge University Press.

Kasarda, John, and Morris Janowitz. 1974. "Community Attachment in Mass Society." *American Sociological Review* 39: 328–39.

Kasperson, Roger E. 1986. "Six Propositions on Public Participation and Their Relevance for Risk Communication." *Risk Analysis* 6: 275–81.

Keeney, Ralph. 1980. *Siting Energy Facilities*. New York: Academic Press.

Keeney, Ralph, and Howard Raiffa. 1976. *Decision Making with Multiple Objectives*. New York: John Wiley.

Keeney, Ralph, Detlof von Winterfeldt, and Thomas Eppel. 1990. "Eliciting Public Values for Complex Policy Decisions." *Management Science* 36: 1011–30.

Kinder, Donald. 1983. "Diversity and Complexity in Public Opinion." In Ada Finifter, ed., *Political Science: The State of the Discipline*. Washington, D.C.: American Political Science Association.

Kinder, Donald R., and D. Roderick Kiewiet. 1979. "Economic Discontent and Political Behavior: The Role of Personal Grievances and Collective Economic Judgments in Congressional Voting." *American Journal of Political Science* 23: 495–527.

———. 1981. "Sociotropic Politics: The American Case." *British Journal of Politics* 11: 129–61.

King, Gary. 1990. "On Political Methodology." In James Stimson, ed., *Political Analysis*. Ann Arbor: University of Michigan Press.

Kingdon, John. 1984. *Agendas, Alternatives, and Public Policies*. Boston: Little, Brown.

Kirschenbaum, Alan. 1983. "Sources of Neighborhood Residential Change: A Micro-Level Analysis." *Social Indicators Research* 12: 183–98.

Kohler, Heinz. 1970. *Economics: The Science of Scarcity*. Hinsdale, Ill.: Dryden Press.

Kraft, Michael E. 1988. "Evaluating Technology Through Public Participation: The Nuclear Waste Disposal Controversy." In Kraft and Vig, eds., *Technology and Politics*. Durham, N.C.: Duke University Press.

Kraft, Michael E., and Bruce Clary. 1991. "Citizen Participation and the NIMBY Syndrome: Public Response to Radioactive Waste Disposal." *Western Political Quarterly* 44: 299–328.

Kraft, Michael E., and Norman Vig, eds. 1988. *Technology and Politics*. Durham, N.C.: Duke University Press.

Kraus, Sidney, ed. 1979. *The Great Debates*. Bloomington: Indiana University Press.

Krislov, Samuel, and David Rosenbloom. 1981. *Representative Bureaucracy and the American Political System*. New York: Praeger.

Krosnick, Jon. 1990. "Lessons Learned: A Review and Integration of our Findings." *Social Cognition* 8: 154–58.

Krosnick, Jon, and Michael Milburn. 1990. "Psychological Determinants of Political Opinionation." *Social Cognition* 8: 49–72.

Krutilla, John. 1981. "Reflections of an Applied Welfare Economist." *Journal of Environmental Economics and Management* 8: 1–10.

Krutilla, John, and Anthony Fisher. 1975. *The Economics of Natural Environments*. Baltimore, Md.: Johns Hopkins University Press.

Kuklinski, James, Daniel Metlay, and W. D. Kay. 1982. "Citizen Knowledge and Choices on the Complex Issue of Nuclear Energy." *American Journal of Political Science* 26: 615–42.

Kuklinski, James, Robert Luskin, and John Bolland. 1991. "Where Is the Schema? Going Beyond the 'S' Word in Political Psychology." *American Political Science Review* 85: 1341–56.

Lane, Robert. 1962. *Political Ideology*. New York: Free Press of Glencoe.

Lasswell, Harold D. 1971. *A Pre-View of Policy Science*. New York: American Elsevier.

Lau, Richard, and David O. Sears, eds. 1986. *Political Cognition*. Hillsdale, N.J.: Lawrence Erlbaum.

Leibenstein, Harvey. 1976. *Beyond Economic Man*. Cambridge, Mass.: Harvard University Press.

Lerner, Melvin. 1980. *The Belief in a Just World*. New York: Plenum.

Light, Paul. 1983. *The President's Agenda: Domestic Policy Choice From Kennedy to Carter*. Baltimore, Md.: Johns Hopkins University Press.

Lilienthal, David. 1963. *Change, Hope, and the Bomb*. Princeton, N.J.: Princeton University Press.

Lindblom, Charles. 1959. "The Science of 'Muddling Through.'" *Public Administration Review* 19: 78–88.

———. 1965. *The Intelligence of Democracy*. New York: Free Press.

———. 1977. *Politics and Markets*. New York: Basic Books.

———. 1979. "Still Muddling, Not Yet Through." Public Administration Review 39: 517–26.

———. 1990. *Inquiry and Change*. New Haven, Conn.: Yale University Press.

Lindell, Michael K., and Timothy C. Earle. 1983. "How Close Is Close Enough: Public Perceptions of the Risks of Industrial Facilities." *Risk Analysis* 3: 245–53.

Linville, Patricia. 1982. "Affective Consequences of Complexity Regarding the Self and Others." In Margaret Clark and Susan Fiske, eds., *Affect and Cognition*. Hillsdale, N.J.: Lawrence Erlbaum.

Lipset, Seymour M., and William Schneider. 1983. *The Confidence Gap*. New York: MacMillan.

Lipsey, R. G., and R. K. Lancanster. 1956–57. "The General Theory of Second-Best." *Review of Economic Studies* 24: 11–32.

Liroff, Richard. 1976. *A National Policy for the Environment: NEPA and Its Aftermath.* Bloomington: Indiana University Press.

Little, I. M. D. 1957. *A Critique of Welfare Economics.* London: Clarendon.

Lodge, Milton, and Ruth Hamill. 1986. "A Partisan Schema for Political Information Processing." *American Political Science Review* 80: 505–40.

Lovins, Amory. 1977. "Cost-Risk-Benefit Assessment in Energy Policy." *George Washington Law Review* 45: 911–43.

Lowi, Theodore. 1969. *The End of Liberalism.* New York: W. W. Norton.

Lowrance, William. 1976. *Of Acceptable Risk.* Los Altos, Calif.: William Kaufman.

———. 1986. *Modern Science and Human Values.* New York: Oxford University Press.

Luttbeg, Norman. 1968. "The Structure of Beliefs Among Leaders and the Public." *Public Opinion Quarterly* 32: 388–409.

Lynn, Frances M. 1986. "The Interplay of Science and Values in Assessing and Regulating Environmental Risks." *Science, Technology, and Human Values* 11: 40–50.

MacIntyre, Angus. 1986. "The Multiple Sources of Statutory Ambiguity: Tracing the Legislative Origins of Administrative Discretion." In Douglas Shumavon and H. Kenneth Hibbeln, eds., *Administrative Discretion and Public Policy Implementation.* New York: Praeger.

MacRae, Duncan. 1976. *The Social Function of Social Science.* New Haven, Conn.: Yale University Press.

MacRae, Duncan, and John Carlson. 1980. "Collective Preferences as Predictors of Interstate Migration." *Social Indicators Research* 8: 15–32.

Maddala, G. S. 1983. *Limited-Dependent and Qualitative Variables in Econometrics.* Cambridge, Eng.: Cambridge University Press.

Majone, Giandomenico. 1989. *Evidence, Argument, and Persuasion in the Policy Process.* New Haven, Conn.: Yale University Press.

March, James, and Johan Olsen. 1989. *Rediscovering Institutions.* New York: Free Press.

March, James, and Herbert Simon. 1958. *Organizations.* New York: John Wiley.

Marcus, George, David Tabb, and John Sullivan. 1974. "The Application of Individual Differences Scaling to the Measurement of Political Ideologies." *American Journal of Political Science* 18: 405–20.

Markus, Gregory. 1988. "The Impact of Personal and National Economic Conditions on the Presidential Vote: A Pooled Cross-Sectional Analysis." *American Journal of Political Science* 32: 137–54.

Markus, Hazel, and Jeanne Smith. 1981. "The Influence of Self-Schemas on the Perception of Others." In Nancy Cantor and John Kihlstrom, eds.,

Personality, Cognition, and Social Interaction. Hillsdale, N.J.: Lawrence Erlbaum.

Marshall, Eliot. 1990. "The Shuttle: Whistling Past the Graveyard." *Science* 250: 499–500.

Martin, J. L. 1981. "Science and the Successful Society." *Public Opinion* 4(3): 16–19, 55–56.

Mason, Richard, and Ian Mitroff. 1981. *Challenging Strategic Planning Assumptions.* New York: John Wiley.

Massart, D. Luc, and Leonard Kaufman. 1983. *The Interpretation of Analytical Chemical Data by the Use of Cluster Analysis.* New York: John Wiley.

Mazmanian, Daniel, and David Morell. 1990. "The 'NIMBY' Syndrome: Facility Siting and the Failure of Democratic Discourse." In Norman Vig and Michael Kraft, eds., *Environmental Policy in the 1990's.* Washington, D.C.: Congressional Quarterly.

Mazmanian, Daniel, and Jeanne Nienaber. 1979. *Can Organizations Change?* Washington, D.C.: The Brookings Institution.

Mazmanian, Daniel, and Paul Sabatier. 1981. "Liberalism, Environmentalism, and Partisanship in Public Policy-Making." *Environment and Behavior* 13: 361–84.

Mazur, Allan. 1981. *The Dynamics of Technical Controversy.* Washington, D.C.: Communications Press.

McEvoy, James, and Thomas Dietz. 1977. *Handbook for Environmental Planning: The Social Consequences of Environmental Change.* New York: John Wiley.

McGraw, Kathleen, and Neil Pinney. 1990. "The Effects of General and Domain-Specific Expertise on Political Memory and Judgment." *Social Cognition* 8: 9–30.

Meier, Kenneth. 1975. "Representative Bureaucracy: An Empirical Analysis." *American Political Science Review* 69: 526–42.

Merewitz, Leonard, and Stephen Sosnick. 1971. *The Budget's New Clothes.* Chicago: Rand McNally.

Merkhofer, M. 1987. *Decision Science and Social Risk Management.* Dordrecht, Holland: Reidel.

Michener, H. Andrew, and Edward Lawler. 1975. "Endorsement of Formal Leaders: An Integrative Model." *Journal of Personality and Social Psychology* 31: 216–23.

Milbrath, Lester. 1984. *Environmentalists: Vanguard for a New Society.* Albany: State University of New York Press.

Miller, Arthur, Martin Wattenberg, and Oksana Malanchuk. 1986. "Schematic Assessments of Presidential Candidates." *American Political Science Review* 80: 521–40.

Miller, G. A. 1956. "The Magical Number Seven, Plus or Minus Two: Some Limits on our Capacity for Processing Information." *Psychological Review* 63: 81–97.

Miller, W. E., and D. E. Stokes. 1963. "Constituency Influence in Congress." *American Political Science Review* 57: 45–56.

Mishan, Ezra J. 1972. "The Futility of Pareto-Efficient Distribution." *American Economic Review* 62: 971–76.

———. 1976. *Cost-Benefit Analysis.* New York: Praeger.

Mitroff, Ian, and Richard Mason. 1982. "On the Structure of Dialectical Reasoning in the Social and Policy Sciences." *Theory and Decision* 14: 331–50.

Moe, Terry. 1984. "The New Economics of Organization." *American Journal of Political Science* 28: 739–77.

Morell, David, and Grace Singer, eds. 1980. *Refining the Waterfront.* Cambridge, Mass.: Oelgeschlager, Gunn, and Hain.

Morgenstern, Oskar. 1972. "Thirteen Critical Points in Contemporary Economic Theory: An Interpretation." *Journal of Economic Literature* 10: 1163–89.

Morone, Joseph G., and Edward J. Woodhouse. 1986. *Averting Catastrophe: Strategies for Regulating Risky Technologies.* Berkeley: University of California Press.

———. 1989. *The Demise of Nuclear Energy? Lessons for Democratic Control of Technology.* Berkeley: University of California Press.

Neisser, Ulric. 1976. *Cognition and Reality: Principles and Implications of Cognitive Psychology.* San Francisco: W. H. Freeman.

Nelkin, Dorothy, ed. 1984a. *Controversy: Politics of Technical Decisions.* Beverly Hills, Calif.: Sage.

———. 1984b. "Science and Technology Policy and the Democratic Process." In James Petersen, ed., *Citizen Participation in Science Policy.* Amherst: University of Massachusetts Press.

Nelkin, Dorothy, and Susan Fallows. 1978. "The Evolution of the Nuclear Debate: The Role of Public Participation." *Annual Review of Energy* 3: 275–312.

Nelson, John. 1977. "The Ideological Connection." *Theory and Society*: 4: 421–45, 573–90.

Nie, Norman, Sidney Verba, and John Petrocik. 1979. *The Changing American Voter.* Cambridge, Mass.: Harvard University Press.

Niemi, Richard, and Herbert Weisberg. 1984. *Controversies in Voting Behavior.* Washington, D.C.: Congressional Quarterly.

Nijkamp, Peter. 1979. *Multidimensional Spatial Data and Decision Analysis.* New York: John Wiley.

———. 1980. *Environmental Policy Analysis.* London: John Wiley.

Nijkamp, Peter, and A. Van Delft. 1977. *Multi-Criteria Analysis and Regional Decision Making.* Leiden: Martinus Nijhoff.

Nijkamp, Peter, and Henk Voogd. 1985. "An Informal Introduction to Multi-Criteria Evaluations." In Gunter Fandel and Jaap Spronk, *Multiple-Criteria Decision Methods and Applications.* New York: Springer-Verlag.

Nisbett, Richard, and Lee Ross. 1980. *Human Inference: Strategies and Shortcomings of Social Judgment.* Englewood Cliffs, N.J.: Prentice-Hall.

O'Brien, David. 1986. "Administrative Discretion, Judicial Review, and Regulatory Politics." In Douglas Shumavon and H. Kenneth Hibbeln, eds., *Administrative Discretion and Public Policy Implementation.* New York: Praeger.

O'Hare, Michael, Lawrence Bacow, and Debra Sanderson. 1983. *Facility Siting and Public Opposition.* New York: Van Nostrand Reinhold.

O'Riordan, Timothy, and R. Kerry Turner. 1983. "Traditional Cost-Benefit Analysis and Its Critique." In O'Riordan and Turner, eds., *Annotated Reader in Environmental Planning and Management.* Oxford: Pergamon Press.

Ostrom, Elinor. 1991. "Rational Choice Theory and Institutional Analysis: Toward Complementarity." *American Political Science Review* 85: 237–43.

Otway, Harry, and Thomas Kerry. 1982. "Reflections on Risk Perception and Policy." *Risk Analysis* 2: 69–82.

Otway, Harry, and Detlof von Winterfeldt. 1982. "Beyond Acceptable Risk: On the Social Acceptability of Technologies." *Policy Sciences* 14: 247–56.

Page, Benjamin I. 1978. *Choices and Echoes in Presidential Elections.* Chicago: University of Chicago Press.

Page, Benjamin, and Robert Shapiro. 1992. *The Rational Public.* Chicago, Ill.: University of Chicago Press.

Peffley, Mark, and Jon Hurwitz. 1985. "A Hierarchical Model of Attitude Constraints." *American Journal of Political Science* 29: 871–90.

Petersen, James, ed. 1984. *Citizen Participation in Science Policy.* Amherst: University of Massachusetts Press.

Petty, Richard, and John Cacioppo. 1981. *Attitudes and Persuasion.* Dubuque, Iowa: William Brown.

———. 1984. "The Effects of Involvement on Responses to Argument Quantity and Quality: Central and Peripheral Routes to Persuasion." *Journal of Personality and Social Psychology* 46: 69–81.

———. 1986. *Communication and Persuasion.* New York: Springer-Verlag.

Pierce, John, and Nicholas Lovrich. 1980. "Belief Systems Concerning the Environment: The General Public, Attentive Publics, and State Legislators." *Political Behavior* 2: 259–86.

Pitkin, Hannah, ed. 1969. *Representation.* New York: Atherton.

———. 1972. *The Concept of Representation.* Berkeley: University of California Press.

Ploch, Louis. 1978. "The Reversal in Migration Patterns: Some Rural Development Consequences." *Rural Sociology* 43: 293–303.

Popkin, Samuel. 1991. *The Reasoning Voter.* Chicago, Ill.: University of Chicago Press.

Popper, Frank. 1983. "LP/HC and LULUs: The Political Uses of Risk Analysis in Land-Use Planning." *Risk Analysis* 3: 255–63.

Price, Don K. 1965. *The Scientific Estate*. New York: Oxford University Press.

Putnam, Robert. 1976. *The Comparative Study of Political Elites*. Englewood Cliffs, N.J.: Prentice-Hall.

Rajecki, D. W. 1982. *Attitudes: Themes and Advances*. Sunderland, Mass.: Sinauer.

Rankin, W. L., and S. M. Nealy. 1978. "Attitudes of the Public About Nuclear Wastes." *Nuclear News* 21: 112–17.

Rayner, Steve, and Robin Cantor. 1987. "How Fair Is Safe Enough? The Cultural Approach to Societal Technology Choice." *Risk Analysis* 7: 3–9.

Redburn, Steve, Terry Buss, Steven Foster, and William Binning. 1980. "How Representative Are Mandated Citizen Participation Processes?" *Urban Affairs Quarterly* 15: 345–52.

Renn, O., H. U. Stegelmann, G. Albrecht, U. Kotte, and H. P. Peters. 1984. "An Empirical Investigation of Citizens' Preferences Among Four Energy Scenarios." *Technological Forecasting and Social Change* 26: 11–46.

Rhoads, Steven. 1985a. "Do Economists Overemphasize Monetary Benefits?" *Public Administration Review* 45: 815–20.

———. 1985b. *The Economist's View of the World*. Cambridge, Eng.: Cambridge University Press.

Ripley, Randall, and Grace Franklin. 1976. *Congress, Bureaucracy, and Public Policy*. Homewood, Ill.: Dorsey.

Robinson, John B. 1982. "Apples and Horned Toads: On the Framework-Determined Nature of the Energy Debate." *Policy Sciences* 15: 23–45.

Rosch, Eleanor. 1975. "Cognitive Representations of Somatic Categories." *Journal of Experimental Psychology* 104: 192–233.

Rosener, Judith. 1982. "Making Bureaucracy Responsive: A Study of the Impact of Citizen Participation and Staff Recommendations on Regulatory Decision Making." *Public Administration Review* 42: 339–45.

Rourke, Francis E. 1984. *Bureaucracy, Politics, and Public Policy*. Boston: Little, Brown.

Rumelhart, David. 1984. "Schemata and the Cognitive System." In Robert Wyer and Thomas Srull, eds., *Handbook of Social Cognition*, vol. 1. Hillsdale, N.J.: Lawrence Erlbaum.

Rumelhart, David, and Andrew Ortony. 1977. "The Representatives of Knowledge in Memory." In Richard Anderson, Rand Spiro, and William Montague, eds., *Schooling and the Acquisition of Knowledge*. New York: John Wiley.

Saaty, Thomas. 1990. "An Exposition of the AHP in Reply to the Paper 'Remarks on the Analytic Hierarchy Process.'" *Management Science* 36: 259–68.

Saaty, Thomas, and Kevin Kearns. 1985. *Analytical Planning*. New York: Pergamon.

Sabatier, Paul. 1978. "The Acquisition and Utilization of Technical Information by Administrative Agencies." *Administrative Science Quarterly* 23: 386–411.

————. 1987. "Knowledge, Policy-Oriented Learning, and Policy Change." *Knowledge: Creation, Diffusion, Utilization* 8: 649–92.

————. 1988. "An Advocacy Coalition Framework of Policy Change and the Role of Policy-Oriented Learning Therein." *Policy Sciences* 21 (Summer and Fall): 129–68.

Sanders, G. S., and R. S. Baron. 1977. "Is Social Comparison Irrelevant for Producing Choice Shifts?" *Journal of Experimental Social Psychology* 13: 303–14.

Scheingold, Stuart. 1974. *The Politics of Rights*. New Haven, Conn.: Yale University Press.

Schulze, William D., and Allen V. Kneese. 1981. "Risk in Cost-Benefit Analysis." *Risk Analysis* 1: 82–88.

Schulze, William, Ralph D'Arge, and David Brookshire. 1981. "Valuing Environmental Commodities: Some Recent Experiments." *Land Economics* 57: 151–72.

Schwartz, Richard. 1978. "Moral Order and Sociology of Law: Trends, Problems, and Prospects." *Annual Review of Sociology* 4: 577–601.

Sears, David O., Richard Lau, Tom Tyler, and Harris Allen. 1980. "Self-Interest vs. Symbolic Politics in Policy Attitudes and Presidential Voting." *American Political Science Review* 74: 670–84.

Sears, David O., and Jack Citrin. 1982. *Tax Revolt*. Cambridge, Mass.: Harvard University Press.

Sears, David O., Leonie Huddie, and Lynitta Schaffer. 1986. "A Schematic View of Symbolic Politics Theory." In Richard Lau and David O. Sears, eds., *Political Cognition*. Hillsdale, N.J.: Lawrence Erlbaum.

Sen, Amartya. 1980. "Description as Choice." *International Economic Review* 21: 353–68.

Sentis, K. P., and E. Burnstein. 1979. "Remembering Schema-Consistent Information: Effects of Balance Schema on Recognition Memory." *Journal of Personality and Social Psychology* 37: 2200–11.

Shibutami, Tamotsu. 1955. "Reference Groups as Perspectives." *American Journal of Sociology* 60: 562–69.

Shumavon, Douglas, and H. Kenneth Hibbeln, eds. 1986. *Administrative Discretion and Public Policy Implementation*. New York: Praeger.

Simon, Herbert. 1957. *Models of Man: Social and Rational*. New York: John Wiley.

————. 1979a. "Information Processing Models of Cognition." In Mark Rosenzweig and Lyman Porter, eds., *Annual Review of Psychology* 7: 363–97.

————. 1979b. *Models of Thought*. New Haven, Conn.: Yale University Press.

————. 1982. "Comments." In Margaret Clark and Susan Fiske, eds., *Affect and Cognition*. Hillsdale, N.J.: Lawrence Erlbaum.

————. 1983. *Reason in Human Affairs*. Stanford, Calif.: Stanford University Press.

Singer, Grace. 1980. "People and Petrochemicals: Siting Controversies on the Urban Waterfront." In David Morell and Grace Singer, *Refining the Waterfront*. Cambridge, Mass.: Oelgeschlager, Gunn, and Hain.

Slovic, Paul, Baruch Fischhoff, and Sarah Lichtenstein. 1980. "Facts and Fears: Understanding Perceived Risk." In Richard Schwing and Walter Albers, eds., *Societal Risk Assessment*. New York: Plenum.

Smith, Eric. 1989. *The Unchanging American Voter*. Berkeley: University of California Press.

Sniderman, Paul, Richard Brody, and Philip Tetlock. 1991. *Reasoning and Choice*. Cambridge, Eng.: Cambridge University Press.

Sokal, Peter, and Robert Sneath. 1963. *Numerical Taxonomy*. San Francisco: W. H. Freeman.

Sorenson, John, Jon Soderstrom, Emily Copenhaver, Sam Carnes, and Robert Bolin. 1987. *Impacts of Hazardous Technology: The Psycho-Social Effects of Restarting TMI-1*. Albany, N.Y.: State University of New York Press.

Sproul, Christopher. 1986. "Public Participation in the Point Concepcion LNG Controversy: Energy Wasted or Energy Well Spent?" *Ecology Law Quarterly* 13: 73–153.

Starr, Chauncey. 1969. "Social Benefit versus Technological Risk." *Science* 165: 1232–38.

Starr, Martin, and Milan Zeleny. 1977. *Multiple Criteria Decision Making*. Amsterdam: North Holland.

Steiner, Henry. 1978. *Conflict in Urban Transportation*. Lexington, Mass.: D. C. Heath.

Stewart, Thomas R., Robin L. Dennis, and Daniel W. Ely. 1984. "Citizen Participation and Judgment in Policy Analysis: A Case Study of Urban Air Quality Policy." *Policy Sciences* 17: 67–87.

Stigler, George, and Gary Becker. 1977. "De Gustibus Non Est Disputandum." *American Economic Review* 67: 76–90.

Stokey, Edith, and Richard Zeckhauser. 1978. *A Primer for Policy Analysis*. New York: W. W. Norton.

Taylor, Serge. 1984. *Making Bureaucracies Think*. Stanford, Calif.: Stanford University Press.

Taylor, Shelley E. 1981. "The Interface of Cognitive and Social Psychology." In John Harvey, ed., *Cognition, Social Behavior, and the Environment*. Hillsdale, N.J.: Lawrence Erlbaum.

Taylor, Shelley E., and Jennifer Crocker. 1981. "Schematic Bases of Social Information Processing." In E. Tory Higgins, C. P. Herman, and M. P. Zanna, eds. *Social Cognition: The Ontario Symposium*. Hillsdale, N.J.: Lawrence Erlbaum.

Tesser, Abraham. 1978. "Self-Generated Attitude Change." In Leonard Berkowitz, ed., *Advances in Experimental Social Psychology*, vol. 11. New York: Academic Press.

————. 1986. "Some Effects of Self-Evaluation Maintenance on Cognition and Action." In Richard Sorrentino and E. Tory Higgins, *Handbook of Motivation and Cognition*. New York: Guilford Press.

Thibaut, J., and L. Walker. 1975. *Procedural Justice: A Psychological Analysis*. Hillsdale, N.J.: Lawrence Erlbaum.

Thomas, K., E. Swatow, M. Fishbein, and H. J. Otway. 1980. "Nuclear Energy: The Accuracy of Policy Makers' Perceptions of Public Beliefs." *Behavioral Science* 25: 332–44.

Thompson, Mark S. 1980. *Benefit-Cost Analysis for Program Evaluation*. Beverly Hills, Calif.: Sage.

Toulmin, Stephen. 1958. *The Uses of Argument*. Cambridge, Eng.: Cambridge University Press.

Tribe, Laurence. 1972. "Policy Science: Analysis or Ideology." *Philosophy and Public Affairs* 2: 66–110.

————. 1973. "Technology Assessment and the Fourth Discontinuity: The Limits of Instrumental Rationality." *Southern California Law Review* 46: 617–60.

————. 1976. "Ways Not to Think About Plastic Trees." In Laurence Tribe, Corinne Schelling, and John Voss, eds., *When Values Conflict*. Cambridge, Mass.: Ballinger.

Tsujimoto, R. N., J. Wilde, and A. R. Robertson. 1978. "Distorted Memory for Exemplars of a Social Structure: Evidence for Schematic Memory Processes." *Journal of Personality and Social Psychology* 36: 1402–14.

Tullock, Gordon. 1982. "More Thoughts About Demand Revealing." *Public Choice* 38: 167–70.

Tversky, A., and D. Kahneman. 1975. "Judgment under Uncertainty: Heuristics and Biases." *Science* 185: 1124–31.

Tyler, Tom. 1984. "Justice in the Political Arena." In Robert Folger, ed., *The Sense of Injustice*. New York: Plenum.

————. 1986. "Justice and Leadership Endorsement." In Richard Lau and David O. Sears, eds., *Political Cognition*. Hillsdale, N.J.: Lawrence Erlbaum.

Tyler, Tom, and A. Caine. 1981. "The Influence of Outcomes and Procedures on Satisfaction with Formal Leaders." *Journal of Personality and Social Psychology* 41: 642–55.

Tyler, Tom, Kenneth Rasinski, and Kathleen McGraw. 1985. "The Influence of Perceived Injustice on the Endorsement of Political Leaders." *Journal of Applied Social Psychology* 15: 700–725.

Tyler, Tom, Kenneth Rasinski, and Nancy Spodick. 1985. "Influence of Voice on Satisfaction with Leaders: Exploring the Meaning of Process Control." *Journal of Personality and Social Psychology* 48: 72–81.

U.S. Council on Environmental Quality. 1979. *Environmental Quality: Tenth Annual Report*. Washington, D.C.: U.S. Government Printing Office.

U.S. Department of the Interior, Water and Power Resources Service. 1980. *Public Involvement Manual*. Washington, D.C.: U.S. Government Printing Office.

U.S. Environmental Protection Agency. 1979. *Siting of Hazardous Waste Management: Facilities and Public Opposition*. Washington, D.C.: U.S. Government Printing Office.

U.S. Executive Office of the President, Council on Environmental Quality. 1979. *Environmental Quality*. Washington, D.C.: U.S. Government Printing Office.

———. 1980. *Public Opinion on Environmental Issues*. Washington, D.C.: U.S. Government Printing Office.

Uslaner, Eric, and Ronald E. Weber. 1983. "Policy Congruence and American State Elites: Descriptive Representation versus Electoral Accountability." *The Journal of Politics* 45: 183–96.

Vig, Norman, and Michael Kraft, eds. 1990. *Environmental Policy in the 1990's*. Washington, D.C.: Congressional Quarterly.

Vlek, Charles, and Pieter-Jan Stallen. 1981. "Judging Risks and Benefits in the Small and Large." *Organizational Behavior and Human Performance* 28: 235–71.

von Winterfeldt, Detlof, and Ward Edwards. 1986. *Decision Analysis and Behavioral Research*. Cambridge, Eng.: Cambridge University Press.

Voogd, Henk. 1983. *Multicriteria Evaluation*. London: Pion.

Ward, J. 1963. "Hierarchical Grouping to Optimize an Objective Function." *Journal of the American Statistical Association* 58: 236–44.

Ward, Lawrence, and James Russell. 1981a. "The Psychological Representation of Molar Physical Environments." *Journal of Experimental Psychology: General* 110: 121–52.

———. 1981b. "Cognitive Set and the Perception of Place." *Environment and Behavior* 13: 610–32.

Warfield, Paul. 1976. *Societal Systems*. New York: John Wiley.

Wason, P. C., and P. N. Johnson-Laird. 1972. *Psychology of Reasoning: Structure and Content*. Cambridge, Mass.: Harvard University Press.

Wasserman, Ira. 1982. "Size of Place in Relation to Community Attachment and Satisfaction with Community Services." *Social Indicators Research* 11: 421–36.

Webber, David. 1983. "Is Nuclear Power Just Another Environmental Issue?" *Environment and Behavior* 14: 72–83.

Weisberg, Herbert, and Jerold Rusk. 1970. "Dimensions of Candidate Evaluation." *American Political Science Review* 64: 1167–85.

Wenner, Lettie McSpadden, and Manfred W. Wenner. 1978. "Nuclear Policy and Public Participation." *American Behavioral Scientist* 22: 277–310.

Wichelman, Allan. 1976. "Administrative Agency Implementation of the National Environmental Policy Act of 1969." *Natural Resources Journal* 16: 263–300.

Wicklund, Robert, and Peter Gollwitzer. 1982. *Symbolic Self-Completion*. Hillsdale, N.J.: Lawrence Erlbaum.

Wildavsky, Aaron. 1966. "The Political Economy of Efficiency: Cost-Benefit Analysis, Systems Analysis, and Program Budgeting." *Public Administration Review* 26: 292–310.

———. 1987. "Choosing Preferences by Constructing Institutions: A Cultural Theory of Preference Formation." *American Political Science Review* 81: 3–22.

Wildavsky, Aaron, and Ellen Tenebaum. 1981. *The Politics of Mistrust: Estimating American Oil and Gas Resources*. Beverly Hills, Calif.: Sage.

Wilkening, E. A., and David McGranahan. 1977. "Correlates of Subjective Well-Being in Northern Wisconsin." *Social Indicators Research* 5: 211–34.

Winner, Langdon. 1986. *The Whale and the Reactor: A Search for Limits in an Age of High Technology*. Chicago, Ill.: University of Chicago Press.

Wolf, Sidney. 1980. "Public Opposition to Hazardous Waste Sites: The Self-Defeating Approach to National Hazardous Waste Control Under Subtitle C of the Resource Conservation and Recovery Act of 1976." *Environmental Affairs* 8: 463–540.

Wood, B. Dan. 1988. "Principals, Bureaucrats, and Responsiveness in Clean Air Enforcements." *American Political Science Review* 82: 213–34.

Woodhouse, Edward. 1983. "The Politics of Nuclear Waste Management." In Charles Walker, Leroy Gould, and Edward Woodhouse, eds., *Too Hot to Handle*. New Haven, Conn.: Yale University Press.

———. 1986. *Averting Catastrophe: Strategies for Regulating Risky Technologies*. Berkeley: University of California Press.

Yager, Ronald. 1978. "Fuzzy Decision Making Including Unequal Objectives." *Fuzzy Sets and Systems* 1: 87–96.

Yates, Douglas. 1982. *Bureaucratic Democracy*. Cambridge, Mass.: Harvard University Press.

Yu, Po Lung. 1984. "Introduction to Decision Dynamics, Second Order Games, and Habitual Domains." In Milan Zeleny, ed., *MCDM: Past Decade and Future Trends*. Greenwich, Conn.: JAI Press.

———. 1985. *Multiple-Criteria Decision Making*. New York: Plenum.

Zajonc, Robert. 1980. "Feeling and Thinking: Preferences Need No Inferences." *American Psychologist* 35: 151–75.

Zajonc, Robert, and Hazel Markus. 1984. "Affect and Cognition: The Hard Interface." In Carrol Izard, Jerome Kagan, and Robert Zajonc, eds., *Emotions, Cognition, and Behavior*. Cambridge, Eng.: Cambridge University Press.

Zaller, John. 1990. "Political Awareness, Elite Opinion Leadership, and the Mass Survey Response." *Social Cognition* 8: 125–53.

―――. 1991. "Information, Values, and Opinion." *American Political Science Review* 85: 1215–38.

Zeleny, Milan. 1982. *Multiple Criteria Decision Making.* New York: McGraw-Hill.

―――, ed. 1984. *MCDM: Past Decade and Future Trends.* Greenwich, Conn.: JAI Press.

Zinke, Robert C. 1987. "Cost-Benefit Analysis and Administrative Legitimation." *Policy Studies Journal* 16: 63–88.

Zuiches, James. 1980. "Residential Preferences in Migration Theory." In David Brown and John Wardwell, eds., *New Directions in Urban-Rural Migration.* London: Academic Press.

―――. 1981. "Residential Preferences in the United States." In Amos Hawley and Sara Mazie, eds., *Nonmetropolitan America in Transition.* Chapel Hill: University of North Carolina Press.

Index

Library of Congress Cataloging-in-Publication Data

Hill, Stuart.
   Democratic values and technological choices / Stuart Hill.
     p. cm.
   Includes bibliographical references and index.
   ISBN 0-8047-1986-1 (alk. paper) :
    1. Technology and state—United States. I. Title.
T21.H47   1992
338.97307—dc20   91-45821
                                   CIP

♾ This book is printed on acid-free paper